# Webbing with Literature

## Creating Story Maps with Children's Books

Karen D'Angelo Bromley

*The State University of New York at Binghamton*

Allyn and Bacon
*Boston    London    Toronto    Sydney    Tokyo    Singapore*

Series Editor: *Sean W. Wakely*
Series Editorial Assistant: *Carol L. Chernaik*
Production Administrator: *Annette Joseph*
Production Coordinator: *Susan Freese*
Editorial-Production Service: *Kailyard Associates*
Text Designer: *Denise Hoffman, Glenview Studios*
Manufacturing Buyer: *Louise Richardson*
Cover Administrator: *Linda K. Dickinson*
Cover Designer: *Suzanne Harbison*

**Library of Congress Cataloging-in-Publication Data**

Bromley, Karen D'Angelo
    Webbing with literature: creating story maps with children's books / Karen D'Angelo Bromley.
        p.        cm.
    Includes bibliographical references and index.
    ISBN 0-205-12610-3
        1. Literature—Study and teaching (Elementary)   2. Language arts
    (Elementary)   3. Children's literature   4. Children—Books and reading.
    I. Title
    LB1575.B73    1991
    372.6'4044—dc20                                                    90-1196
                                                                       CIP

Printed in the United States of America

10 9 8 7 6 5 4 3        95 94 93 92

*Dedicated to Joan Nelson-Herber*
*for her support and the outstanding model she provides*

*and to Christopher, Westra, Karen, and Hanlon*
*for their special response to literature*

# contents

# preface

This handbook explores webbing as a way children can share and respond to literature. It is written for K–8 classroom, reading, language arts, and resource room teachers who want to connect their students with stories and poems written especially for children and youth. Webbing enhances the understanding, enjoyment, and appreciation of the literature we read to students and the books they read themselves. It is a springboard for discussing literature. Webbing also provides students with a visual display of the important ideas, information, and relationships in a story or book and helps students understand the way an author uses literary elements. Webbing promotes comprehension, links reading and writing, invites students to learn, and increases enjoyment of literature.

This handbook explores webbing and its use in classroom instruction. The ideas suggested here, however, are only a starting point. As you and your students use webbing, you will find ways to adapt and build on what you find here, thus making this strategy a useful learning tool and integral part of your classroom.

There are two parts to the book. Part I explains semantic webbing, story elements, and the elements of quality in literature. It provides practical ideas for using webs in the classroom and includes seventy-five actual webs for books. It includes suggestions for effectively sharing literature and exploring responses to literature, especially writing.

Part II includes annotations and webs for 50 books, as well as annotations for 145 other books, all of which include Caldecott and Newbery Medal and Honor books, International Reading Association's Children's Choice books, titles chosen by the Children's Book Council as outstanding science and trade books, and other examples of quality literature for K–8 children and youth. Titles include books about children and youth with handicaps and various heritages, including African, Asian, European, Hispanic, and Native American.

In the annotations and webs for the 50 titles, each includes the following sections: *Summary, Setting, Characters, Theme, Vocabulary, Illustrations,* and *Grade Level/Content Area* (grades for which the book is appropriate and specific themes or units in science, social studies, math, etc.

for which the book can be used are included). Each web is accompanied by ideas for its use with students. Many of the annotations and webs come from teachers who have used them in their classrooms. For the 145 other titles, only *Summary* and *Grade Level/Content Area* are provided. These books lend themselves as well to webbing and integration with the K-8 curriculum.

## Acknowledgments

For their contributions, I want to especially thank the teachers and graduate students whose work appears throughout this book. Lisa Milano, Carol Cedarholm, Mary Johnson, Charlotte De Almeida, Yvonne Caravaglia, Regina Mardex, Kate Giblin, Terri Judge, Jill Zavelick, Suzanne French, Liz Harris Ginrich, Stephanie Horowitz, Mary Bonner, Wendy Hughes, Mary Stratton, Kris de Vente, Valerie Myers White, Chris Czarnecki, Helen Hermann, Penny Zandy, Betty Brewer, and Nancy Mangialetti all freely contributed their ideas, observations, and enthusiasm about webbing.

I am also grateful to the children who used webbing in all variety of ways and allowed me to use their work here. My special thanks also go to the following reviewers: Judith Hakes at Angelo State University, Jerry Watson at the University of Iowa, Sheila Shapiro at Northeastern Illinois University, and M. Lee Manning at Columbia College. Their thoughtful suggestions helped me see the reader's perspective and then write a more useable book.

For his support and editorial help throughout the project, I am grateful to Sean Wakely.

# chapter 1

# Semantic Webbing

This chapter discusses a flexible instructional strategy called *semantic webbing* that many teachers use daily in their classrooms for a variety of purposes and with a myriad of outcomes. The chapter explores different types of webs and the versatility of webbing for building literacy. It includes examples of how teachers use webs with children's literature as they integrate language arts and learning across the curriculum.

## Webbing Defined

In nature, a web is a network of fine threads that a spider weaves. This network forms a complicated structure that is the means by which the spider snares its prey. A web can also be a complicated work of the mind that represents objects or concepts and the relationships a person perceives among them. In a classroom, the term *web* borrows something from both definitions. A semantic web, used as an instructional tool in a classroom, is a graphic representation or visual display of categories of information and their relationships.

Of course, the dictionary provides definitions other than a spider's web and the web created in the mind. A web can also be a woven fabric, a membrane of skin joining together an animal's fingers or toes, or a large roll of newsprint. In the classroom, just as in the dictionary, webs are referred to in a variety of ways. They are sometimes called semantic webs, concept maps, semantic networks, structured overviews, or diagrams. In the classroom, the process of creating a web is called webbing or semantic webbing, mapping, semantic mapping, networking, or concept mapping. The variety and number of names for both the process and the product indicate that the strategy is versatile and useful for many purposes.

The basic structure of a web (Freedman & Reynolds, 1980) usually consists of a *core concept* or idea at the center of the web (see Figure 1.1). *Web strands* are placed at various points beyond the core to represent different categories of information related to the core. Each web strand is tied to the core with a *strand support* containing facts or information to support the web strand. *Strand ties* represent supporting details or relationships among strands. Of course, not all webs look exactly like this, but this is the basic structure.

Webbing or mapping is used as a flexible instructional strategy at all instructional levels. In a college or university chemistry class, a concept map helps students organize and represent information about the element tritium, for example, so they can more easily understand and learn about its properties. In an education course, a student creates a literature web to represent and organize a variety of purposes and activities for studying the interdependence of plants and animals, using books like *The Lorax* by Dr. Seuss. In a sixth-grade classroom, a teacher uses a web to represent the causes of the Civil War and to show his students how the North and South participated in

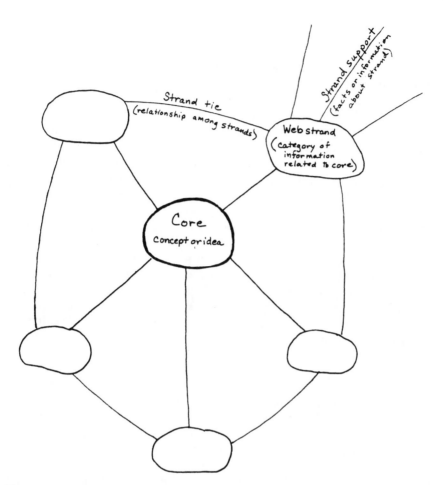

**Figure 1.1** The basic structure of a web.

creating the conflict that resulted in that war. In a third-grade classroom where students are learning about a community in Brazil, children brainstorm topics for written reports about that community while their teacher constructs a web of the topics. In a first-grade classroom, a teacher uses a web to show children the stages in the life of a monarch butterfly.

## Rationale for Webbing

Both research and theory support the notion that generating illustrative material, such as semantic webs, enhances comprehension and learning (Davis & McPherson, 1989; Flood & Lapp, 1988; Heimlich & Pittelman, 1986; Pearson & Johnson, 1978). Webbing is suggested as a way to help children identify important issues in children's books (Cleland, 1981), as an alternative to the directed reading activity (Bromley, 1988), to enrich basal reading lessons (Freedman & Reynolds, 1980), and to enhance understanding and apprecia-

3

tion of literature (Norton, 1985; Reutzel & Fawson, 1989). Visual displays such as webs are also suggested to help students understand the main ideas, supporting details, and organization of expository material found in content texts (Alvermann, 1986; Flood & Lapp, 1988).

The many benefits of webbing with literature are highlighted in Figure 1.2, which presents a visual display of the ideas discussed next. The core concept is "webbing with literature," and beyond the core are web strands, such as "promotes enjoyment," which represent different categories of information related to the core. Each web strand is tied to the core with strand supports, such as "builds appreciation" and "provides enrichment," which contain the information to support the web strand. Strand ties represent supporting details or relationships among strands. In this web, the idea that ties the strands together is the function that webbing performs.

Four major reasons for using semantic webs with literature are discussed further here. Of course, you should remember that webbing is only one of many ways to connect children with literature, and overuse will certainly dilute its effectiveness. But when used appropriately, it is a rich avenue for sharing and responding to literature.

## Promotes Comprehension

Webbing promotes comprehension because it allows the new to be related to the known. Webs are often used by teachers to assess and organize students' prior knowledge about a topic before teaching a lesson or unit. By questioning students to determine what they already know about energy consumption and creating a web that represents this knowledge, a fifth-grade teacher can motivate students for the lesson and lay excellent groundwork for what she hopes students will learn as they read about the topic in their science texts or information books from the library. Her students can see where the new information fits into what they already know, by reviewing the web they created before reading.

Schema theory tells us that what we comprehend and learn from what we read or hear is directly related to what we already know and bring to a given situation. So the background knowledge, *schema* (singular) or *schemata* (plural), that fifth-grade students possess about energy consumption is important to assess if the teacher wants to help them relate new information to what they already know. When new information meshes with known information, it clicks into place, is more firmly based, and is also easier to remember because it makes sense to the learner.

Webbing promotes comprehension because it builds personal involvement with text. When a third-grade student reads or listens to a biography of Christopher Columbus and helps create a web or complete a partially constructed web representing problems and solutions Columbus faced in his lifetime, she has a purpose for comprehending and interacting personally with text. As she learns about the milestones in Columbus's life, she can relate

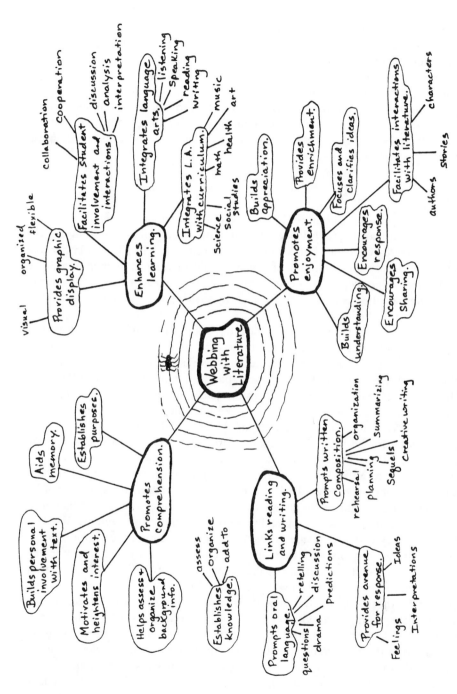

**Figure 1.2** Using webs with literature serves many functions.

them directly to the problems he experienced. For example, she learns that before Columbus landed in America, the king of Portugal and Queen Isabella of Spain turned down his requests for help, forcing him to prepare to go to the king of France for aid. With the help of a web highlighting problems and solutions, the student can see clearly that Columbus was a risk taker and problem solver. In choosing among ideas or information to complete a web, she reads with heightened interest and understanding about Columbus's commitment to his goal and his solutions to problems, and thus her comprehension is enhanced.

## Enhances Learning

As well as promoting comprehension, webbing enhances learning. From the literature on learning theory, we know that organizing information into some sensible or logical order helps us learn and remember it. We also know that seeing a visual representation of organized information aids memory. Since webs display concepts and relationships among concepts in a visibly structured format, they enhance the probability that we will learn and remember what is read or heard.

Webbing also promotes student interaction and learning. It allows for the kind of interaction between students that can be a catalyst for rich responses. When a class or group of students works together to develop a web, there is a high degree of student participation, involvement, and interaction that increases their chances for learning. Each student hears and sees what other students feel, believe, and know about a topic, and each student has an opportunity to add his beliefs and knowledge to the collective knowledge represented in the web. Webbing also provides rich opportunities for students to critically interpret and analyze what they read or hear in light of what they know and what others perceive. So the creation of webs allows for the growth of collective wisdom by promoting interaction among students.

Webbing integrates the language arts and requires the use of listening, speaking, reading, and writing skills. Webbing requires students to *use* language as they *learn* language. After listening to a story about Robin Hood, second-grade students who help their teacher build a web of words to describe Robin Hood first talk about the story and Robin's character. Then they identify adjectives that describe Robin and phrases from the story that support their adjectives, which they write on a web or dictate for their teacher to write. Students then read and reread the words and phrases from the web as they search for other additions to complete the web. Finally, they use information from the completed web to retell the story or write a brief character sketch of Robin. In this example of the webbing process, these students listen, speak, read, and write as they use and learn oral and written language simultaneously.

Webbing also integrates language arts learning with learning in other areas of the curriculum. Webbing lends itself easily to content-area lessons in science, social studies, math, health, music, and physical education and, in fact, simplifies the learning of most subject material because it provides a system for organizing information and showing relationships. Because of the flexibility of webs, they are used to develop vocabulary, organize information by imposing structure, differentiate main ideas and details, solve problems, identify relationships, and build oral and written language as content is learned.

## Links Reading and Writing

While reading and writing are not identical processes, they share many features, and when they are taught together, they can enhance children's literacy learning. We know that it is not necessary to wait until young children can read before encouraging them to write (Calkins, 1986). In fact, young children possess quite a bit of knowledge about writing, and when given opportunities to write, they begin to experiment with and organize their literacy knowledge. Shanahan (1988) says that for students of all ages, it is important to teach reading and writing in meaningful contexts that emphasize communication as well as content and process knowledge. Webbing is a strategy that fills these requirements.

Webbing links reading and writing as part of the process of making meaning from print and with print. If you create a web with children as a prewriting exercise to assess and organize their knowledge before they read a story or book, children can read what they have dictated to you and what you have written. When you add new information obtained in reading to this web or change it as children direct you to, then what you write directly connects children with what they have read and with their own oral language.

When children create their own webs before, during, or after they read, the reading-writing link is even more direct. Webs can be used as springboards for discussing a story or retelling it in its entirety. Webs can also help children plan and organize thoughts and ideas for writing about a book or story. Children can compose webs as a response to what they read and as a way of reviewing and sharing their thoughts with others after reading and before writing. They can interpret the content of what they read through webs and explore their feelings as they use the elements or structure of a story to guide their writing.

Webbing involves children in writing as a process because in creating a web, children are planning what they will include in their written piece. Webs aid planning by serving as outlines or skeletons for writing. Creating a web can help children recall and represent information and ideas about a particular topic in a few words or phrases that can later be expanded and elaborated into complete sentences and paragraphs for a report. In this way, a web provides structure for a written composition. The advantage of using a web as an outline or structure for writing is that a web is a nonlinear representation of information, whereas an outline is linear. If an idea is omitted in the creation of an outline, it must be squeezed into the outline later or an arrow used to identify where it fits. With a web, an idea or piece of information can be recorded on each strand without attention to order or proper sequence. Before writing, the writer can number each strand in the order in which it is to be included in the written piece. In this way, webbing allows the writer to think and record ideas in random order but sequence in a logical way.

### Promotes Enjoyment

Last, and just as important as the other major reasons for using webbing, is the idea that it promotes the enjoyment and appreciation of literature. Webbing structures and clarifies prose by helping students identify elements and ideas they might not normally be aware of. Webbing helps ensure that students understand what they have read so that they can then relate personally to it. In the process of webbing, students interact with each other and their teacher in ways that are different from the traditional teaching mode of teacher-question and student-response. By allowing students to react to what they have read and to share those reactions, webbing extends the opportunities for understanding and enjoying literature from a variety of perspectives. And because of the tangible ways that webbing promotes comprehension, enhances learning, and links reading and writing, it extends and enriches student response to literature and so promotes enjoyment as well.

From the examples and discussion provided so far, you can see that webbing has broad versatility and rich potential for instruction. It is used in a variety of subject areas, with a variety of types of students, at a range of grade levels, and in a multitude of ways, depending on the purposes of teachers and students. The possibilities for using webs are limited only by your imagination and creativity.

## Flexibility with Webs

Webbing is one of the most versatile strategies a teacher can learn to use and teach children how to use. Its flexibility is the subject of the rest of this chapter.

Webbing is an excellent strategy to use when you want to foster enjoyment and appreciation of literature and help children become involved with literature as they interact with each other to learn. You can organize ideas for teaching a content-area unit with a web. You can represent the elements, structure, or relationships in a story with a web, which will make children's understanding of the story easier and thus their responses richer. You can also help children organize their own ideas and information with webs.

Teachers often use webs to help them organize their ideas and their instructional plans. The literature web in Figure 1.3 shows how Wendy Hughes,

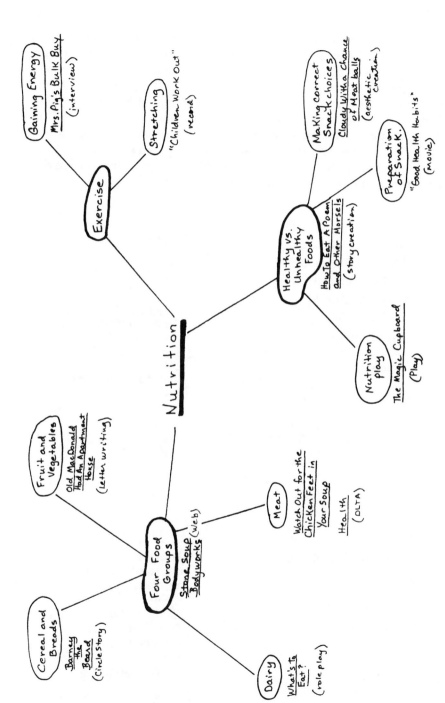

**Figure 1.3** A literature web.

a second-grade teacher, incorporated literature into her health unit on nutrition. The web includes nutrition topics Wendy wanted the children to learn about as well as titles of children's books appropriate to each topic and teaching activity. The science concept web in Figure 1.4 shows how Valerie Myers-White, a fourth-grade teacher, wove literature and language arts into her unit on the interdependence of plants and animals. Valerie's web includes opportunities for the children to experience content through listening, speaking, reading, writing, and appropriate children's literature. Huck, Helper, and Hickman (1987) and Norton (1985; 1987) provide further explanations of literature webs for the interested reader.

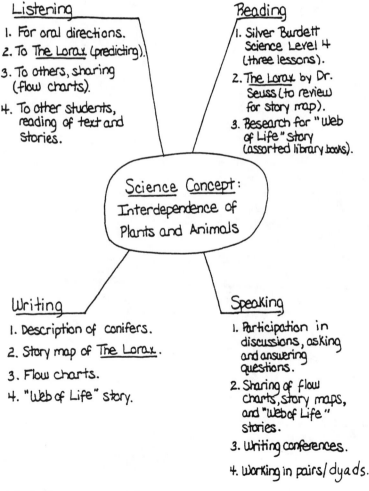

**Figure 1.4**  A science concept web.

Children often create webs to represent their ideas or information they have learned on a specific topic. Matt, a second-grader, made the food groups web in Figure 1.5 near the end of the unit on nutrition, and Wendy (Ms. Hughes) responded with a personal note.

A variety of different kinds of webs can be created to represent the content, elements, and relationships found in literature. You can develop children's appreciation and understanding of literature by modeling the use of these webs. Children can then become familiar with the process of webbing and can use webs themselves with literature. Webs can be used before, during, or after students read or listen to a story. The teacher can construct a web, students can create them, or webs can be developed cooperatively by teacher and students or small groups of students working independently.

The kinds of webs illustrated in the next seven figures can fit a variety of instructional purposes. Each of the these webs is based on the book *Rachel and Obadiah* (Turkle, 1978), an example of historical fiction that can be shared with children in grades 2–4 for pure enjoyment or to enrich a study of

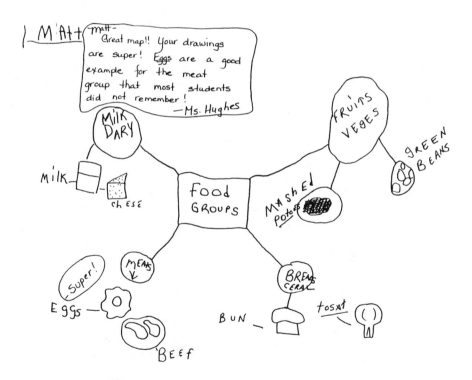

**Figure 1.5** A web of the four food groups made by a second-grade child.

early colonists, an island community, whales and the whaling industry, or the changing roles of women. The story is of two young Quaker children who both want to be the one to report the news of the next whaling ship's return to Nantucket harbor, thereby earning a silver coin. Obadiah challenges Rachel to a race that has a surprise result, and the reader is shown, in full-color, authentic drawings, the gentle Quaker atmosphere of old Nantucket. With an open-ended conclusion, the story lends itself to divergent thinking and different interpretations. Here are some ideas for creating and using various webs:

1. Before reading this story, you might partially create the web in Figure 1.6 as a way of introducing the story to children and establishing what they know

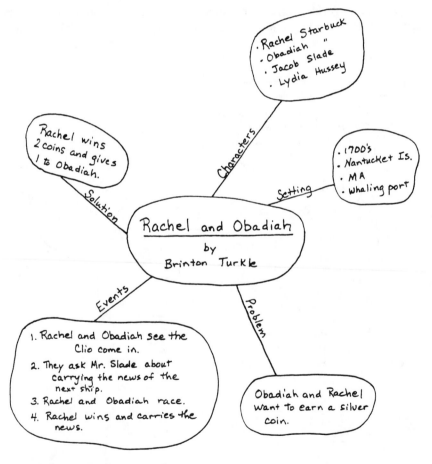

**Figure 1.6** A story elements web.

about the setting. Present children with the "characters" and "setting" strands, including any further information on setting supplied by the children, who may have been to Nantucket or other ocean communities. After reading the story and encouraging children to respond and talk about what happened, they can dictate the "problem," "events," and "solution" for you to fill in.

2. After hearing the story, you can involve children in webbing to reinforce vocabulary and spelling. You might have four groups of children each brainstorm and list the important vocabulary words that fit the categories of "objects," "characters," "scenes," and "old words." Each list can be included in a completed web that might look something like the one in Figure 1.7. This web can spark further discussion and even research. For example, the special language used in the story might be an avenue for learning more about the Quakers.

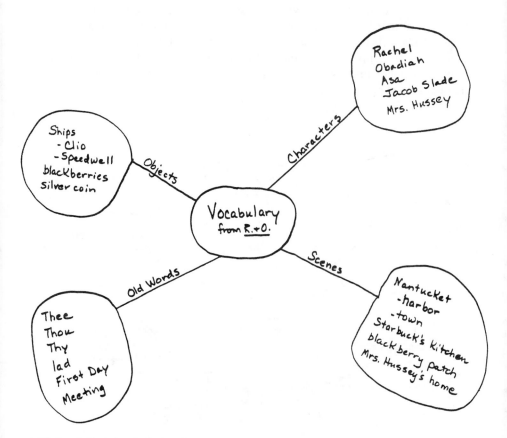

**Figure 1.7** A vocabulary web.

3. Following the reading of this story, if children do not notice and comment on it themselves, you might ask whether Obadiah got a coin. The last page says "Rachel put one coin in her pocket. She would keep it forever. And she knew just what to do with the other one." This open-ended conclusion lends itself to the creation of a web of other possible conclusions, which some third-graders created in Figure 1.8.

4. After hearing the story, the same third-grade class created the character web in Figure 1.9 to represent Obadiah's character. This teacher required her students to use descriptive words other than *good, bad,* and *nice,* which she felt were overused and bland. Creating this web expanded vocabulary, provided an outline or skeleton for writing a brief character sketch, and involved children in a character analysis that could enhance a dramatization of the story.

5. The feelings web in Figure 1.10 is based on one suggested by Galda (1987) as a way to teach higher-order reading and thinking skills with literature. The directions of the arrows in this web denote how one character feels towards another character. For example, during the course of the story Rachel feels "hurt, mad, loyal, and kind" towards Obadiah, and he feels "confident, fair, superior, and angry" towards Rachel. A web of this kind can produce a richer understanding of the story by encouraging analysis of the characters' feelings for each other.

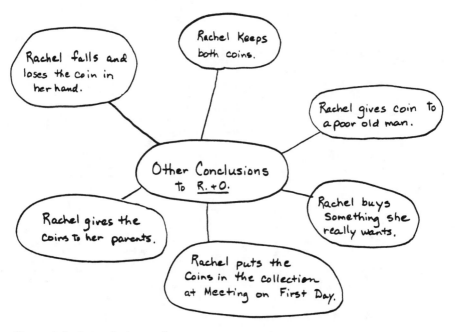

**Figure 1.8** A conclusions web.

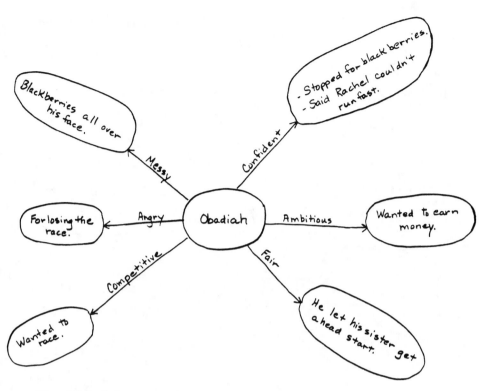

**Figure 1.9** A character web.

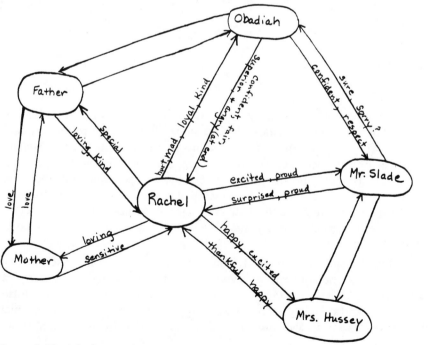

**Figure 1.10** A feelings web.

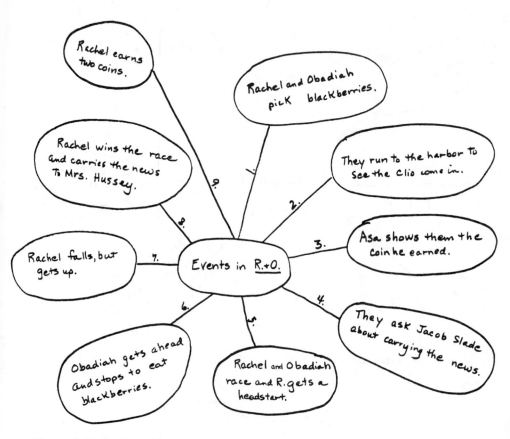

**Figure 1.11**  A plot web.

6. After listening to the story, the plot web in Figure 1.11 can be constructed by the class as a whole, in two steps to encourage recall and accuracy in sequencing events. First ask students to recall events in approximately the order of their occurrence. Then if there are questions about sequence, have students check the story and number the events. Events do not necessarily need to be remembered and included on the web in exact order. By adding numbers after events that have been remembered, the proper sequence can be established and students with less accurate memories have a better chance for success.

7. A fourth-grade teacher used a blank version of the comparison web in Figure 1.12 with her students to help them see the similarities and differences between the fable by Aesop and *Rachel and Obadiah*. She read both stories to her class and then had students work in pairs to complete the web, which then served as a basis for discussion of the two stories. Items for comparison

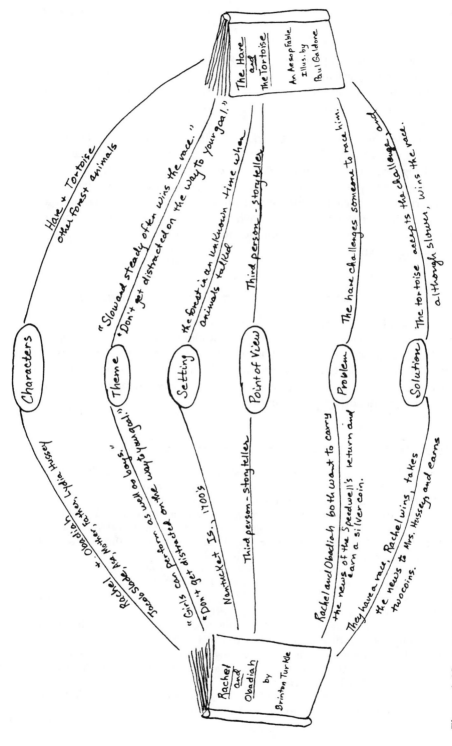

**Figure 1.12** A comparison web.

could change depending on your purpose. For example, two fairy tales illustrated by different artists might be compared on the basis of illustrations; thus, the categories in the middle of the web might be "color," "line," "shape," "texture," "arrangement," and "total effect."

Examples of webs are to be found in the remaining chapters of this book, and the 50 webs found in Part II include many more types and varieties. They provide a beginning place to explore the flexibility of webs for enhancing the ways you teach and use children's literature. Each web in Part II was created by a teacher and/or a group of children from the content and structure of the book or selection on which it is based. So there are many different types, depending on the unique story elements of the book or genre the book represents.

## Summary

Webbing can be as versatile and flexible a teaching tool as you allow it to be. You can make it fit your needs and your students' needs by adapting and modifying the process to suit your purposes and the content or structure of a particular book, selection, or genre. As well as promoting comprehension, enhancing learning, and linking reading and writing, webbing promotes children's enjoyment and appreciation of literature.

## REFERENCES

Alvermann, D. E. (1986). Graphic organizers: Cuing devices for comprehending and remembering main ideas. In J. S. Baumann (Ed.), *Teaching Main Idea Comprehension*. Newark, DE: International Reading Association.

Bromley, K. (1988). *Language Arts: Exploring Connections*. Boston: Allyn and Bacon.

Calkins, L. M. (1986). *The Art of Teaching Writing*. Portsmouth, NH: Heinemann.

Cleland, C. (1981). Highlighting issues in children's literature through semantic webbing. *The Reading Teacher, 34*(6), 642–646.

Davis, Z. T., & McPherson, M. D. (1989). Story map instruction: A road map for reading comprehension. *The Reading Teacher, 43*(3), 232–243.

Flood, J., & Lapp, D. (1988). Conceptual mapping strategies for understanding information texts. *The Reading Teacher, 41*(8), 780–783.

Freedman, G., & Reynolds, E. (1980). Enriching basal reading lessons with semantic webbing. *The Reading Teacher, 33*(6), 677–684.

Galda, L. (1987). Teaching higher order reading skills with literature. In B. Cullinan (Ed.), *Children's Literature in the Reading Program* (pp. 54–58). Newark, DE: International Reading Association.

Heimlich, J. E., & Pittelman, S. D. (1986). *Semantic Mapping: Classroom Applications*. Newark, DE: International Reading Association.

Huck, C. S., Helper, S., & Hickman, J. (1987). *Children's Literature in the Elementary School* (4th ed.). New York: Holt, Rinehart & Winston.

Norton, D. E. (1987). *Through the Eyes of a Child: An Introduction to Children's Literature* (2nd ed.). Columbus, OH: Merrill.

_____. (1985). *The Effective Teaching of Language Arts*. Columbus. OH: Merrill.

Pearson, P. D., & Johnson, D. D. (1978). *Teaching Reading Comprehension*. New York: Holt, Rinehart & Winston.

Reutzel, D. R., & Fawson, P. C. (1989). Using a literature webbing strategy lesson with predictable books. *The Reading Teacher, 43*(3), 208–215.

Shanahan, T. (1988). The reading-writing relationship: Seven instructional principles. *The Reading Teacher, 41*(7), 636–647.

## Children's Literature

Aesop. (1962). *The Hare and the Tortoise*. New York: McGraw-Hill.

Geisel, T. (1971). *The Lorax*. New York: Random House.

Turkle, B. (1978). *Rachel and Obadiah*. New York: Dutton.

# *Identifying Story Elements*

The purpose of this chapter is to describe story elements of each of the genres of literature. As you read, keep in mind that when story elements are represented in webs these networks provide students with rich opportunities to better understand and respond to literature.

## Story Elements Defined

Story elements are the common components or similar structures of stories or books from a particular genre of literature. Every story or selection from a genre contains some common elements that represent its structure and each genre contains some elements that are unique to that genre. Folktales, fantasy, realistic fiction, historical fiction, biography, poetry, and information books each contain some common components that we will call story elements. Many of the following elements can be found in each genre of literature:

- setting
- character
- problem, conflict, or goal
- plot, sequence of events, or attempts to solve the problem
- solution, resolution, or accomplishment of goal
- theme, moral, or lesson
- point of view or narrator
- style or tone

You and the children you teach will discover other elements that fit a genre of literature or may be characteristic of two particular books from one genre that you have read and want to compare.

Until recently, we thought that knowledge of story elements was developmental, with older children and adults possessing a more elaborate concept of what constitutes a story than younger children. To some extent this is true. A recent study by Lehr (1988), however, suggests that even kindergarten children have quite well-developed senses of story and can summarize plots, react to characters, and identify and match themes in related stories.

It is important to realize that not every story or selection possesses all the traditional story elements. Information books and poetry are two literary genres that do not. As an example, *Mad as a Wet Hen! And Other Funny Idioms,* by Marvin Terban, is a collection of idioms, their definitions, their contemporary usage, and illustrations of their literal meanings. *A House Is a House,* by Mary Ann Hoberman, is a poem about the many different kinds of houses in our environment. Neither book is a story in the usual sense, and neither book contains the usual main and secondary characters or explicitly stated problem. But both books contain many of the other story elements listed previously.

The theme of *Mad as a Wet Hen!* is that our language is colorful and cannot always be taken literally. In this book, the narrator is the author, and his style of writing is concise and to the point. The unstated problem is that many phrases in our language are often misunderstood, which the author attempts to clear up. The theme of *A House Is a House* is that all of the things in our environment actually have a place, or "house." In this poem, the setting is the world around us, the unstated goal is to identify a house for each of the live and inanimate objects included, and the resolution is the identification of the houses. The poem is written from the point of view of an author with a creative eye, and the style involves a distinctive use of rhyme and repetition.

We know from the research literature that knowledge of story elements may aid children's comprehension and memory of stories. Reutzel (1984) found that integrating story maps into a reading lesson helps readers attend to details as well as to relationships among story elements before, during, and after reading. Reutzel (1985) also reported that story mapping significantly improved fifth-grade students' comprehension. Sinatra and others (1984; 1985; 1986) found that visually presenting story elements with semantic maps helped promote the reading comprehension of learning-disabled students and poor readers. Idol (1987) also reported that the comprehension of third- and fourth-graders, including learning-disabled and unskilled readers, was improved using a group story-mapping strategy.

We also know that one good way to assess children's literacy knowledge and comprehension abilities is to involve them in retelling stories after they listen or read. Marshall (1983) suggests that a retelling performance checklist using the elements of story helps teachers assess comprehension. Children with sophisticated literacy skills and good comprehension often have an easier time identifying story elements and using them to tell a story that they have just heard or read than children who have little knowledge of story elements.

Knowledge of story structure can improve writing abilities as well. Fitzgerald and Teasley (1986) found that instruction focusing on forming a mental picture of a story's structure and understanding of story parts improved less able fourth-grade readers' organization and the overall quality of their compositions. Olson (1984) found that the writing of good book reports is made easier when second- and fifth-grade children are aware of and use story structure as an aid in their writing.

There are two cautions about the use of story elements that Schmitt and O'Brien (1986) note and are worth discussing here. First, teaching children the knowledge of structure is not necessary for comprehension of a story. In fact, we know that even young children who have no knowledge of story elements can recall and understand stories. But awareness of how story content is organized and interrelated may promote comprehension. Second, when structure is the focus in discussions of literature, we risk losing the most important aspect of the experience—appreciation and enjoyment of literature. But we do know that most readers can be helped to develop their sense of story not so much by direct instruction in story elements as by giving them many "opportunities to experience a rich variety of stories in an organized fashion using the grammar as a foundation" (Schmitt & O'Brien, p. 5). In this way, we enhance students' abilities to interact with characters and authors and thus better understand, appreciate, and enjoy stories.

## Story Elements in the Genres

Because webs represent the organization of text into categories and relationships among categories, and because webs are adaptable and flexible, they have potential for representing and clarifying the elements of story in children's literature. Cleland (1981) suggests webbing as a way to help children identify important issues in children's books. Galda (1987) describes how teachers can use webbing to help children better understand characters in literature. Bromley (1988) provides ideas for using webs and diagrams as ways of representing various aspects of literature to enhance reading comprehension. This text goes beyond these sources in exploring the use of webs with story elements and provides you with the understanding and familiarity necessary to begin using webs regularly in your classroom.

Seven different genres of literature, each including picture books as well as books without pictures, are described in the following pages. The special story elements of each genre are identified.

### Folktales

Folktales deal with the legends, superstitions, customs, and beliefs of ordinary people. *Why Mosquitoes Buzz in People's Ears,* by Verna Aardema, is an example of an African folktale that was originally spoken and passed on from one generation to another. *The Paper Crane,* by Molly Bang, is an example of a modern tale that is based on a Japanese folktale about a magic crane. Folktales are timeless in their appeal, reflecting universal human feelings and desires.

Folktales include four special kinds of stories. *Fairy tales* are stories that usually contain an imaginary being with some sort of special or magical power, such as the fairy godmother in "Cinderella." *Fables* are brief stories that illustrate a moral or lesson and include animals or inanimate objects that have been personified with human traits. Arnold Lobel's *Fables* is an example of a collection of modern day fables. Each is a one-page story about a particular animal that concludes with a one-sentence statement or moral. Fables are attractive to both children and adults, perhaps because they are simple and concise lessons on human behavior. *Myths* are stories that answer questions about something people cannot explain. They describe a cosmic phenomenon, strange natural happenings on earth, the start of civilization, or the origins of a custom. They often include gods and goddesses, mystical universal forces, and magic. *Epics* are long folktales or collections of tales about legendary heroes who personify the best human traits and represent the ideals of a nation. Homer's *Iliad* and *Odyssey* are examples of epic poems.

Most folktales possess the story elements discussed previously, but with slight modifications. In the web for *The Paper Crane* by Molly Bang (Figure 2.1), many of the following story elements can be found:

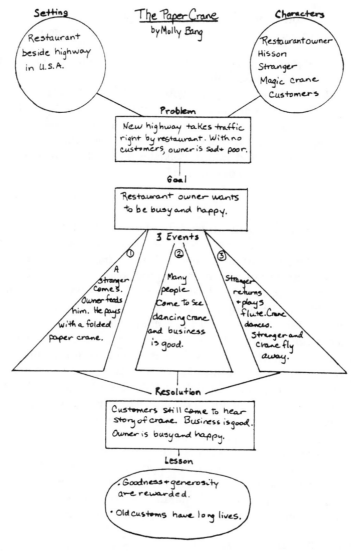

**Figure 2.1** The elements of a folktale, including three important events, are shown in this web.

- a brief introduction in which the setting, characters, and problem are included
- one-dimensional characters that possess an obvious trait (e.g., good, evil, envious, etc.)
- a problem, conflict, or goal
- a fast-paced plot with attempts to solve the problem or reach the goal
- a conclusion that quickly follows the climax
- the number *three* (e.g., three sons, three wishes, three attempts to win favor, etc.)
- a theme, lesson, or moral with universal appeal
- a style or tone using vocabulary and folkways of the common people

Folktales help children see that good often wins out over evil, that cleverness triumphs over strength and might, and that the plain and simple are often rewarded for their honesty and goodness. Folktales let children experience fast-paced action, sometimes violent and horrible acts, but all in the guise of stories, which often contain elements of magic or fantasy, that happened long ago. Through folktales, children can learn about human problems, solutions, morals, and values. Folktales show children how different cultures have contributed to our own society.

## Fantasy

Fantasy is fiction that contains an element of unreality. Fantasy twists or manipulates reality, often using fast action, humor, magic, and imaginary events or characters. Maurice Sendak's *Where the Wild Things Are* and *Outside over There* are two examples of fantasy for younger readers. Lynne Reid Banks's *The Indian in the Cupboard* and *The Return of the Indian* are examples of fantasy that older students enjoy. *Hey, Al*, by Arthur Yorinks, is an example of fantasy that concludes with a moral and is enjoyed by all ages.

*Science fiction* is a special kind of fantasy that is set in other worlds and deals with the future. These stories are based on known scientific facts but they explore the technology of the future and raise questions about the future of humanity. For example, Madeleine L'Engle's *A Wrinkle in Time* is created around the concept of the *tesseract,* which is a scientific term that means the fifth dimension. The story involves three children's travel by "tessering" through time to the planet Comatzoz and the help they receive from three imaginary characters named Mrs. Who, Mrs. Whatsit, and Mrs. Which.

In order for fantasy to be good, the impossible must be believable within the context of a logical and consistent story framework. In most fantasy, one or more of the common elements of literature is manipulated, and because of these twists it appeals to the imagination. Fantasy includes:

- a setting that may be enchanted
- characters that include humanlike animals, stereotypes of good and evil, heroes and heroines with magical powers, or extraterrestrial beings

- a problem, goal, or conflict, sometimes between forces of good and evil
- a plot that may include adventures of the characters, or, in science fiction, a heroic battle for the common good
- a climax, resolution of conflict, or accomplishment of the goal
- a theme or universal truth
- a point of view or a narrator
- a tone or style that is special in some way

Fantasy provides adventures into worlds of unreality for children, and it can help children understand the difference between fiction and fact. Figure 2.2 shows a web for *Hey, Al*, by Arthur Yorinks, in which the vocabulary for the real and unreal worlds is the focus. Fantasy is often humorous and enter-

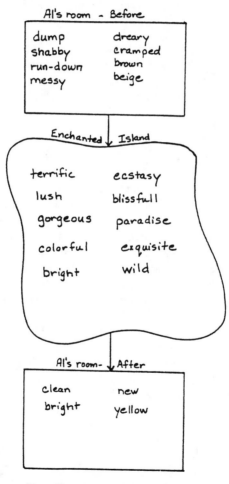

**Figure 2.2** In the fantasy *Hey, Al*, setting is manipulated as it moves from the reality of a cramped apartment to an enchanted island in the sky and finally back to Al's apartment.

taining. It allows children to use their imaginations and explore with characters who often have special powers. For these reasons, it is one of the most popular genres.

## Realistic Fiction

Realistic fiction stories are true to life. They are set in a time period that children know and understand. They can be about people in other countries as well as the United States. This genre includes realism in stories about animals, mysteries, sports, and adventures, as well as stories about those involved in the dilemmas and social issues of today's world. Topics include divorce, death, drugs, handicapping conditions, peer relationships, family problems, school failure, survival, and so on. The special elements of realistic fiction are:

- a setting that is real and believable
- characters who reflect those found in everyday life
- a believable problem, goal, or conflict
- a plot that may not always end happily, but reflects reality and may contain humor
- a theme or universal truth
- a particular point of view or narrator
- a tone or style that is special in some way

Realistic fiction shows students they have the power to change their lives. For example, *Dear Mr. Henshaw,* by Beverly Cleary, humorously helps middle-grade readers see how a young boy who lives with his mother and rarely sees his father copes with that situation while adjusting to a new school. In *Park's Quest,* Katherine Paterson sensitively portrays a young boy who desperately wants to know about his father, who was killed in Vietnam. The web for *The Flunking of Joshua T. Bates,* by Susan Shreve, (Figure 2.3) shows the feelings Joshua has as he is tutored by his third-grade teacher and then is promoted to the fourth grade.

These stories help children know and learn about their world by allowing them to see that people are more alike than different. Realistic fiction can give children insight into their own problems and help them understand the feelings of others. It shows students that their emotions and experiences are not unique. Realistic fiction also helps students rehearse roles they may have in the future.

## Historical Fiction

Historical fiction is based on facts and grounded in history but not restricted by it. It is realistic for the time period depicted and contains convincing dialogue between characters. Good historical fiction also contains accurate descriptions of settings and happenings that further children's knowledge of

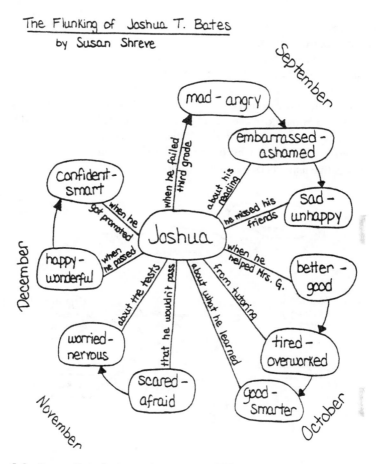

**Figure 2.3** For realistic fiction to be good, characters must be as believable as Joshua is in this web, which shows how third-graders depicted the changes in his feelings.

other times and places. Jean Fritz's *Shh! We're Writing the Constitution* is an example of this genre for older children, and *Dakota Dugout*, by Ann Turner, is an example for younger children. When authors of historical fiction take care to research their subjects, as these two authors have, the authenticity, quality, and realism of their stories are clearly apparent.

Historical fiction contains realistic and believable dialogue and accurate factual information, as well as these elements:

- a setting that is authentic to a particular historical period
- characters that act, speak, and have values that are true to the historical period
- a believable problem, goal, or conflict
- a plot or sequence of events

- a theme or universal truth that may include such things as loyalty, friendship, or courage
- a point of view or narrator
- a tone or style that is special in some way

Historical fiction can make the past come alive for students. It can make content-area learning more interesting by providing related knowledge about people, places, and events in history. It also can help students become aware of their own heritage. The web in Figure 2.4 realistically represents the positive and negative aspects of living in a dugout or in a clapboard house.

**Figure 2.4** These webs of life in the dugout versus life in the clapboard house show how third-graders related to this authentic and believable example of historical fiction.

## Biography

Biography is considered nonfiction that deals with the history of a person's life. Autobiographies are written by a person about his or her own life; biographies are written by writers who research and read about their subjects in order to accurately and interestingly portray the person's life the way it was. Evidence that information included in a biography is authentic makes it more believable.

Among some of the most accurate and entertaining biographies are those written by Jean Fritz. *And Then What Happened, Paul Revere?*, *What's the Big Idea, Benjamin Franklin?*, and *Why Don't You Get A Horse, Sam Adams?* are three of her books enjoyed by middle readers that represent realism and accuracy.

Biography contains realistic and believable dialogue and accurate factual information within these elements:

- an authentic setting where the main character lived or worked
- characters (political heroes or heroines, sports figures, explorers, scientists, musicians, writers, actors or actresses, etc.) who act, speak, and have believable values
- a believable problem or goal
- a plot or sequence of events substantiated by factual information that leads to an achievement or contribution
- a theme or universal truth
- a point of view or narrator
- a tone or style that is special in some way

Biography, like historical fiction, teaches children about other times, places, and people. Biographies such as *Jesse Jackson: I Am Somebody*, by Paul Westman, provide role models whom students can identify with and learn from. Biographies may help students think about setting personal goals and aspirations as well. Books of this genre relate real happenings of real people to children, and so biography has a special allure. The character web in Figure 2.5 shows the variety of roles Jesse Jackson plays in his life as a politician.

## Poetry

Poetry is an expression of a writer's inner thoughts and feelings and his or her relationship to the world and to others. Poets, more often than other writers perhaps, build sensory images through the use of *simile* ("shrill as a whistle"), *metaphor* ("the sun was an egg yolk"), *alliteration* ("leaping lizards lured me"), *onomatopoeia* ("slushing and slurping her slops"), or other techniques to produce a particular thought or feeling in the reader.

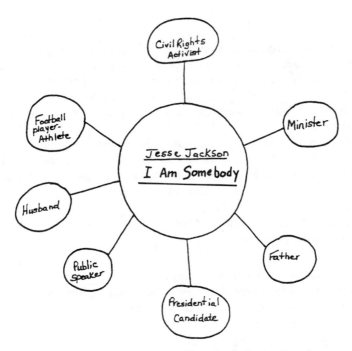

**Figure 2.5**  A web for *Jesse Jackson: I Am Somebody* depicts Jesse's many roles.

Poetry uses sensuous and concise language that appeals to children's emotions and intellects by giving new or special meaning to everyday events, people, or places.

Because poems often contain rhyme, rhythm, and repetition, which enhance their message and impact, they should be read aloud to be fully enjoyed. Paul Fleischman's *Joyful Noise: Poems for Two Voices* is a collection of poetry about insects that can be read aloud chorally by two individuals or groups. Lee Bennett Hopkins's *More Surprises, Read Aloud Rhymes for the Very Young*, by Jack Prelutsky, and Shel Silverstein's *Where the Sidewalk Ends* or *A Light in the Attic* are examples of collections of poems on a variety of topics that children enjoy hearing and that many teachers keep close by for reading when they have a few minutes.

Many of the elements of literature listed with the other genres can be found in poetry:

- a setting
- a character or characters
- a theme or universally understood message

- a point of view or speaker
- a special style or tone
- creation of visual and/or sensory images
- use of rhyme, rhythm, and/or repetition

Poetry allows children to experience the world in new and different ways. It provides opportunities to hear, see, and live in the everyday world with new insights. It also allows students to explore the world of the unknown and exercise their imaginations, while learning about and appreciating the rhyme and rhythm of language. The web in Figure 2.6 for *Read Aloud Rhymes for the Very Young*, by Jack Prelutsky, identifies the special characteristics of his poetry and invites children to supply the titles of poems that fit those characteristics.

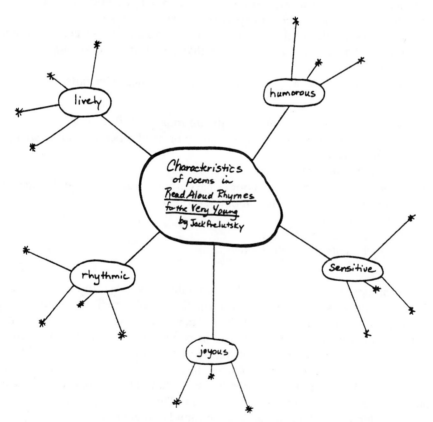

**Figure 2.6** After hearing a poem read aloud, children can decide which characteristic it demonstrates and add the title at the asterisk (*).

## Information Books

Information books are nonfiction books written to inform and explain. For young children there are concept books on a variety of topics, from dinosaurs to word opposites. Alphabet books, like *David McPhail's Animals A to Z* or Tana Hoban's *A,B,See!* provide the very young with an introduction to the letters of the alphabet. Number books, like John Reiss's *Numbers*, or Mitsumasa Anno's *Anno's Counting Book*, help teach and reinforce numeration. For older students, information books are written on all sorts of topics, from molecules and cats to drugs and the management of wildlife.

Two important things to consider when choosing an information book are how recently it was written and whether the information included is accurate. Often, the facts and concepts in older books are not up to date, especially if the topics are science or technology or other areas where our knowledge expands so rapidly that books become quickly outdated. One way to determine accuracy is to look at the author's credentials and/or experiences that allow him or her to be an expert on the subject. Another way is to read several books on the topic to compare the information and concepts they contain for similarities and differences that could indicate accuracy or authenticity.

Information books may contain some or all of these elements:

- an authentic setting from which the information is drawn
- characters who explain the information or exhibit behaviors that share it in some way
- a central issue or problem
- a sequence of events or account of accurate factual evidence that may or may not result in the solution of the problem
- a theme or main idea
- a point of view or narrator
- a tone or style that is distinctive

Information books provide children with knowledge and quench their thirst for answers to questions. Information books support content-area learning in science and social studies. They provide children with specific facts and information often not found in content texts, and the information they contain is often more current than in content texts. Information books written about topics from the sciences, history, sociology, the arts, and the humanities allow children to broaden their horizons as they learn about other people, places, and things. The web in Figure 2.7 for *Snakes*, by Sylvia Johnson, depicts the factual information found in that book.

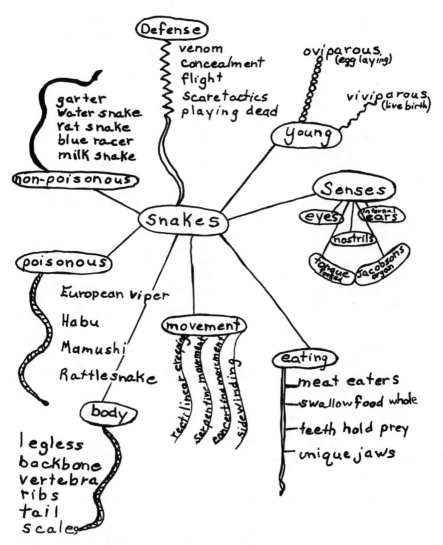

**Figure 2.7** The information in Sylvia Johnson's book *Snakes* is both recent and accurate.

================================================================ *Summary*

Each genre of literature possesses elements of structure. Some of these elements are common to books in all genres, and some are only found in books that represent one genre. With semantic webs, you can help children identify these elements and encourage rich responses to literature. Awareness and understanding of these common structures or elements make books more comprehensible, enjoyable, and inviting for children.

## REFERENCES

Bromley, K. (1988). *Language Arts: Exploring Connections.* Boston: Allyn and Bacon.

Cleland, C. (1981). Highlighting issues in children's literature through semantic webbing. *The Reading Teacher, 34*(6), 642–646.

Fitzgerald, J., & Teasley, A. B. (1986). Effects of instruction in narrative structure on children's writing. *Journal of Educational Psychology, 78*(6), 424–432.

Galda, L. (1987). Teaching higher order reading skills with literature. In B. Cullinan (Ed.), *Children's Literature in the Reading Program* (pp. 54–58, 89–96, 121–124). Newark, DE: International Reading Association.

Idol, L. (1987). Group story mapping: A comprehension strategy for both skilled and unskilled readers. *Journal of Learning Disabilities, 20*(4), 196–205.

Lehr, S. (1988). The child's developing sense of theme as a response to literature. *Reading Research Quarterly, 23*(3), 337–357.

Marshall, N. (1983). Using story grammar to assess reading comprehension. *Reading Teacher, 36*(7), 616–620.

Olson, M. W. (1984). A dash of story grammar and . . . Presto! A book report. *The Reading Teacher, 37*(6), 458–461.

Reutzel, D. R. (1985). Story maps improve comprehension. *The Reading Teacher, 38*(4), 400–404.

_____. (1984). Story mapping: An alternative approach to comprehension. *Reading World, 24*(2), 16–25.

Schmitt, M. C., & O'Brien, D. G. (1986). Story grammars: Some cautions about the translation of research into practice. *Reading Research and Instruction, 26*(1), 1–8.

Sinatra, R., Berg, D., & Dunn, R. (1985). Semantic mapping improves reading comprehension of learning disabled students. *Teaching Exceptional Children, 17*(4), 310–314.

Sinatra, R., Stahl-Gemake, J., & Berg, D. (1984). Improving reading comprehension of disabled readers through semantic mapping. *The Reading Teacher, 38*(1), 22–29.

Sinatra, R., Stahl-Gemake, J., & Morgan, N. (1986). Using semantic mapping after reading to organize and write original discourse. *Journal of Reading, 30*(1), 4–13.

### Children's Literature

Aardema, V. (1975). *Why Mosquitoes Buzz in People's Ears.* New York: Dial.

Anno, M. (1977). *Anno's Counting Book.* New York: Crowell.

Bang, M. (1985). *The Paper Crane.* New York: Greenwillow.

Banks, L. R. (1982). *The Indian in the Cupboard.* New York: Doubleday.

_____. (1986). *The Return of the Indian.* New York: Doubleday.

Cleary, B. (1983). *Dear Mr. Henshaw.* New York: Morrow.

Fleischman, P. (1988). *Joyful Noise: Poems for Two Voices.* New York: Harper & Row.

Fritz, J. (1973). *And Then What Happened, Paul Revere?* New York: Coward-McCann.

_____. (1974). *Why Don't You Get A Horse, Sam Adams?* New York: Coward-McCann.

_____. (1976). *What's the Big Idea, Benjamin Franklin?* New York: Coward-McCann.

_____. (1987). *Shh! We're Writing the Constitution.* New York: Scholastic.

Hoban, T. (1982). *A,B,See!* New York: Greenwillow.

Hoberman, M. A. (1984). *A House Is a House for Me.* New York: Viking.

Hopkins, L. B. (1987). *More Surprises.* New York: Harper & Row.

Johnson, S. A. (1986). *Snakes.* Minneapolis, MN: Lerner.

L'Engle, M. (1962). *A Wrinkle in Time.* New York: Farrar, Straus, & Giroux.

Lobel, A. (1980). *Fables.* New York: Harper & Row.

McPhail, D. (1988). *David McPhail's Animals A to Z.* New York: Scholastic.

Paterson, K. (1988). *Park's Quest.* New York: Dutton.

Prelutsky, J. (1986). *Read Aloud Rhymes for the Very Young.* New York: Knopf.

Reiss, J. (1971). *Numbers.* New York: Bradbury.

Sendak, M. (1963). *Where the Wild Things Are.* New York: Harper & Row.

_____. (1981). *Outside over There.* New York: Harper & Row.

Shreve, S. (1984). *The Flunking of Joshua T. Bates.* New York: Scholastic.

Silverstein, S. (1974). *Where the Sidewalk Ends.* New York: Harper & Row.

_____. (1981). *A Light in the Attic.* New York: Harper & Row.

Terban, M. (1987). *Mad as a Wet Hen! And Other Funny Idioms.* New York: Clarion.

Turner, A. (1985). *Dakota Dugout.* New York: Macmillan.

Westman, P. (1985). *Jesse Jackson: I Am Somebody.* Minneapolis, MN: Dillon.

Yorinks, A. (1986). *Hey, Al.* New York: Farrar, Straus, & Giroux.

# chapter 3

# Selecting Quality Literature

No discussion of children's books is complete without considering the characteristics of quality literature. This chapter will help you choose quality books to: share with children through oral reading or storytelling, make available in the classroom for children to read, and use with webbing to encourage your children's responses and promote their learning.

================================ *Popularity versus Quality*

To stimulate interest, enjoyment, and appreciation of books and to celebrate Children's Book Week, an elementary school library media specialist and reading teacher carried out a special week-long project. This cooperative project, called "Characters and Books—A Winning Ticket," occurred in the fall of an election year and was meant to educate students for a democratic citizenship.

A brief account of some of the activities follows. Students in grades K–3 nominated their favorite book characters, and in grades 4–6, students nominated their favorite books. They participated in a variety of campaign activities to promote their class's favorite nominees—by writing and reading their ads to each other, making placards and carrying them through the halls, drawing pictures for hallway walls, sharing their books through oral reading and book talks, making puppets and giving puppet shows, and making collages and art projects. They used real voting machines to register their ballots. After tallying the votes and announcing the grade-level winners and runners-up, a storyteller and puppeteer made special presentations. Videotapes of the entire week's activities allowed each class to see itself on camera and know what others had done.

It was an exciting week for these elementary school students, and both the library media specialist and reading teacher reported high levels of enthusiasm for "Winning Ticket" books, book characters, and reading in general. Other teachers made similar observations and noted that students who had been apathetic in their independent reading were actually reading books, and not just nominated books.

Why begin a discussion of quality in the selection of literature for students with a description of this project? Because as it turned out, "Winning Ticket" books were hardly those that the teachers in this school thought represented quality. Garfield, Clifford, and Roger Rabbit were three of the most popular book characters among younger children. The winning titles among older students were popular paperbacks that students had recently purchased from book club lists.

The library media specialist and reading teacher, though surprised and a little disappointed, rationalized that at least these students were reading and were excited about reading. They took Charlotte Huck's statement (1983) to heart: "I think children do not find the good books unless somebody helps them. That somebody can be a librarian, it can be an enthusiastic teacher, it can be a parent" (p. 3). The results of their collaboration helped these two teachers see that they needed to work with students, classroom teachers, and parents to expose students to quality literature.

## Characteristics of Quality

In a recent study of fifth- and sixth-grade students and classic books, Wilson and Abrahamson (1988) encouraged students to read three or more books from a list of 27 classics that had survived at least one generation. Students were then asked what their favorite book was and why. *Charlotte's Web,* by E. B. White, *The Borrowers,* by Mary Norton, *The Lion, the Witch, and the Wardrobe,* by C. S. Lewis, and *Little House in the Big Woods,* by Laura Ingalls Wilder, were their favorites. Students' comments about their reasons for selecting *Charlotte's Web* suggest that they were able to identify some aspects of quality literature:

- "I liked the story because it is not possible for something like that to happen, yet it seems so real."
- "I loved the story because it touched me. It made me sad in parts and happy in others."
- "I like the book because the animals could talk."
- "It was well written. The author made me feel like I was there with Charlotte and Wilbur." (p. 410)

But when students are not fed quality literature, do they recognize it and seek it out to read themsleves? Experience tells us that many of them do not. They probably need more guidance and direction in differentiating between popular and quality literature than we realize.

Much of what influences children in their book selection and reading habits probably is related to the reading habits of admired peers and teachers. Peers and teachers exert a powerful influence on children's book preferences. For example, at the school described in the beginning of this chapter, where the "Winning Ticket" project occurred, the characters nominated in the early grades reflected books that the teachers had read orally. Children's choices in the later grades reflected popular titles purchased by students through monthly book clubs or at a fall book fair held in the school.

While peers play an important role in determining what children read, teachers have a special impact on shaping children's preferences. At all grade levels, the books teachers introduce to children, read to them, or read themselves are often those that are read or reread by students. Many teachers who read children's books, perhaps during a special time set aside each day when everyone in the class reads, report that children clamor for these books when the teacher finishes them.

In an attempt to provide teachers with titles of popular books children choose to read, each year the International Reading Association (IRA) publishes a list of 100 books, called *Children's Choices*, in the October issue of *The Reading Teacher*. From the 4,000 or so books published yearly for children the IRA and Children's Book Council (CBC) choose 500 books, which are selected as examples of good books for recreational reading and teaching reading. These selections are then tested in five school districts around the country, and children vote for their favorites. In addition to the list, a graded and annotated bibliography of the 100 most popular books is published every year.

In general, as adults we have different criteria for defining quality literature than do children. Two terms that often appear in discussions of quality in children's literature by adult experts are *excellence* and *permanence* (Cullinan, 1989). Excellence is the degree of specialness, tastefulness, or superiority a book possesses. Permanence is the ability of a book to endure over time. In order for a book to stand the test of time it must be memorable and of universal interest. Books that are lasting favorites with children are often high-quality books. With a newly published book it is impossible to know for sure if it has that quality of permanence, but you may be able to make a guess based on your perception of the book's excellence and your personal response to it.

As well as excellence and permanence, *personal appeal* is a third characteristic of quality literature that both adults and children include when they talk about books they especially like. The personal appeal a book has is its power to connect with a reader, to make a link in some way with the experiences, attitudes, or beliefs of the reader. A good book is one an individual can relate to and respond to in some way, whether or not that response is overt and observable. A good book allows us to experience some of it and be changed in some way because of that experience.

While younger children may not be able to articulate quite as clearly as can older students about what appeals to them in a particular book, we can get clues by observing what they read. Younger children often want a particular book read over and over to them, which Don Holdaway (1983) says is a child's way of telling us what is good for him or her: "A good book is one that a child will turn to again and again" (p. 3). Dorothy Butler (1983) believes that "A good children's book is a book which is an experience for a child, an enjoyable experience, a literary experience" (p. 3). So we know that personal response is a critical component in judging what a good book is, especially for younger readers.

Adults are probably more sensitive than children to characteristics of excellence and permanence in children's literature because they have had broader and richer experiences with books and life in general. Children are probably more sensitive to the way a book appeals to them personally, and young children often show this preference by continually turning to favorite books. Often these books are so repetitive or predictable that they are not adult favorites. But it is from rereading them over and over again that children begin to learn language patterns, vocabulary, and the elements of story, among a host of other things.

## Quality in Story

You can help children learn to understand and appreciate quality by identifying a favorite book and focusing on their personal reactions and responses to that book. You can also begin to educate young children to the criteria of excellence and permanence in their favorite books. Help them ask and answer questions like the following about a favorite book:

- Why do you like it?
- What things make it excellent or special?
- How enjoyable is it?
- Is it worth remembering? Why or why not?
- Would other children like and appreciate it?
- Does it have a theme(s) that everyone can understand?

You can also encourage children to judge quality of text by answering questions about some specific story elements. When children are aware of these elements they can more easily respond to a book in terms of them.

Not all genres possess the same elements, as you know from reading Chapter 2. For instance, poetry is best judged by answering the more general questions just mentioned. When you help children judge information books you can ask these questions: How accurate is the information? How current is the book? and What are the author's credentials? Questions such as How accurate is the information? and Did the author do any research? will encourage children to evaluate historical fiction and biography. For further discussions of specific genres the reader is directed to Cullinan (1989), Norton (1987), or Sutherland and Arbuthnot (1986).

The following list can serve as a guide as you help children ask questions that build their awareness of the elements of quality in story. You can help them ask other questions about specific genres by looking back to the discussion in Chapter 2 of the elements of these genres.

*Setting*
- Where and when does the story take place?
- Is it appropriate to the story?

*Characters*
- Who are they and how are they developed?
- Do they seem real, or are they convincing?

*Point of View*
- Who tells the story?
- How does the narrator tell about characters and actions? Is it effective?

*Plot*
- What happens in the story?
- What are the actions? Do they keep you interested?
- What is the conflict or problem? Does the solution make sense?

*Style*
- Is the writing special in some way?
- How does the author express ideas?

*Tone and Mood*
- What is the author's attitude?
- What special feelings do you get from the book?

*Theme*
- What is the main message or big idea of the story?
- What did you learn from the story?
- Can everyone understand and appreciate it?

Whether for an adult or a child, good literature possesses unique language that truly delights the senses and develops the knowledge of those who read it or hear it read. Literature shows children and adults how others live and have lived, and as we understand the lives of others, we develop a better understanding of ourselves and the people in our own world.

Learning to appreciate and love literature should be a positive and enriching part of a child's school experience. Learning to love reading and to enjoy literature as a child can be the start of a lifelong habit that brings pleasure and knowledge (Sutherland & Arbuthnot, 1986). Children are not born with a preference for quality literature, and many will not receive encouragement or experience the joy of reading at home. For these children, the reading beliefs and behaviors you exhibit, as well as your use of literature in the curriculum, are critical. When you use and read books of high literary quality and give children the opportunity to read books of their choice, then you help children develop a taste for quality. Children can then begin to compare and contrast different traits in books and become appreciative readers of quality books.

There are a number of awards that provide recognition for outstanding quality in children's literature. The Newbery Medal was named for John

Newbery, the first English publisher of books for children, and is given yearly to the book considered the most distinguished contribution to literature for children. The Caldecott Medal was named for Randolph Caldecott, an English illustrator, and is given yearly to the most distinguished picture book for children. The Children's Book Council publishes two listings: Outstanding Science Trade Books for Children and Notable Children's Trade Books in the Field of Social Studies. Lists of books that have received some of these awards are found in the Appendix.

## Quality in Pictures

We know that high-quality pictures, as well as high-quality text, contribute to a book's excellence, permanence, and personal appeal. Each of us has observed a child at one time or another who is completely mesmerized by the pictures an illustrator has created to tell a story. Spellbound attention, wide-eyed wonder, eager page turning, exclamations of delight and appreciation, and sometimes even a disinterest in print characterize these events. Pictures that have the power to connect with a reader and communicate messages in these ways possess some aspect of quality, whether the illustrations enhance the content of the story for the reader or elicit children's feelings and responses, or both (see Figure 3.1).

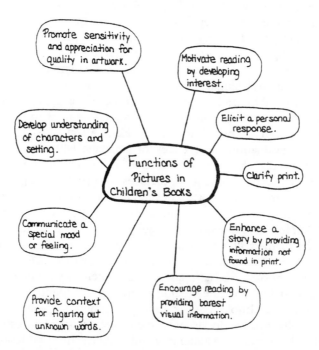

**Figure 3.1** Illustrations and artwork in children's books serve several functions.

Cianciolo (1973) tells us that four major factors affect the ways in which children perceive and evaluate the illustrations in picture books. First, a child's age and stage of cognitive and social development impact what he or she perceives. Second, the way that adults have prepared a child for an experience with a picture book is critical to the child's perception. Third, the child's emotional and psychological state at the time the book is read is important. Fourth, a child's exposure to a book or the number of times a child has looked at the pictures affects his or her interpretation and evaluation. All of these factors account for differences in children's perceptions and responses and the many ways in which pictures in books function for children.

Good pictures have the power to communicate with children and encourage their personal responses to a story. Sometimes pictures tell a story on their own and allow children to understand that story without reading the text, such as the pictures in *King Bidgood's in the Bathtub*, by Audrey Wood. In books like *The Magic Schoolbus at the Waterworks*, by Joanna Cole, pictures enrich the printed story and contain a second story themselves. In other books, like *Owl Moon* by Jane Yolen, the pictures reflect most, but not all, of the story; that is, the text is more complete than the pictures.

Traditionally, there are six aspects of art—color, line, shape, texture, arrangement, and total effect—that contribute to its impact. We should consider these six aspects when we make judgments about the quality of pictures in children's books. We can also help children become sensitive to these aspects of good art as they begin to make their own decisions about the quality of the pictures in the books they read.

While building children's awareness of quality in pictures you can, at the same time, develop their *visual-verbal literacy*. This is a term Stewig (1988) uses to mean the ability to decode messages in pictures and encode these ideas in coherent oral language. While many children can easily tell you which illustrations they prefer, most have trouble expressing why they like certain illustrations. Stewig compares this to the adult who says, "I don't know anything about art, but I know what I like." A lack of background upon which to make evaluations and a lack of language with which to express preferences handicap children and adults alike. But children and adults can learn to identify aspects of quality in pictures they prefer and put a value on them when they are given opportunities to engage in these activities.

Caldecott Medal and Honor books are especially good for developing visual-verbal literacy, as these books are judged and awarded this distinction on the quality of their illustrations. (The Appendix contains a list of these books.) This is not to say that children cannot learn to read pictures from other children's books, a basal reader, or a content text, but the Caldecott books are a valuable and dependable source of excellent illustrations. Although many picture books appear appropriate only for younger children, the thinking skills involved in visual-verbal literacy make pictures from these books challenging for upper elementary and middle school students as well.

You can ask children questions about the pictures in books to help them learn to determine what constitutes the kind of quality that appeals personally to them. Of course, you should remember first that the most important question concerns whether or not the pictures fit the story and communicate information, ideas, a mood, or feelings to the reader. Beyond this basic requirement, you can help children examine the visual message of a picture by exploring the six aspects of art in more depth.

## Color

- What colors do you see?
- Are the colors bright, soft pastels, or something else?
- Where and when are colors used?
- Do the colors match the mood or content of the story or help it in some way?

To help children become sensitive to color and how an illustrator uses it effectively, you can show them a book like *Arrow to the Sun,* by Gerald McDermott, which is done in bright yellows, oranges, and other colors in contrast to black. Or use *Why Mosquitoes Buzz in People's Ears,* by Verna Aardema and illustrated by Leo and Diane Dillon, which is done in pastel shades in contrast to white and black backgrounds. Or use *Frog and Toad Are Friends,* by Arnold Lobel, in which only soft shades of green and brown appear. The comparison web in Figure 3.2 shows how color and the other five aspects of art are used in *Arrow to the Sun,* by Gerald McDermott, and in *Frog and Toad Are Friends,* by Arnold Lobel.

When children can describe the colors in one book's pictures you can show them two or three books that use color in different ways. Then children begin to see similarities and differences and learn how to make comparisons in the way illustrators use color in a variety of books. Comparing observations of two or three books that contrast with each other is often easier than evaluating a single book.

You can help children understand that the bright yellows and oranges of *Arrow* realistically depict the heat and sun of the desert where this Pueblo Indian tale originates. The full range of softer pastel shades used in *Why Mosquitoes* helps give this funny African folktale some of its warmth and humor. In *Frog and Toad,* the soft shades of brown and green are the colors of the two animals on which this quiet story of friendship focuses.

You might ask children why they think the illustrator did not use shades of green and brown for *Arrow* or why *Frog and Toad* was not done in bright primary colors. You might also ask children why they think *Arrow* begins with shades of yellow, orange, and rust, and then the yellow intensifies as the story progresses and other bright colors, such as pink, green, and blue, are added. It is with questions like these that you can help children see how color enhances the content and moods of stories differently.

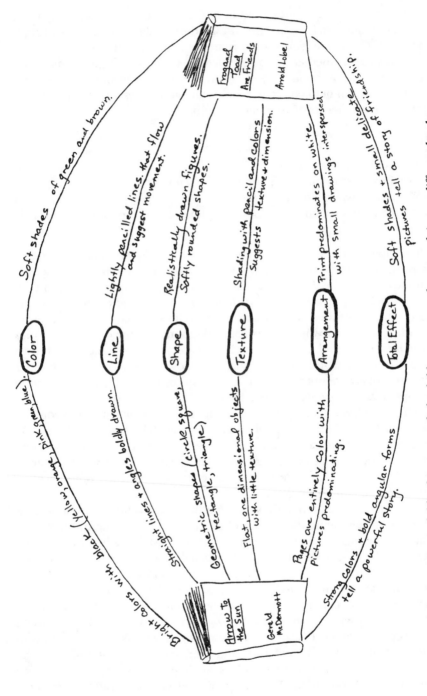

**Figure 3.2**  Creating a web like this one can help children compare the artwork in two different books.

## Line

- Do you see lines in the pictures?
- Are the lines thick or thin, dark or light?
- When and where do you see lines?
- Do the lines do something special for the pictures?

To help children gain an understanding and appreciation of how illustrators use line in their pictures, again you need to ask questions that help children identify how line is used in individual books. Next, children can compare books that contain contrasting uses of line for the variety of ways line is used to communicate with the reader.

You might begin to help children see how some black and white illustrations use line in very obvious ways. Silverstein's books *The Missing Piece* and *A Light in the Attic* are good examples of an illustrator's use of line to create pictures. Silverstein uses no color and little texture but is able to create simple, humorous drawings with black line and white background only. In *Castle,* by David Macaulay, black lines are used to create each illustration of a medieval castle (see Figure 3.3).

**Figure 3.3** Black line drawings are a perfect medium for communicating the architect's or engineer's perspective in the information book, *Castle*, by David Macaulay.

Some illustrators use line to make one-dimensional, cartoon-style drawings that they add color to. James Marshall in both *Miss Nelson Has a Field
Day* and in *The Cut-Ups* (see Figure 3.4) uses black ink lines to create his cartoon-like drawings. James Stevenson in *What's Under My Bed?* seems to use
pencil in cartoon-like pictures that look more obviously sketched. In *How a
Book Is Made,* Aliki Brandenberg uses a delicate line and adds cartoon bubbles in which are printed conversations among the various cat characters.

You can also show children how illustrators use line for the special effect it achieves. In *Python's Party,* Brian Wildsmith uses both thick and thin
lines to give a sense of texture. The thicker, crayon-look lines show the heavy
foliage of the jungle, and the thinner, pen-and-ink lines show the wiry hair of
a goat and the softer fur of a fox. In *Why Mosquitoes Buzz in People's Ears,*
Leo and Diane Dillon use white to outline the bold cut-out shapes and patterns of this African tale. In *Owl Moon,* illustrated by John Schoenherr, the
lines are delicate and soft.

**Figure 3.4** This cartoon-style line drawing with color added from *The Cut-Ups,* by
James Marshall, has appeal for children.

Again, you might ask children some questions that require them to evaluate the effectiveness of an illustrator's use of lines. Ask children if they think Wildsmith's *Python's Party* would be as good if it were done with the cartoon-style drawings that Aliki uses in *How a Book Is Made*. You might ask them how well they think Silverstein's use of line would fit the story of *Why Mosquitoes* or *Owl Moon*.

Asking children a few questions like these can help them begin to become sensitive to how artists use line to communicate and achieve special effects. Once children become aware of this aspect of artwork, they can identify it in almost any illustration and then speculate on how line adds distinctiveness to the content or mood of the story.

## Shape

- Do you see any special shapes?
- What shapes do you see?
- Are shapes distinct or subtle? Simple or ornate? Realistic or abstract? Free-flowing or rigid?
- Do they match the story or help it in some way?

Even very young children can learn to identify the variety of shapes that illustrators use. Initially, you can help children identify distinct shapes—circles, squares, rectangles, and triangles—such as those in *Arrow to the Sun*. You might ask children why they think McDermott used these geometric shapes and whether or not they match the story or help it in some way. In contrast, a book that contains subtle shapes is *Dawn*, in which Uri Shulevitz uses softer, less distinct shapes to communicate the quiet and subdued mood of a peaceful time of day.

Some illustrators create collages that use realistic shapes. Molly Bang, in *The Paper Crane*, uses paper cutouts and a variety of other materials in the collages that accompany the story of a paper crane that comes alive and changes the fortunes of an old man. Ezra Jack Keats, in *The Snowy Day* and other works, uses oils and collage to tell simple stories about Peter, a young black child. Eric Carle's artwork in *Why Noah Chose the Dove*, by Isaac Bashevis Singer, uses paint and collage and a touch of the abstract to create bold but simply shaped animals and people. The shapes in these collages might be compared to the use of shapes in *Dawn* to help children understand and appreciate the variety of possibilities an illustrator has for using shape to clarify or enhance a story. The web in Figure 3.5 compares the color, shape, effect, and texture aspects of the collage art in *The Paper Crane* and *The Snowy Day*.

You can introduce children to other examples of how artists use shape. Graeme Base's *Animalia*, an animal alphabet book with a surrealistic look, contains a myriad of ornately detailed animals and objects on each page that

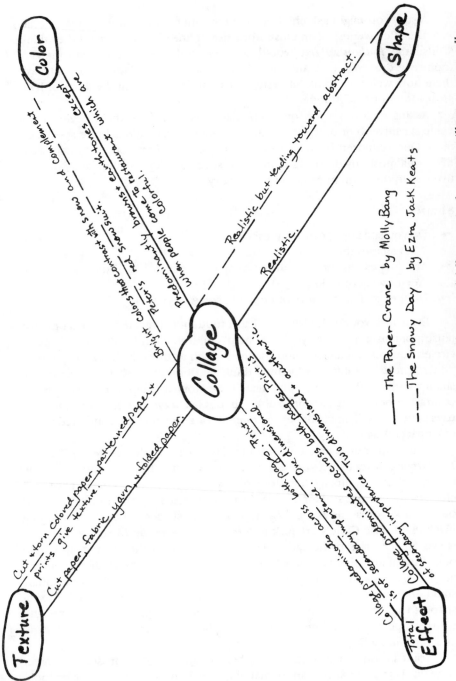

**Figure 3.5** A web such as this helps children identify the similarities and differences in the way two illustrators use collage.

**Figure 3.6** Realistic shapes and soft texture help tell this story of a magical train ride to the North Pole on Christmas eve in Chris Van Allsburg's book *The Polar Express*.

all begin with the same letter of the alphabet. Mitsumasa Anno uses abstract shapes as an appropriate complement to the content of *Anno's Alphabet: An Adventure in Imagination*. Chris Van Allsburg, in *The Polar Express*, uses realistic shapes and forms in muted pastels to tell a story about the meaning of Christmas (see Figure 3.6). To help children understand the way these artists use shape, you can ask why they think Base's detailed shapes fit his subject, or how Anno's abstract shapes allow the reader to pretend and imagine more easily than photographs might allow.

## Texture

- Do the surfaces of the things in the pictures look different from each other in any way?
- Do objects look like they feel a certain way? Rough or smooth? Furry or jagged? Solid and heavy or light?
- What makes the objects or pictures look like they might feel a certain way?

To help children appreciate and understand how an illustrator creates the visual sensation of feeling or texture, you can first show them pictures that contain little or no texture. A book like *The Missing Piece,* by Shel Silverstein, with its simple outline drawings, shows children effective art in which no texture has been created.

Then you can share pictures in which the illustrator manipulates color, line, or shape to create texture or a pattern that suggests texture. In *Owl Moon,* John Schoenherr uses many fine lines to give the bark on the trees a rough look and the owl's feathers a soft, full, ruffled look. In *The Snail's Spell,* by Joanne Ryder, Lynne Cherry uses many fine lines and shades of colors to create a real-looking turtle with a plated shell, a toad with rough, bumpy skin, furry chipmunks, and a snail with soft skin and a smooth shell (see Figure 3.7). Shades of color combined with geometric patterns in *Arrow to the Sun* give depth to pictured objects in this story. In *Python's Party,* Brian Wildsmith expertly combines layers of brilliant color, fine lines, and smudged, indistinct shapes to create scenes of the jungle and wild animals that are effectively textured. With pencil drawings in tones of black, gray, and white, Chris Van Allsburg achieves wonderful texture and realism in *Jumanji* that include hairy monkeys, an exploding volcano, and a snake and chair upholstery that share the same bold pattern.

The mediums of collage and woodcut also allow an illustrator to give the sensation of texture. Ezra Jack Keats, Leo Lionni, Eric Carle, and Molly Bang

On the top of your head
you have two long feelers.
You can stretch and stretch
these feelers
till they look like
long, long horns.

**Figure 3.7** Soft natural colors and fine lines depict the world of a snail in a garden in *The Snail's Spell,* written by Joanne Ryder and illustrated by Lynne Cherry.

**Figure 3.8** Ezra Jack Keats uses a variety of patterns and textures in the collages in his story *The Snowy Day.*

all use collage to achieve dimensionality and visual differences in objects. Lionni uses collages composed of crayoned shapes, torn newspaper, wallpaper, and tissue paper overlays with color to provide texture in *Frederick* and *Alexander and the Wind-Up Mouse.* Marcia Brown in *Once a Mouse* uses woodcuts in subdued colors to portray texture. Ed Emberley in *Drummer Hoff* uses simple, three-color stylized woodcuts to accompany this tale. Figure 3.8 shows Ezra Jack Keats' use of collage in *The Snowy Day.*

By giving children opportunities to look at and compare different illustrators and their styles, you encourage their awareness of how color, line, and shape are manipulated to achieve texture. Then children will better appreciate the pictures in the books they read and the impact these illustrations have on the content and mood of stories.

## Arrangement

- Where do you find the print on the pages?
- Where do you find the pictures on the pages?
- Do you think the print and pictures go together in a special way for some reason?

Sometimes the arrangement of pictures and text in a book seems to have no rhyme or reason, but often with close observation, you and your children can discover that there is a special design or composition to a book. Caldecott Medal books such as *Arrow to the Sun* by Gerald McDermott in Figure 3.9 and Caldecott Honor books are especially good to use when you begin to help build your children's knowledge of arrangement, or composition. These books are chosen specifically for excellence in artwork, and arrangement is often carefully orchestrated.

Maurice Sendak's *Where the Wild Things Are,* one of the most popular and best-selling books for younger children, possesses an arrangement of print and pictures that enhances the story. Print is found on a white back-

**Figure 3.9** Bright colors and geometric shapes similar to the artwork of native Americans of the Southwest fill entire pages and predominate over the text of Gerald McDermott's *Arrow to the Sun.*

ground on the left side of each double page from the beginning of the story, when Max is at home in his bedroom, until he sails "in and out of weeks and almost over a year to where the wild things are." Initially, pictures occur on the right side of each double page, with the first picture quite small, but they increase in size as the story progresses. By the time Max is ready to sail away, the picture has become so large that it covers the entire right page and a third of the left page. When Max reaches the land of the wild things and while he is there among the monsters, the print appears across the bottom third of both double pages and pictures are found across the upper two-thirds of both facing pages. After Max makes friends and is proclaimed king, the "wild rumpus" is shown on three entire double facing pages with no print at all. When Max sails back home, the print again appears on the left-hand side of each page, with pictures gradually shrinking in size until he finds a hot dinner waiting on the table in his room.

Sendak uses the size and placement of pictures and the placement of print as the story progresses to heighten the reader's involvement in the journey that results in Max's confrontation and conquest of the wild things. Sendak carefully arranges text and pictures to convey sequence of events and mood in this fantasy.

As you help children notice the way a few good books are designed, they will more easily be able to see the design and composition in other books they read. Understanding how authors and illustrators arrange print and pictures can help children appreciate and articulate their reasons for preferring one book over another.

## Total Effect

- How do color, line, shape, texture, print, type, pictures, end papers, and cover fit together?
- Are they all related in some special way? How?
- Do all the artistic aspects blend together to create a special design or composition?

The total effect or impact a book has on a reader is determined first by the way in which the story is complemented by the illustrations and format, and secondly, by how the reader is able to relate to the whole package. Sometimes the effect a book has is clear from the look of wonder or smile of satisfaction on a child's face. Sometimes effect can be measured by the repeated requests or reading of a particular book. Sometimes effect can be seen in the number and type of questions asked or observations made.

We can teach children about the elements that contribute to the effect or impact of a book. Again, good examples of the total effect of content interwoven with the aspects of art discussed previously are often found in Caldecott Medal and Honor books.

Don't overlook the possibility of enlisting the help of your school's art teacher in developing children's understanding and appreciation of how color, line, shape, texture, and arrangement combine to make pictures and the books in which they occur appealing. With a background knowledge in art, an art teacher can help deepen your children's understanding and sensitivity about what makes high-quality pictures and books.

## Summary

Quality literature can be described as books that possess excellence, permanence, and personal appeal. Adult choices of quality literature often differ from books children identify as their favorites or the books that are most popular. Helping children understand what makes a quality story and how color, line, shape, texture, arrangement, and the story itself affect the quality of the pictures can help them appreciate, understand, and enjoy literature.

## REFERENCES

Butler, D. (1983). In *What's A Good Book?* Weston, CT: Weston Woods.

Cianciolo, P. (Ed.). (1973). *Picture Books for Children.* Chicago: American Library Association.

Cullinan, B. E. (1989). *Literature and the Child.* New York: Harcourt Brace Jovanovitch.

Holdaway, D. (1983). In *What's A Good Book?* Weston, CT: Weston Woods.

Huck, C. S. (1983). In *What's A Good Book?* Weston, CT: Weston Woods.

Huck, C. S., Helper, S., & Hickman, J. (1987). *Children's Literature in the Elementary School* (4th ed.). New York: Holt, Rinehart & Winston.

Norton, D. E. (1987). *Through the Eyes of a Child: An Introduction to Children's Literature* (2nd ed.). Columbus, OH: Merrill.

Stewig, J. W. (1988). *Children and Literature* (2nd ed.). Boston: Houghton Mifflin.

Sutherland, Z., & Arbuthnot, M. H. (1986). *Children and Books* (7th ed.). Glenview, IL: Scott, Foresman.

Wilson, P. J., & Abrahamson, R. F. (1988). What children's literature classics do children really enjoy? *The Reading Teacher, 41*(4), 406–411.

### Children's Literature

Aardema, V. (1975). *Why Mosquitoes Buzz in People's Ears.* New York: Scholastic.

Aliki (Brandenberg). (1986). *How a Book Is Made.* New York: Harper & Row.

Allard, H. (1985). *Miss Nelson Has a Field Day.* New York: Scholastic.

Anno, M. (1975). *Anno's Alphabet: An Adventure in Imagination.* New York: Harper & Row.

Bang, M. (1985). *The Paper Crane.* New York: Scholastic.

Base, G. (1987). *Animalia.* London: Harry N. Abrams.

Brown, M. (1982). *Once a Mouse.* New York: Macmillan.

Cole, J. (1986). *The Magic Schoolbus at the Waterworks.* New York: Scholastic.

Emberley, E., & Emberley, B. (1967). *Drummer Hoff.* Englewood Cliffs, NJ: Prentice-Hall.

Keats, E. J. (1962). *The Snowy Day.* New York: Scholastic.

Lewis, C. S. (1950). *The Lion, the Witch, and the Wardrobe.* New York: Macmillan.

Lionni, L. (1967). *Frederick.* New York: Pantheon.

_____. (1970). *Alexander and the Wind-Up Mouse.* New York: Pantheon.

Lobel, A. (1971). *Frog and Toad Are Friends.* New York: Scholastic.

Marshall, J. (1984). *The Cut-Ups.* New York: Viking.

Macaulay, D. (1977). *Castle.* New York: Houghton Mifflin.

McDermott, G. (1974). *Arrow to the Sun.* New York: Viking.

Norton, M. (1953). *The Borrowers.* New York: Harcourt Brace Jovanovitch.

Ryder, J. (1988). *The Snail's Spell.* New York: Penguin.

Sendak, M. (1963). *Where the Wild Things Are.* New York: Harper & Row.

Shulevitz, U. (1974). *Dawn.* New York: Farrar, Straus, & Giroux.

Silverstein, S. (1976). *The Missing Piece.* New York: Harper & Row.

_____. (1981). *A Light in the Attic.* New York: Harper & Row.

Singer, I. B. (1987). *Why Noah Chose the Dove.* New York: Farrar, Straus, & Giroux.

Stevenson, J. (1983). *What's Under My Bed?* New York: Greenwillow.

Van Allsburg, C. (1981). *Jumanji.* Boston: Houghton Mifflin.

_____. (1982). *Ben's Dream.* New York: Houghton Mifflin.

_____. (1985). *The Polar Express.* Boston: Houghton Mifflin.

White, E. B. (1952). *Charlotte's Web.* New York: Harper.

Wilder, L. I. (1932). *Little House in the Big Woods.* New York: Harper.

Wildsmith, B. (1974). *Python's Party.* New York: Franklin Watts.

Wood, A. (1985). *King Bidgood's in the Bathtub.* New York: Harcourt Brace Jovanovitch.

Yolen, J. (1987). *Owl Moon.* New York: Scholastic.

# chapter 4

# Sharing Literature

This chapter takes a brief look at some ways to share literature with children and gives suggestions for integrating webbing into your plans. The ideas presented here are meant as a starting place for using webs to make your sharing more effective and to stimulate your children's understanding, enjoyment, and appreciation of literature.

## Reading Aloud

Much sharing of literature that is done in classrooms occurs when teachers read aloud to students. Most primary-grade teachers establish a special time each day when they read aloud to their class, and this storytime is usually looked forward to with eagerness. Teachers who read daily to children report that when they overlook reading aloud for one reason or another, children miss it and voice their complaints. Reading aloud may be less common in intermediate grades, perhaps because teachers feel that students are too old for the practice or they feel the pressures of a crowded curriculum and find little time for it. But time for reading aloud can and should be set aside at all grade levels, since it is pleasurable and relaxing as well as potentially beneficial in a number of other ways.

There are many benefits that come from reading aloud to children. First, listening to stories read aloud is a pleasurable and enjoyable experience. Mendoza (1985) found that 94 percent of primary students and 73 percent of intermediate students enjoyed being read to. Frick (1986) contends that reading aloud to middle-grade students is just as important as it is with lower elementary-grade children. She notes that listening skills improve, motivation to read increases, it inspires writing, and it is a pleasurable and relaxing experience. Through reading aloud, children can use their imaginations and broaden their experiences as they hear about places, people, and things they might not have the chance to learn about otherwise. Hearing books read aloud can answer personal questions children have or put their uncertainties to rest by affirming their own experiences. Children can escape from the realities of everyday life and become involved in satisfying and enjoyable experiences.

As well as enjoyment, children can gain an appreciation of good literature and language use by being read to. You can select quality books to read, and through your involvement and direction help children appreciate why the books you read are good. Reading aloud from a variety of genres and styles of writing within one genre exposes children to many different language patterns and writing styles. It also introduces children to genres they might not normally choose to read themselves, such as historical fiction or biography. Just as children learn to value their experiences with literature through read-aloud times, they also learn to appreciate and value the kinds of books you expose them to.

Both theory and research support the notion that reading aloud results in measurable benefits to learning. Reading achievement, measured in terms of comprehension, vocabulary, decoding abilities, and readiness, improves as a result of listening to literature read orally (Cullinan, Jaggar, & Strickland, 1974; Kimmel & Segel, 1983; Walker & Kuerbitz, 1979). Reading aloud allows both nonreaders and readers to develop good reading behaviors. As well as learning about themselves and each other from listening to literature, children's knowledge bases broaden, their vocabularies increase, they develop a sense of story, and they learn to listen. For many children, the only way they will experience good books is if someone reads to them.

## Guidelines

When you read orally, there are several things that promote children's enjoyment, appreciation, and learning and ensure that your oral reading is effective and interesting. What follows are eight guidelines (Bromley, 1988) for selecting literature and reading it aloud.

1. *Choose literature you enjoy that is well-written.* Your enjoyment and involvement with a story communicates itself and more easily draws an emotional response from children. In addition, when you choose a well-written selection, one with a fairly fast-paced storyline and smooth-flowing syntax, reading aloud is more comfortable (Sutherland & Arbuthnot, 1986).

Share a wide range of reading materials from every genre, and seek out new books and stories so that you do not always share old favorites year after year. A blend of old and new is a treat for you and your children.

Consult an anthology of children's literature or a library media specialist if you are looking for books to read on special topics. References such as *Children's Books in Print* and *The Bookfinder*, found in children's libraries, and books such as *Adventuring with Books: A Booklist for PreK–Grade 6* (Monson, 1985) and *Children's Literature: An Issues Approach* (Rudman, 1984) provide annotations for books according to topics. *The New Read-Aloud Handbook* (Trelease, 1989) contains annotations of good fiction books and *Eyeopeners* (Kobrin, 1988) contains annotations of good nonfiction for reading aloud.

2. *Read the literature before sharing it with children.* To avoid surprise or embarrassment over a concept or word that is offensive, read the story or book first before sharing it. If you are uncomfortable with language or ideas in a book, either omit those particular sections or do not read the book at all. If the use of questionable material is justifiable, then inquire about your school's policy on censorship and consider obtaining parental permission before sharing the material.

3. *Practice the piece of literature.* Especially if oral reading is new for you, practicing a selection before reading it to a group is a must. Familiarity with a story ensures its enjoyment by both you and your children. Reading, skimming, or previewing a book or story has other advantages. You determine the author's style and tone, make mental note of how to interpret various charac-

ters, and identify critical points in the story so that you know where to stop and start for best effect. As you gain experience and confidence in reading orally, you may find that skimming or previewing suffices. An exception to this is poetry, which should *always* be practiced before reading aloud since it is written for the ear and the mind.

Ross (1980) believes that a story should *never* be read aloud unless it has first been read aloud to oneself. If you practice in front of a mirror you will discover how to use eyes, voice, and facial expressions effectively. By varying the intonation, juncture, stress, and pace you create mood, heighten suspense, and generally read with better expression.

Using inappropriate phrasing or stumbling over words creates a potential comprehension problem for those who listen to you and also dampens interest. Fluent reading is not only more comfortable to hear, it also demonstrates a model of good oral reading for children.

4. *Arrange the setting so children can comfortably hear and see you.* Position yourself front and center so that children face you or can comfortably turn to see and hear you. Sit on a chair or desk so that you too are comfortable and enjoy the reading. When you read to a small group, sit on a low chair and hold the book close to or at the children's eye level. Minimize distractions so that every child enjoys and appreciates what is read.

5. *Show pictures in ways that enhance the story.* If you read a picture book, either master the art of reading from the side so that children can see pictures at all times or read the text first and then show the pictures. You can also show the pictures first to prepare for the text and not show the pictures while reading, and then let children look at the pictures later as they reread the book. Or use a combination of methods. Since so much of a picture book's appeal is the pictures, place yourself close enough to children that they can see the pictures. Even older children enjoy seeing the few illustrations in books written for them. Walk the book around the room for everyone to see these smaller drawings, since this additional visual input enriches and broadens responses. The audience and story determine how best to share text and pictures.

6. *Encourage reexamination and rereading of the book.* After you read a book, children enjoy rereading all or parts even though they have just heard it. Let them examine pictures closely. When making the book available, include it in a display with other books by the same author and illustrator or other books on the same topic.

Working with some books in depth and reading the same story on several occasions to your children broadens and strengthens response (Beaver, 1982). Just as adults reread favorite poems or novels, so do children enjoy hearing stories read to them more than once. Deeper insights into characters and events develop when children are already familiar with plot structure. Also, an author's particular style is sometimes not evident or appreciated until the second or third reading.

7. *Observe children's responses.* Watch for spontaneous responses such as a smile, grimace, rapt attention, or other changes in facial expression that coincide with characters' actions, story mood, or plot. These responses signal emotional involvement with the story and are the basis for interpreting and evaluating literature. Accept, encourage, and extend these observed responses with questions and discussion when the situation is right (Sutherland & Arbuthnot, 1986).

An observed response or remark a child makes, such as a comment about a setting that sounds like his grandmother's house or a value judgment about how one should act in the real world compared to a character's actions, often triggers discussion. The responses you note and extend are often critical to the development of deeper and more insightful responses.

8. *Be aware of reasons for poor listening.* If children are not listening or are disruptive while you read, ask yourself some questions. Do you like the story? Is it well-written, interesting, and fast-paced enough to maintain attention? Can children understand it? Were you familiar with the story before you read it? Did you practice it? Is your voice well-modulated and do you use appropriate facial expressions? Are conditions in the classroom conducive to listening? If your answers are affirmative, then perhaps you need to talk with children about how to listen effectively or place disruptive children close to you and the book.

Now let's look at some classrooms where literature is shared orally with children and explore some possibilities for using webs while reading orally to enhance this sharing.

## Book Sharing with Webs

■ In a first-grade classroom, a group of children participate with their teacher to tell the story *The Grey Lady and the Strawberry Snatcher,* by Molly Bang. They look closely at the pictures and talk together to identify what is happening.

■ A class of third-graders sit quietly as their teacher reads *Abraham Lincoln* by I. and E. D'Aulaire. She stops occasionally to make comments and ask questions and students offer observations and opinions.

■ In a sixth-grade classroom, a teacher reads from *Tuck Everlasting* by Natalie Babbitt, stopping occasionally to ask students to identify similes, metaphors, and other elements of style that Babbitt uses.

In each of these situations, students became involved with literature as they responded to what they heard and saw. How might these teachers use webbing to share literature more effectively and promote their students' understanding and enjoyment? Here are some ideas.

The first-grade teacher might create two simple webs, such as those in Figure 4.1, to introduce the characters before children look at the book. After reading the story together, children can add other descriptive words to the webs and then share these webs in a retelling of the story to the class. The webs extend and reinforce vocabulary and allow a book that is too small for whole-class sharing to be enjoyed by everyone together.

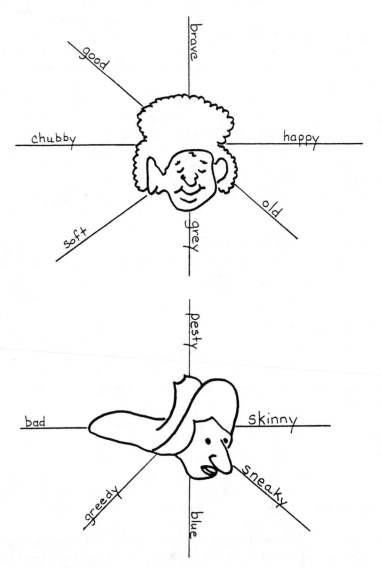

**Figure 4.1** These vocabulary webs for *The Grey Lady and the Strawberry Snatcher,* by Molly Bang, can introduce the story and children can add words after they hear it.

Before reading to her third-grade class, this teacher could create a web such as the one in Figure 4.2. She can use it to introduce the story and children can add important occurrences to the web at each stop on Abe's journey from the wilderness to the White House. A web like this one can help students remember and clarify the major events in Lincoln's life that helped him become president. If the book is read in conjunction with a social studies unit on the Civil War, for example, children can add other information to the web as they integrate what they learn from their content text with the knowledge they gain from literature.

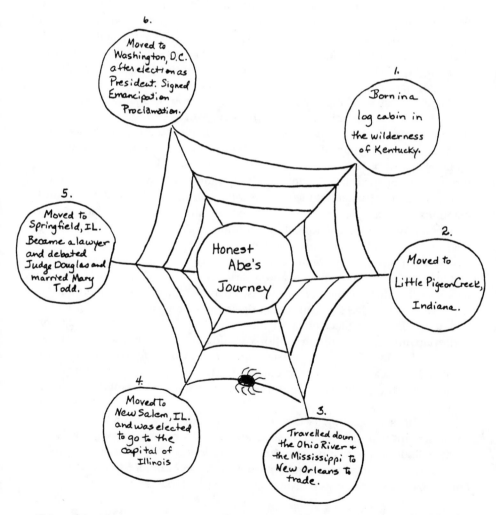

**Figure 4.2** This web provides an overview of the setting for I. and E. D'Aulaire's story *Abraham Lincoln*, which can be shared before oral reading.

The sixth-grade teacher might share the elements of "point of view," "style," "setting," and "characters" from the web in Figure 4.3 to set the stage before reading *Tuck Everlasting*. Students can then add the information on "plot" and "themes" as they listen to the story. This web of literature elements can serve as a basis for a written book report as well as ensuring comprehension and promoting discussion.

There are many other ways to use webbing as you share literature. You can use webbing before reading to assess and organize the knowledge children have about a certain topic. By creating webs before reading or listening, you provide a framework into which children can put new information and ideas that come from what they hear. Webbing allows for new information to be attached to known information, and thus ensures comprehension and learning. Webbing before reading also plays a role in developing interest in the book to be read. In many cases, the more students know about a plot, theme, setting, or characters, the better the chances are they will want to hear the book, listen carefully as it is read, and understand and remember what they have heard.

You can use webbing in a number of ways as you read aloud to children. Creation of a vocabulary web or a web of key words can focus attention on new vocabulary as it occurs in a story or reinforce it after the story has been read. Students can identify important words and classify them in different sections of a web. As students hear a story, they can make a web to represent the relationships among concepts or ideas in the selection, chapter, or story. As a web is constructed, students have opportunities to discuss events and emotions, for example, which can help ensure that they understand what is happening in a story. Then, as they continue to listen to a story, what they hear tends to make more sense to them.

You can also use webbing after reading as a way of summarizing and highlighting important concepts and information. Webs that contain the elements of literature, sequence of events, characters' feelings, causes and effects, and so on give students visual diagrams of critical story components and allow them to reflect on what they have heard. Making interpretations and evaluating stories and an author's writing style is thus made easier for students. Following reading, students can predict what will happen next in a story and make a web of these predictions. This web can establish purposes for listening and focus listening during the next day's read-aloud session as well.

Prior to asking students to use webbing with their own silent reading, you will want to use webbing in a variety of ways before, during, and after reading aloud to them. It is important that students feel comfortable creating webs with you and then in small groups with peers before being asked to finish a partially created web or make their own independently.

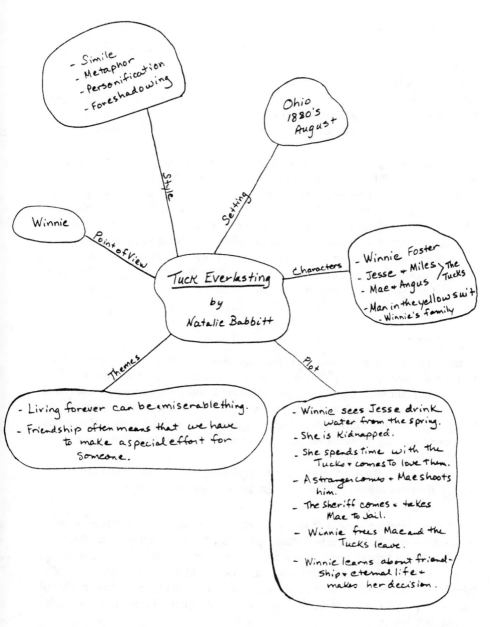

**Figure 4.3** Presenting part of a web of *Tuck Everlasting* by Natalie Babbitt before reading will set the stage for the story, and students can add information as they listen.

## *Storytelling*

Storytelling is another excellent way to share literature. Many teachers who enjoy reading and read often to children have a fear of storytelling. But contrary to popular belief, you do not need special talents or skills to be a storyteller. If you stop to think about it, you practice storytelling every time you tell someone about something you have seen or done. Storytelling is just retelling a story, whether an actual event or a tale once told by someone else and now written down.

Storytelling provides a different forum for sharing literature than does reading aloud. When telling a story, you can use your hands and body in ways that are not possible if you are holding a book. A storyteller also can use drama and props to add interest and power to a story. A storyteller, unlike a reader, can hold the audience's attention with uninterrupted eye contact. A storyteller can make print come alive for children by removing the print from the interaction that occurs between the reader and the story. For these reasons, telling stories has a special place in the sharing of literature and you may want to explore it with your students.

## Guidelines

A number of the guidelines for reading aloud also apply to storytelling. Choose a story you enjoy that is well-written, read and practice the story so you are familiar with it and your presentation is smooth, vary your voice and pacing for maximum effect, arrange the setting so that children comfortably hear and see you, and observe children's responses and be aware of reasons for poor listening. Remember, you do not need to memorize a story or tell it word for word.

When you tell a story, there are several things that ensure effective storytelling. Bromley (1988) outlines five guidelines for storytelling:

1. *Choose stories with a linear or circular plot and strong characterization.* A story with a clearly defined plot that builds steadily to a climax is best. Focus on folktales at first since they are short and contain fast-paced action and characters with one basic trait. Moss and Stott (1986) group folktales by the physical journeys characters make: (1) linear stories that begin in one setting and conclude in another and (2) circular stories that conclude where they began.

2. *Learn the story as a whole.* Read the entire story several times, preferably aloud. Then close the book, introduce the characters and setting, and tell the actions in the sequence in which they happen. Though your retelling does not include such information, if you imagine what your characters look

like, how the characters might act in different situations, and how each character feels about the other characters, your portrayal will be more vivid during the retelling. If the story uses repetitions or unique wording, memorize these as a way to help retain the story style and original flavor. Remember that communicating the meaning of the story is the most important thing.

3. *Allow time each day to practice.* It may take a few hours to learn a folktale and somewhat longer to learn a narrative tale. Practice that is spaced out over two to three weeks is more effective than trying to learn something all at once. Use a mirror to watch yourself, and then practice on a friend who can give you important feedback. A tape recorder is helpful and a video camera even more so because with it you can evaluate the effect of body language as well as your voice.

4. *Slow down and breathe.* The single most helpful suggestion for beginning storytellers may be to slow down (Farnsworth, 1981). The listener better comprehends the spoken word and the speaker produces with more clarity when pace slows. If tension makes you speak quickly and garble your words, stop and regulate your breath intake and outflow before you continue. Often, just taking two or three deep breaths before you begin helps pace your delivery.

5. *Use your voice and body naturally.* Observe yourself in a mirror and have a friend observe what you do with your body during storytelling. Do your head, eyes, hands and arms move to emphasize points? You help children visualize the story when you raise a hand to shade your eyes as you look into the distance while saying, "And he looked up the road and he looked down the road." Let your hands establish some of the story emphasis by moving them naturally to strengthen points, depict actions, and add interest.

Children can also learn to tell stories themselves using these guidelines. As well as folktales, wordless picture books and predictable books with repetitive language or cumulative story events make for easier storytelling.

## Storytelling with Webs

Many teachers find that telling a story from the pictures in a book helps them feel comfortable as a storyteller. For example, a pre-kindergarten teacher believed strongly in daily read-aloud periods and tried to read to her class from the first day of school in September. But she found that the children were not ready, interested, or able to sit still and listen to even the simplest of books. So she began by telling the story in her own words and using the pictures to support her storytelling. She found that this was successful and used it to prepare her children for listening to formal read-aloud sessions. When her children were able to listen, one of the books she read was *Whale in the Sky*, by Anne Siberell, a folktale about the origin of the totem pole. She then created the picture web of events in Figure 4.4 to aid their recall of what they had heard and to support their retellings of the story to each other.

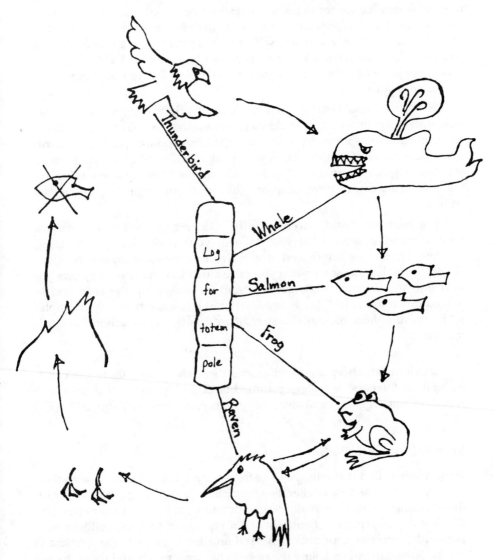

**Figure 4.4** The fast-paced action and few characters in this northwest Indian folktale, *Whale in the Sky* by Ann Siberell, lend themselves to storytelling with a picture web.

You can also use a web to enhance your telling of a story. A standard literature web or plot web provides you with all the necessary elements to include as you relate the story to a group of children. You can use puppets, flannel board figures, or other visuals to introduce a story, maintain interest, strengthen a point, or otherwise enrich your children's understanding and appreciation of stories you tell.

Webs can help children of all ages become storytellers. When telling stories themselves, children gain confidence by first reading a book, then creating a web of important ideas and information either by drawing pictures or using written words and phrases, and finally telling the story by referring to the web. Webs can help ensure that the storytelling is organized and inclusive. Often, a few ideas included on the web will trigger children's memories and they will be able to relate much richer and more elaborate stories than they might if they relied on their memory alone.

## Giving Booktalks

You can encourage your students to read books that support their content-area units of study and quality books that you think your students will enjoy by giving booktalks. A *booktalk* is a short presentation designed to help someone learn about a book and be inspired to read it. Booktalks are enthusiastic personal pitches to sell books, using a combination of verbal and visual modes in no prescribed format. You may or may not have read the books you talk about and introduce to your class. Of course, the most successful booktalks are those done on books you have read and genuinely like. The rationale for booktalks is twofold. First, many children are immediately interested in a book their teacher suggests or has read and likes. Second, a teacher can share many books quickly with a class through booktalks and pique student interest in reading.

One sixth-grade teacher found that booktalks paid dividends in student interest and increased the amount of actual reading they did. She asked the school librarian to identify a number of books to accompany her class's social studies unit on ancient Egyptian civilization. She then spent several minutes each day introducing a few of these books to her class in short booktalks. By skimming, surveying, and sometimes reading an entire book, she employed a variety of booktalk ideas, some of which are listed below.

- Use a web to discuss the elements of the story.
- Introduce an author and tell about his or her special expertise with the topic.
- Use a theme and share several books on a topic.
- Show a picture that relates to the book in some way.
- Draw a web, picture, or map that fits the story.

- Share a real object that is relevant to the story.
- Use a puppet to introduce the plot or characters.
- Read a first paragraph or interesting part.
- Make a web of key vocabulary words.
- Create an acrostic with the title or character's name.
- Roleplay one of the characters.
- Read information on the book's flap orally.

Once you have modeled booktalks, students can do their own. When a child gives a booktalk it should be done on a book the child has read and wants to endorse. Children will know these books well and can talk easily about them. A web is one method of telling a little about a book to sell it. With a web, such as the one in Figure 4.5 made by a fourth-grade student, a booktalk can be organized and presented in a somewhat structured and related way. Webbing gives students practice in representing key information and relationships in a concise visual display. As students become comfortable using webs to structure their presentations, they become more adept at using webs to structure their writing as well.

## Summary

When reading aloud, storytelling, or giving booktalks, there are some basic guidelines to keep in mind to be most effective. Whether listening to stories or telling their own stories, children's understanding and enjoyment of books

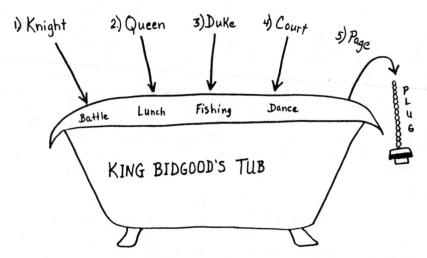

**Figure 4.5** This web, made by a fourth-grader to use in a booktalk she gave before her class, contains both important vocabulary and the sequence of events in Audrey Wood's story, *King Bidgood's in the Bathtub*.

can be enhanced when webs are used. Webs used by teachers and children can promote children's listening and reading and have rich potential for sharing literature effectively.

## REFERENCES

Cullinan, B., Jaggar, A., & Strickland, D. (1974). Language expansion for black children in the primary grades: A research report. *Young Children, 29,* 98–112.

Beaver, J. M. (1982). Say it! Over and over. *Language Arts, 59*(2), 143–152.

Bromley, K. (1988). *Language Arts: Exploring Connections.* Boston: Allyn and Bacon.

Farnsworth, K. (1981). Storytelling in the classroom: Not an impossible dream. *Language Arts, 58*(2), 162–167.

Frick, H. A. (1986). The value of sharing stories orally with middle grade students. *Journal of Reading, 29*(4), 300–303.

Kimmel, M. M., & Segel, E. (1983). *For Reading Out Loud!* New York: Delacorte.

Kobrin, B. (1988). *Eyeopeners.* New York: Penguin.

Mendoza, A. (1985). Reading to children: Their preferences. *The Reading Teacher, 38*(6), 522–527.

Monson, D. L. (1985). *Adventuring with Books: A Booklist for PreK–Grade 6.* Urbana, IL: National Council of Teachers of English.

Moss, A., & Stott, J. C. (1986). *The Family of Stories: An Anthology of Children's Literature.* New York: Holt, Rinehart & Winston.

Ross, R. R. (1980). *Storyteller* (2nd ed.). Columbus, OH: Merrill.

Rudman, M. K. (1984). *Children's Literature: An Issues Approach* (2nd ed.). New York: Longman.

Sutherland, Z., & Arbuthnot, M. H. (1986). *Children and Books* (7th ed.). Glenview, IL: Scott, Foresman.

Trelease, J. (1989). *The New Read-Aloud Handbook.* New York: Penguin.

Walker, G. H., & Kuerbitz, I. E. (1979). Reading to preschoolers as an aid to successful beginning reading. *Reading Improvement, 16,* 149–154.

*Children's Literature*

Babbitt, N. (1975). *Tuck Everlasting.* New York: Farrar, Straus, & Giroux.

Bang, M. (1980). *The Grey Lady and the Strawberry Snatcher.* New York: Four Winds.

D'Aulaire, I., & D'Aulaire, E. (1957). *Abraham Lincoln.* Garden City, NY: Doubleday.

Siberell, A. (1982). *Whale in the Sky.* New York: Dutton.

Wood, A. (1985). *King Bidgood's in the Bathtub.* San Diego: Harcourt Brace Jovanovitch.

# chapter 5

# Responding to Literature

This chapter explores differences in children's responses to literature. It discusses ways in which webbing can aid in the creation of a literate environment, in reading stories interactively with children, and in engaging them in drama. You will see how webs can help structure responses and serve as springboards for different kinds of responses.

## Differences in Response

Both research and theory tell us that responses to literature grow from interactions with print and are highly personal (Mikkelson, 1984; Purves & Monson, 1984; Solsken, 1985; Sutherland & Arbuthnot, 1986; Tchudi, 1985). Rosenblatt (1985) identifies two different kinds of personal response. One is an *efferent response*, in which the reader focuses on the information to be acquired in the reading. The second is an *aesthetic response*, in which the reader attends to what is read and what he is living through as he reads. Rosenblatt believes that when a transaction occurs between a reader and a text, it falls somewhere on a continuum between efferent and aesthetic.

What one child identifies with and remembers is often quite different than what another sees as most important or memorable. Each child brings his own special background and experiences to literature and so each child can potentially have a different literary transaction and response to a story or poem.

Children interact emotionally with literature and often respond in ways that are immediate and clearly observable. When a six-year-old and four-year-old listened to the circular story *If You Give a Mouse a Cookie*, by Laura Numeroff, the six-year-old enthusiastically retold the story by looking at the last picture, which includes objects from each of the important events in the story. When he finished his retelling, without encouragement he told a sequel, another adventure about the mouse who receives a toy motorcycle from the boy. This child's obvious delight in the mouse's escapades and his understanding of the story and how to link a chain of events are clear from his response.

Children often respond in ways that are not so immediate or observable, however. The four-year-old who listened to the story, along with her six-year-old brother, was riveted to the book's pictures as the story was read and looked closely at each illustration. She listened as her brother retold the story, adding an occasional comment. An hour later, she looked at the book again and brought it to her mother to show that she had found the mouse's tiny green backpack on the last page, a detail her brother omitted in his retelling of the story. Then she retold the story from the last picture, asked for crayons and paper, and drew a picture of the boy and mouse in a kitchen baking cookies together. The four-year-old's response to the story is not as immediately evident as the six-year-old's, but quietly and in her own time she did respond. The responses of both children fall somewhere between efferent and aesthetic.

So you can see that there are differences in when and how children respond to literature. It may be that the four-year-old needed her brother to model a response for her to imitate. It may be that she felt more comfortable interacting alone with her mother about the book. It may be that her response is very different than her brother's. Or it may be that a combination of factors was at work.

An adult who reads a book and then talks with someone else about it often finds that his idea of theme conflicts with the other person's idea. Each adult brings different experiences, values, beliefs, and knowledge to the book. Any teacher who has read a story to a class or group of children has observed that some students easily relate personal experiences to the story or disagree with each other in their evaluations of what the author means, while other students sit quietly and do not enter into the discussion. Children also bring different experiences, values, beliefs, and knowledge to literature. These and a host of other differences account for the variety in children's responses to literature.

Although many children respond to literature in immediate and observable ways, some children's responses are not evident at all or are difficult or impossible to determine because they have trouble articulating them. In interviews with children who read a book that gave them a special feeling for a long time afterward, Cramer (1984) reports that the magic of special books is sometimes hard to express and difficult to relate to others, but it was definitely there for each child. In many cases you may need to seek out children's responses. For young children, drawing is often a way to begin to explore response. Older students can more easily respond in writing.

Children's comprehension of print occurs at various levels, which may be seen from their responses. For example, in Figure 5.1, Christopher comprehends the story literally by writing "Squanto brads [brings] gifts," which is an efferent response. He also shows evaluative comprehension or one kind of aesthetic response when he draws pictures of other ocean dwellers that he thinks Squanto brought to the Pilgrims. In Figure 5.2, Jessica interprets Max's taming of the monsters in *Where the Wild Things Are* and responds aesthetically when she identifies herself as "baws [boss] of the land." In Figure 5.3, the student demonstrates literal comprehension and an efferent response in entries 1-18, 1-21, and 1-24, and interpretive comprehension or an aesthetic response in 1-16.

While a child's response to literature is essentially individual and personal and is shaped by her experiences and perceptions, there are other factors, such as the environment and the people in it, that influence what the child reads and how she responds. We know that children influence each other's reading and response and so does the teacher (Hickman, 1984).

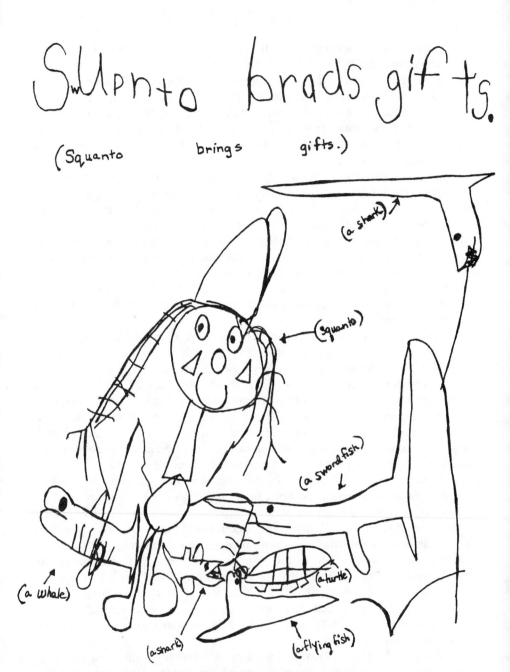

**Figure 5.1** Six-year-old Christopher's drawing in response to what he thinks Squanto brought to the first Thanksgiving based on his knowledge of ocean dwellers.

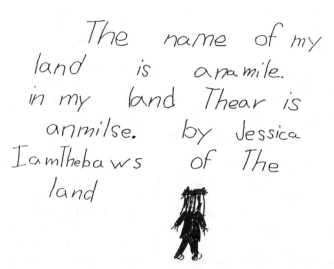

The name of my
land is a pa mile.
in my land Thear is
anmilse. by Jessica
I amThebaws of The
land

**Figure 5.2** A pre-first-grade child relates to Max's power. She draws a queen with a veil and says she wants to be "baws" of the land.

1-16

I don't think that she will want to forget that she can swim because he father taught her how to swim when she was able to walk. I don't think that She is a witch either I think that he was trying to protect her because if she swam again they would be sure she was a witch because witches float.

1-18

The rich people came by paying there own way but poor people came by giving up their freedom for a few years.

1-21

The pilgrims were poor and were farmers but the puritans were rich and were also farmers only they were skilled. The pilgrims were travelers and came for freedom of religion. The Puritans also came for freedom of religion.

1-24

I liked the class, I learned stuff about the pilgrims and puritins that I didn't know before.

**Figure 5.3** These journal entries made by a sixth-grader after he heard his teacher read *The Witch of Blackbird Pond*, by E. G. Speare, show his personal response.

Children model their responses for each other, sharing favorite parts of stories or appealing passages, drawing pictures, making puppet plays, designing game boards, and otherwise rethinking and representing stories in different ways for each other. Children in a class form a community of readers who show each other how to act like readers and respond personally to the books they read.

You can use the Literature Response Inventory in Figure 5.4 to help determine how a child responds to literature. This inventory includes a range of behaviors that occur on a response continuum from efferent to aesthetic. The three levels of reading comprehension traditionally identified in basal readers and used by teachers appear on this inventory. Retelling the story requires *literal comprehension* (reading the lines), or an efferent response. Making inferences requires *interpretive comprehension* (reading between the lines), a response that is both efferent and aesthetic. Making a judgment or evaluating requires *evaluative comprehension* (reading beyond the lines), a response that is closer to the aesthetic than the efferent. Of course, you can expand the inventory by adding responses that you value. When using an inventory such as this one be sure to reassess children regularly since their abilities to respond can change and develop over time as a result of exposure, practice, and a variety of other factors.

Purves (1986) also suggests the use of a grid-type assessment device and interviews to determine student attitudes and interests. He reminds us that we want to not only develop students' knowledge through literature but also affect their attitudes in a positive way so that they want to read and do read. Purves and Monson (1984) also discuss response to literature and you may want to consult them for more ideas about measuring response.

You also play a critical role in developing children's responses to literature. The teacher who reads, enjoys what he reads, and shares this with children becomes a model that children can imitate. This teacher regularly reads aloud to children and reads children's books independently as well. He lets children see him reading and tells them about the books he reads. He asks children for their opinions of certain characters or authors and tells children why certain books are his favorite. He makes time each day for silent reading and makes sure there is a variety of materials at a range of grade levels available for children to read, and he encourages activities that foster responses. He is a skillful discussion leader, guiding talk about books and characters so that children arrive at new meanings. In all of these ways and many more, a teacher can foster children's responses to literature.

## Creating a Literate Environment with Webs

The classroom environment you create can inhibit or encourage children's responses to literature. With some forethought and planning in the way you organize and structure your classroom, you will find many ways to involve

When the child reads or listens does s/he:

| | Folktales | Fantasy | Realistic Fiction | Historical Fiction | Biography | Poetry | Information Books |
|---|---|---|---|---|---|---|---|
| Show enjoyment. | | | | | | | |
| Take part in discussion. | | | | | | | |
| Ask questions. | | | | | | | |
| Draw pictures. | | | | | | | |
| Take part in drama. | | | | | | | |
| Write about it. | | | | | | | |
| Retell the story. | | | | | | | |
| Identify special uses of language. | | | | | | | |
| Identify the elements of story. | | | | | | | |
| Make inferences in relation to a broader context. | | | | | | | |
| Make a judgment or evaluate. | | | | | | | |
| Prefer certain types of books. | | | | | | | |

+ = Almost always

 = Sometimes

− = Never

**Figure 5.4** A Literature Response Inventory

children with literature and help them feel comfortable and better able to respond.

First, it's important to create a literate environment that is rich in print. You need to make books and other printed materials readily available in your classroom and allow time for children to read. Some teachers find that establishing a classroom library is the first step. The library can include books you own yourself and books you periodically borrow from the public library to use in your classroom, as well as magazines, comics, and the newspaper. Public libraries often have a wider range of books than school libraries and will allow classroom teachers to borrow them for longer than the usual period of time.

You can locate your library in one corner or part of the room—perhaps with a filmstrip projector, tape recorder, and materials for drawing and writing, such as different types of paper, pencils, crayons, and felt-tip pens—and call it the Literacy Center, Reading Corner, or Reading-Writing Area. There are many children's books available on tape or filmstrip with accompanying tapes that unskilled or reluctant readers may particularly enjoy. Locating writing materials in the same area as books helps children make the connection between reading and writing.

When you give children time to read and write and some direction with publishing, you will find that they love to write and publish their own books. Several resources provide indepth information on student book publishing. In *Gifts of Writing: Creating Projects with Words and Art,* Susan and Stephen Judy share a collection of activities that encourage creative writing and its attractive presentation. In *How to Make Your Own Books* by Harvey Weiss, readers are shown how to make personal, one-of-a-kind books that anyone can put together. In *How to Make Books with Children,* Joy Evans and Jo Ellen Moore provide easy-to-follow instructions and a variety of designs for making books.

Don't confine the print you make available for children to what is written by adults. Children are often just as eager to read what other children have written. If you use one large bulletin board in your classroom for children's writing and display everyone's writing, not just the few you identify as the best, you will do much to enhance self-esteem and ownership of writing as well as promote children's reading of each other's work. You can also include the books your students have written in your classroom library.

Belonging to a monthly book club can provide your classroom library and students with inexpensive paperback books. Each month a company like The Trumpet Club (PO Box 604, Holmes, PA, 19043) or Scholastic Books (730 Broadway, NY, 10003) will send you order forms and brochures advertising books they have for sale. If children order books and you send in their order, you are eligible for credits that can be used toward free books for your classroom. In this way, you build the reading habit and encourage children to own their own books while you increase your classroom library.

Webbing can be helpful in the creation of a literate environment. When you and your students create a web before, during, or after reading to represent the structure or elements in a particular book, try to use large chart paper and a felt marker rather than the blackboard. A web created on the blackboard is often lost when it is erased, but if you create your web on chart paper, it can be posted near the reading-writing area to encourage retelling or discussion of the story using the web. Using webs in this way can promote story enjoyment and comprehension as well as oral language development.

In addition, if you use cooperative learning—encouraging children to work with buddies or partners as they read, retell, draw, and write—you promote student-student interactions. We know from current professional literature and research that there are many benefits to working cooperatively in pairs or small groups. Children talk, question, argue, defend, develop social skills, and learn from each other. As an example, Figure 5.5 shows a web made by two first-grade boys to map out a story they created about Frog and Toad. Their teacher used webbing almost daily with the class in one way or another and had just read *Frog and Toad Together,* by Arnold Lobel. She then had "cooperative partners" plan sequels to the story to tell the class.

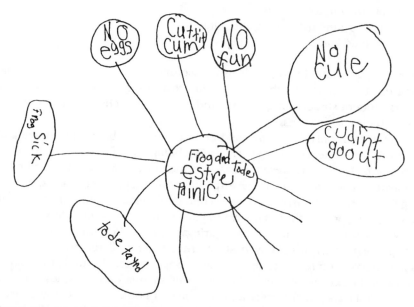

**Figure 5.5** David and Todd respond to stories about Frog and Toad with their own web for a new story called "Frog and Toad's Easter Picnic."

From the web they had created, these boys told their story of Frog and Toad getting ready for Easter. The text of their story exactly as they wrote it follows.

### Frog and Tade estre Pinick

Frog and Tode wrae getting.
rede for estre thay wint to bed.
erley the nxst marnig thay loke.
but thay did not hav eggs.
wat wile we do sed toad i dant no.
we will salv it but toad dinint.
fele good wat will i do now
I will mall the estre buney a llder
so he roght the leter the
estrbune get the leter so the
nxt nit the strebuy wint to the
hose and gave teme eggs
But that onley savt one prblum
toad was not well
so he toce care of toad.
he gave him chikn sup and jello
thn toad wint to bed erly
and got up the nxt mornig and felt betr
Then toad and frog wint to the estre pinick

Their story contained two problems and solutions for both problems, something the teacher felt neither boy could create independently. So webbing fosters student-student interactions and can inspire children to grow and stretch their imaginations.

Teachers report that many children freely use webbing without being directed to. These teachers regularly use webbing with their classes to brainstorm, organize, and represent ideas. When children have a model to imitate and materials to use, you will be surprised at their spontaneous use of webbing for a variety of purposes. One second-grade teacher found her students webbing on newsprint with markers to plan a story they wanted to write.

Webs can also be useful for sharing literature in thematic units. One third-grade teacher uses a web structure on her bulletin board with the theme "Books About . . ." as the core idea. She changes this topic to promote interest in books that are related to her content-area units of study, the seasons, or holidays. Each web strand is an actual book jacket borrowed from the school librarian's file or a book jacket made by a child. She also occasionally uses the web structure as a record of good books children have read. As children finish books, they write short advertisements and illustrations for them, and each of these becomes a strand in a "We Recommend . . ." theme web.

## ══════════ *Interactive Story Reading and Webbing*

In a literate classroom environment, teachers foster the freedom to respond to books. These teachers make children feel that their opinions will be accepted and valued whether or not they match those of the teacher or other students. They give children the freedom to agree or disagree as long as they can support their opinions with rational ideas and information. When the classroom atmosphere is open for discussion and the airing of opinions, then children will feel free to offer their thoughts and responses to books as they interact with each other.

In this environment, it is important that you see students as participants in the story-reading process. By encouraging students to participate when stories are read, you promote a personal emotional response, the processing of information, and direct involvement that can have a positive effect on enjoyment and comprehension. There are several ways to promote interactive story reading.

First, you might begin by constructing a web with children to represent what they already know about the setting or theme of what is to be read. In this way, you enhance comprehension by cooperatively constructing meaning into which new information fits.

Second, respond personally to books and share your responses and interpretations freely with children, encouraging children to do the same. For example, when you let your children know how a story makes you feel, what you did or did not like about it and why, what you think the author meant, and the kinds of pictures the story helps you create in your mind, you provide children with a model of personal responses to imitate and value. By telling children how *Owl Moon,* by Jane Yolen, reminds you of the special relationship you had with your father when you were finally old enough to go fishing with him, you share a personal response. When you communicate how the cold stillness of a winter night in this book reminds you of skating on a frozen pond under the moon, you can help free children's memories and promote their ability to relate their own experiences to this story.

Third, make story reading a cooperative venture among you and your students. While pauses to comment or ask a question about a story can be distracting and have less than positive effects on listeners if carried to the extreme, stopping occasionally at appropriate points to look closely at a picture and discuss it or share a feeling, observation, or interpretation can significantly enrich story enjoyment and comprehension for many children. There are a variety of strategies you can use to affect the kind and quality of children's responses:

- Ask Why . . . ?, What do you think . . . ?, and How . . . ? questions. These questions foster personal interpretations and evaluations, and children will sometimes use literal information to respond, making it unnecessary to ask literal questions.
- Restate what children have said and probe for an elaboration.

- Offer positive feedback or praise for opinions whether or not you agree with them.
- Add or give information yourself that extends a student response or knowledge related to the story.
- Provide clues or cues to tease out children's understanding or perceptions of a story.
- Clarify uncertainties by relating examples of something children know to what they have trouble grasping.
- Listen and allow student-student dialogues.
- Encourage children to add new information to a web as a story is read and they discover facts and ideas that are appropriate.

Some teachers who do not like to interrupt their story sharing or reading will read the entire story through once, and then during a rereading encourage children to discuss the story, interact more fully with each other, and perhaps generate a web. Whether you encourage cooperative interactions and use webbing during a first or second reading, remember that through cooperatively constructing meaning with a web you can enhance children's enjoyment and appreciation of literature.

Fourth, recognize the healthy benefits of prediction. An elementary school librarian, who was reading aloud a chapter a day of Natalie Babbitt's *Tuck Everlasting* to a group of students, found that at the end of each chapter they enjoyed making predictions about what would happen next. Making a web of predictions about what might happen to Winnie Foster and how the Tuck family's problem might be resolved gave these students a real way to be a part of the story. Making educated guesses helped involve these students in what they were listening to and built their anticipation and comprehension of the story as well. Even young children can participate in story reading in this way and reap similar benefits. A first-grade teacher reports that she uses prediction and webbing so much in her read-aloud sessions that her children now routinely hypothesize and predict as they read stories in the basal and selections from their science books. Both teachers routinely represent their students' predictions in webs that provide records so that predictions can be revisited and checked for accuracy.

When you provide opportunities to hear, read, talk about, and respond in a variety of personal ways to literature, you help children develop responses to their full potential (Huck, Hepler, & Hickman, 1987). In addition, when you give them time to respond through talk, writing, art, drama, and other means, you help them know and enjoy literature (Kiefer, 1988).

## Drama and Webbing

It was an exciting day in the third-grade class where children were preparing to put on a play they had written about an ant colony. The class had been studying communities and the ant culture was one that had intrigued them.

In fact, they had a classroom ant colony they had been observing for several weeks and they had read and reported to each other on every trade book about ants in the local libraries. Two other classes and the parents of the children involved had been invited and were seated in the classroom eagerly awaiting the production. A video camera was set up to record the play and the classroom atmosphere was alive with anticipation.

The same sort of electricity was crackling in a pre-first-grade classroom where these children were about to act out the song/picturebook *Old Mac-Donald Had a Farm* (Mills, 1969) with puppets they had made. They used scraps of felt glued to potholders to make the animals, and their teacher had sewn loops of elastic onto the backs of the potholders for their hands so they could manipulate the puppets.

In a sixth-grade classroom down the hall, students were planning a video documentary on the history of their community, which is located at the confluence of two rivers. They had read accounts by local historians of important events that had occurred, biographies of past local leaders, and historical fiction that described what might have happened. Plans were for one student to take film footage of his classmates interviewing older residents of the community, other students would film historic buildings and evidence of the rivers' impact on the community, and others would film various collections of art and artifacts in the local museum. They were all involved in writing, revising, and editing their own sections of the narrative that would accompany the documentary.

Through dramatic involvement supported by webbing, all of these students were responding to literature in various ways. Creative drama includes both informal, spontaneous drama like the roleplaying that the children did as they dramatized the farm animals and their actions. It also includes formal, scripted drama like the ant colony play. It may include an audience, as with the ant colony play and the documentary that would ultimately have an audience. Or it may not include an audience, as with the pre-kindergarten children who were all involved. Spoken language is sometimes improvised, as with Old MacDonald and the ants, and sometimes written language is read interpretively, as with the narrative that accompanied the historical documentary. Stewig (1983) describes the many uses of drama in the elementary school classroom.

All of the planning for the dramatic activities in these three classrooms was enhanced with webbing. The third-grade teacher used webbing to organize various sections of the play and make sure that the factual information and insights the children had gained about ants were included. The pre-first teacher used a sequenced picture web to help children know when it was their turn to act out the song. The sixth-graders used webbing as a prewriting strategy before drafting each section of the narrative for their documentary.

You can use webbing to plan and organize several forms of creative drama in which you can easily involve your students as you promote their personal response, understanding, and appreciation of literature.

## Pantomime

Pantomime uses gestures and actions without words to communicate meaning. While students do not speak or use any kind of verbal language during enactment, pantomime (or mime) does require purposeful talk about the task or topic in order to plan or carry out the drama. When children pantomime they learn the importance of nonverbal or body language and facial expressions to demonstrate feelings and thoughts. They see how important gestures and the face can be in communicating meaning.

Children love to imagine and act out the situations they hear or read about in stories. For example, when young children have heard the story *The Snail's Spell*, by Joanne Ryder, they can make a web of the snail's characteristics and easily imitate the boy as he pretends to be a snail in a garden. Children can then use webs to identify the characteristics and actions of other animals from the story: a rabbit, chipmunk, tortoise, bird, mouse, toad, butterfly, or mole. Then children can improvise from their webs the ways these animals move through the garden as they eat various vegetables. After hearing *The Snail's Spell*, Jeff, a third-grader, imagined that he was a cougar and created the web in Figure 5.6, wrote and printed on the computer the poem in Figure 5.7, and drew the picture in Figure 5.8 to accompany the poem.

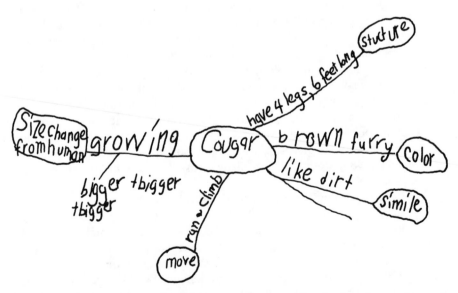

**Figure 5.6** After webbing the snail's characteristics, Jeff, a third-grader, made a web about a cougar and pantomimed its behavior.

The Cougar's Spell
By Jeffrey R. Long

Imagine
you are furry
and have strong bones inside you.
Imagine
you are brown,
the color of coffee.
Imagine
you are growing,
bigger
and
bigger
and
bigger.
Imagine
You are six feet long,
lying under a green tree,
all furry and brown.
Imagine
you have four powerful legs now.
You seldom walk.
Instead,
you run, and climb trees,
and make your own tracks.
It is easy to move this way,
and it feels fast and cool.

**Figure 5.7** From the web in Figure 5.6, Jeff created this story on the computer.

**Figure 5.8** The picture that accompanied Jeff's story.

Older students also enjoy pantomime. One sixth-grade class, in which wildlife and the environment were the focus of a month-long study, completed their unit with a pantomime festival, or "mime fest." Students wrote definitions for key vocabulary in web formats. Each web was written on a piece of paper, and then groups of students picked a web out of a hat and pantomimed the vocabulary word for everyone to guess. They thought of original and creative ways to mime such terms as water cycle, biodegradable, hibernation, and shelter. These students were mentally and physically involved as they acted out and guessed the concepts they had learned about and webbed as they responded to literature.

## Charades

Charades is a game where titles, quotations, or names are acted out and the audience tries to guess what is being said. Charades are a good way to involve both the presenters and the audience, since those who do the acting try to represent words with action and movement, and those who do the guessing try to match words with what they see.

Some of the students in a fourth-grade class where the topic for science study was electricity chose to read biographies of U.S. scientists who had contributed to our knowledge and eventual use of electricity. One group of students read *Benjamin Franklin*, by Ingri and Edgar D'Aulaire, and chose to make a web of Ben's character traits. Then each student acted out one trait for the rest of the class. These students were involved in another kind of nonverbal response to literature supported by webbing.

## Improvisation

Improvisation is drama with dialogue but no script. Material for improvisation can come from stories that children know or have just heard or read. Entire stories or situations from a story or book can be improvised. To involve your entire class you need to choose a selection that contains a number of characters or modify a selection so that there are enough parts for everyone. Then make a web of the various characters or parts, numbering each character as it is to appear in the improvisation. In the ant colony improvisation mentioned earlier, the students made stick puppets and used them to portray their parts in the play. Other students were responsible for backstage aspects of the production, for example, introduction, music, set, and curtain. Their web contained every child's name and responsibility in the play.

Children get closer to a piece of literature and more intimately involved with it through improvisation than they might normally. Their enjoyment and understanding of what took place and how characters felt is heightened when they act it out and speak as the characters would.

One of the advantages of improvisation is that dialogue is ad-libbed and does not have to be memorized or said in exactly the same way each time the drama unfolds. Children are free to interpret characters and action in more personal ways than they might in a scripted play. Also, the original work can be followed closely, referred to occasionally, or modified by enlarging or omitting a part or adding parts.

Improvisation provides experience that can lead students to perform more formal plays, in which they deliver lines they have learned, wear costumes, make or collect props, and take part in all the other tasks that are part of a formal dramatic production. If your goal in using drama is to encourage children to personally respond to literature and enjoy and appreciate it, then you will probably want to make use of improvisation, or at least the less formal plays in which children deliver lines they make up themselves as the play progresses. Memorizing and presenting scripted dialogue, at least for younger students, may do more to dampen their enjoyment of literature than you realize.

## Readers Theater

When a group of readers performs a work of literature by reading it orally, this oral interpretation is called readers theater. Performances can be done without a narrator or with one who fills in the setting and action. Performers learn how to use their voices and how to change their tone, pitch, volume, and rate of delivery to communicate meaning. They also learn to use gestures to enhance meaning.

Readers generally sit on stools, chairs, or the floor facing the audience and hold the material from which they will read in front of them. The audience imagines the action and characters, and usually there are no props or costumes.

This technique can be used with children as young as first grade. One prerequisite is that children be able to read the material independently, otherwise they will struggle with word recognition and be unable to read fluently and with expression. A second requirement is that the story or poetry offer action, drama, and excitement so that it can be interpreted and dramatized. Readers theater needs little preparation and so webbing does not support it in the same way as it does an acted play or improvisation.

## Choral Speaking

When a group of children reads or recites a poem or piece of rhymed prose together, the performance is usually called choral speaking. An entire class can speak together, or you can divide the class in half, with the halves responding to each other. You can include solos, duets, quartets, or other types of groupings that make sense. There are four types of choral speaking:

- *Refrain:* the leader speaks most of the lines with the group repeating the refrain.
- *Line-at-a-time:* one student or a small group of students speaks a line or two lines, then another student or small group speaks a line or two, and so on.
- *Antiphonal:* two or more groups of speakers alternate in speaking a piece. Sometimes females and males are grouped together or voices are grouped according to pitch. The groups can be alternated or combined for effect.
- *Unison:* an entire group speaks lines together with no subgrouping.

A combination of some of these forms of choral speaking with an improvisation can be interesting. For example, one group of third-graders studying the weather had read Judi Barrett's *Cloudy with a Chance of Meatballs* and decided to share this book with the class. They acted out the story, adding poems about foods that fell from the sky. The poems grew from a web they had made of all the possible foods that might fall from the sky. Some of the poems were spoken by everyone in unison and some by pairs of children who took turns speaking lines. Each student found a poem about a different food and made a copy for the person they recited with so that there was no memorization involved. The class liked this creative way of sharing this humorous book.

## Videotaping

The video documentary mentioned earlier that was created by the sixth-graders is an example of students' dramatic involvement with content-area literature. Videotaping a show such as this was wonderful motivation for them to read, interact with what they read and each other to create webs, and collect snapshots to weave into the videotaped history of their community.

Videotaping has a range of possibilities for involving students in literature and learning. Some teachers have found that their students enjoy videotaping reenactments of books or stories they have read. Improvised dialogue and narration coupled with costumes and rudimentary props make it a creative experience for students. Other teachers find that creating and videotaping a documentary motivates students to read historical fiction, biography, and other content-area materials.

## Puppets

The hand puppets the pre-kindergarteners used in their enactment of the song/picturebook about Old MacDonald are only one of a variety of puppets children enjoy using. Puppets made from paper and sticks, paper bags, socks, cardboard cylinders, boxes, tagboard and straws, gloves, and mittens are easy ways to help your children respond to what they read or hear.

After hearing folktales of the Northwestern Indians, two third-grade girls created a web from which they made up their own folktale and then used simple stick puppets to dramatize their story. They tied a cord across the corner of the classroom from the crank handle of a window to the knob of a closet door and draped a sheet over it. The girls knelt behind the sheet and improvised the dialogue and actions to accompany their story. This kind of puppet is simple to make, and even older students enjoy using them as a way of sharing books or stories.

Puppets provide shy children with a way to express themselves. Puppets give all children a chance to be creative in their responses and interpretations. Puppets can be used by the teacher or children as an aid to storytelling, as a way to roleplay or retell a story, or to help in improvising a new story.

## Art and Music

Children can also respond to literature through art and music. Although many teachers leave instruction in art and music to the teachers of these subjects, you can provide opportunities in your classroom that encourage children's artistic and musical responses to books. Some teachers work closely with the art teacher so they know what media and ideas the children are being exposed to in art class, and together they explore ways that classroom learning and/or book sharing can be integrated into the art curriculum. Often, the music teacher can suggest songs and records that correlate with the mood or setting of the literature your children read.

For young children, drawing pictures after listening to a story is an excellent way to encourage a response to literature. We know that a picture can stimulate oral language, and that often children have very involved stories to tell about pictures they have drawn. Creating webs serves the same function. With the support of a web they have drawn, even young children can tell stories with a beginning, middle, and end that are thoughtfully connected. The drawing and scribbling that young children do signals emergent literacy and is a precursor to the development of formal writing. So you not only enhance responses to literature when you allow children to draw but you aid the development of expressive skills in general.

Music learning also can support what is going on in the classroom. For example, a fourth-grade teacher enlisted the help of the music teacher, who taught the students several pioneer songs that were included in their enactment of a play based on one of Laura Ingalls Wilder's books about the prairie. Most improvisations or plays are more enjoyable and creatively performed with the addition of music. Don't overlook the fact that there is much good music that your music teacher can suggest or provide to authenticate or accompany your reading or your children's reading of literature. It is often through music that children's creative senses are touched.

When these kinds of cross-overs happen, you can integrate the learning that occurs in school and enrich your children's responses and appreciation of books. Music and art allow for a fuller range of enjoyment and understanding of literature.

## Summary

We know that responses to literature are highly personal and grow from interactions with print. These interactions occur when a child brings various meanings and background knowledge to print as he creates a new personal experience from reading. Responses range from the efferent to the aesthetic and depend upon some level of comprehension. You can promote fuller and richer responses by encouraging children to use webs to interact with each other and story characters. You can use webbing to create a literate environment, practice interactive story reading, and involve children in a variety of dramatic forms.

## REFERENCES

Cramer, B. B. (1984). Bequest of wings: Three readers and special books. *Language Arts, 61*(3), 253–260.

Evans, J., & Moore, J. E. (1985). *How to Make Books with Children.* Monterey, CA: Evan-Moor.

Hickman, J. (1984). Research currents: Researching children's responses to literature. *Language Arts, 61*(3), 278–284.

Huck, C. S., Hepler, S., & Hickman, J. (1987). *Children's Literature in the Elementary School* (4th ed.). New York: Holt, Rinehart & Winston.

Judy, S., & Judy, S. (1980). *Gifts of Writing: Creating Projects with Words and Art.* New York: Scribner's Sons.

Kiefer, B. (1988). Children's literature: Lighting up the reading program. In *The Leadership Letters.* Columbus, OH: Silver Burdett & Ginn.

Mikkelson, M. (1984). Talking and telling: The child as storymaker. *Language Arts, 61*(3), 229–239.

Purves, A. C. (1986). Testing in literature. *Language Arts, 63*(3), 320–323.

Purves, A. C., & Monson, D. L. (1984). *Experiencing Children's Literature.* Glenview, IL: Scott, Foresman.

Rosenblatt, E. M. (1985). The transactional theory of the literary work: Implications for research. In C. R. Cooper (Ed.), *Researching Response to Literature and the Teaching of Literature: Points of Departure* (pp. 33–53). Norwood, NJ: Ablex.

Solsken, J. W. (1985). Authors of their own learning. *Language Arts, 62*(5), 491–499.

Stewig, J. (1983). *Informal Drama in the Elementary Language Arts Classroom.* New York: Teachers College Press.

Sutherland, Z., & Arbuthnot, M. H. (1986). *Children and Books* (7th ed.). Glenview, IL: Scott, Foresman.

Tchudi, S. (1985). The roots of response to literature. *Language Arts, 62*(5), 463–468.

Weiss, H. (1974). *How to Make Your Own Books.* New York: Crowell.

## Children's Literature

Babbitt, N. (1978). *Tuck Everlasting.* New York: Farrar, Straus, & Giroux.

Barrett, J. (1978). *Cloudy with a Chance of Meatballs.* New York: Macmillan.

D'Aulaire, I., & D'Aulaire, E. (1950). *Benjamin Franklin.* New York: Doubleday.

Lobel, A. (1972). *Frog and Toad Together.* New York: Scholastic.

Mills, A. (1969). *Old MacDonald Had a Farm and Other Funny Songs.* New York: Scholastic.

Numeroff, L. J. (1985). *If You Give a Mouse a Cookie.* New York: Harper & Row.

Ryder, J. (1988). *The Snail's Spell.* New York: Penguin.

Sendak, M. (1963). *Where the Wild Things Are.* New York: Harper & Row.

Speare, E. G. (1958). *The Witch of Blackbird Pond.* Boston: Houghton Mifflin.

Yolen, J. (1987). *Owl Moon.* New York: Scholastic.

# chapter 6

# Writing as Response

This chapter addresses writing as an important response to literature and discusses the connection between reading and writing. It explores webbing as an aid to writing and provides examples of the use of webs to promote planning, organizing, notetaking, reporting, reacting, and keeping track of what has been read.

## Literature Models

Writing allows children to interact with literature in different ways than oral language, drama, or art and music allow. When literature is a springboard for children's writing, they have the luxury of spending more time than oral language permits to create something new and very personal that is relatively permanent. When children write in a classroom where a process approach to writing (Calkins, 1986; Graves, 1983; Harste, Burke, & Short, 1988) is used, they are encouraged to rehearse and plan what they will write before they draft; to reread and revise their work, and to help their peers do the same, with an eye to communicating the message effectively; and to share or publish their work. Webbing supports a written response to literature and the process approach to writing in several ways.

If children are to write well, it is commonly accepted that they need exposure to good literature models. We know that the best writing of all for children is that found in quality literature written especially for them. We also know that to help children become good writers, we must surround them with the best books and stories, help them see themselves as authors by becoming authors, and make the reading-writing connection real for them. Several experts elaborate on the links between reading and writing:

- "The reading-writing connections that matter most belong to the quiet moments when a writer is snuggled up, reading a book" (Calkins, 1986; p. 232).
- "Writing is learned by writing, by reading, and by perceiving oneself as a writer" (Smith, 1982; p. 199).
- "Studies show almost consistently that . . . better writers tend to read more than poorer writers" (Stotsky, 1983; p. 636).
- "Students draw upon what they read as a source of knowledge when they write" (Cullinan, 1987; p.13).
- "All children need literature. Children who are authors need it even more" (Graves, 1983; p. 67).

For some children, making the jump from reading good literature to writing good prose comes easily. For other children, however, one does not necessarily follow the other. These children need help bridging the gap and making the connection between reading and writing.

As a teacher, you can help children read with a writer's eye—to explore the impact, look, and sound of good writing. You can introduce them to authors and make sure they understand that authors are real people. You can provide them with a variety of materials, plenty of time, positive reinforcement, and encouragement to write. You can write yourself and share your problems and successes with them. You can also guide children to use strategies that make writing easier and more pleasurable for them.

Teachers who use literature as a model for teaching writing—clarifying the elements of story and structure—encourage children to imitate specific literary structures, to write in the same ways and using the same forms as the authors of the selected books and stories. The remainder of this chapter provides suggestions for getting children to actively participate with webbing when writing in different literary genres.

## Planning with Webs

Webbing is one way to make the reading-writing connection real for children. Webbing can do for older students what drawing a picture does for the very young child. When a young child draws a picture, the picture is a stimulus for talking about a topic. The picture serves as a springboard for oral composition by providing the child with content to talk about. The picture is the child's way of rehearsing and planning for what he will say when he shares his picture with his peers. As children become more verbal and gain writing skills, the drawings they use to stimulate their writing become more sophisticated. Webs allow children to represent and organize graphically some rather sophisticated ideas and relationships and then to write or talk about what they have drawn.

By creating a web from what they have read or heard, students rehearse and plan for what they can talk or write about. After reading a story, students can sequence the events in a web format and use the structure to retell the story or write a summary of it. In this way, responses to literature grow from webbing. Younger children can help you create a web, while older students can learn to create their own webs with your guidance.

In one school, two teachers collaborated on a project to stimulate and develop the writing of their students. A fifth-grade class adopted a class of second-graders and taught them how to write letters and keep buddy journals. One of the things the fifth-graders were eager to do was write stories and make books for the younger students. Betty, the fifth-grade teacher, had seen a web on chart paper in the second-grade classroom (see Figure 6.1) that Penny had made with her children's direction after they heard *If You Give a Mouse a Cookie,* by Laura Numeroff. The web gave Betty an idea for helping some of her reluctant and less skilled writers.

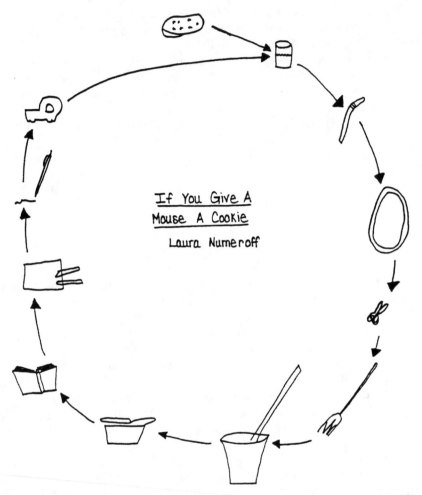

**Figure 6.1** A second-grade teacher's picture web for *If You Give a Mouse a Cookie* by Laura Numeroff.

She borrowed the web, shared it with her students, and showed them how to use it as a model for writing their own stories for the second-graders. First, Betty read *If You Give a Mouse* to her students, and together they webbed the elements of the story (see Figure 6.2). Then Betty helped her students create a new web by changing the setting and action. They changed the setting to "the mouse's home" and made a new web for the action to reflect the chain of events that might occur when a boy visits a mouse's home and the mouse gives the boy a piece of cheese. In this way, they used webbing to plan a new story. Figures 6.3 and 6.4 show a web and original story that grew from this lesson.

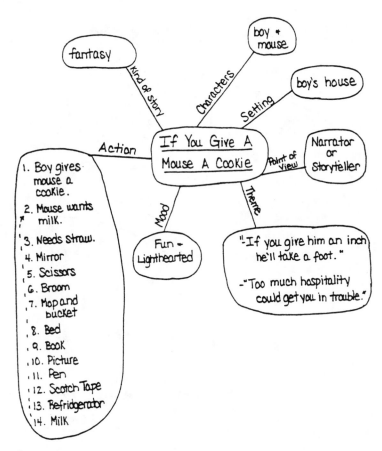

**Figure 6.2** A fifth-grader's web of *If You Give a Mouse a Cookie.*

Betty did some professional reading and found an article on predictable books (Heald-Taylor, 1987) that gave her some more ideas. She shared with her students another book that had a circular plot, *One Fine Day* by Nonny Hogrogian, and three other predictable books, *The Big Sneeze* by Ruth Brown, *The Napping House* by Audrey Wood, and *My Mom Travels a Lot* by Caroline Bauer. She suggested that these stories could be rewritten in the same way. Students could web these stories, like they had webbed *If You Give a Mouse,* modify the webs by changing one or two aspects of their structure, and then write sequels or new stories. In fact, she told them, with webs to help them, they could write interesting sequels to any story they knew the second-graders had read and liked. With this preparation, a few books to read and use as models, and some unlined paper on which to draw their webs, her students excitedly started their book-writing project.

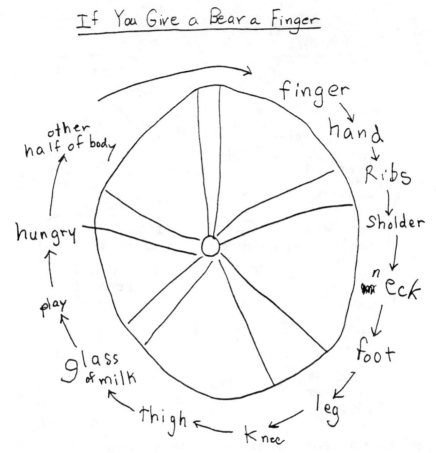

**Figure 6.3** A fifth-grader's web for a modified version of *If You Give a Mouse a Cookie.*

Two weeks later, Betty's class had completed cloth-cover books that contained some of the best writing Betty had seen her students do. Penny's class eagerly listened as a few fifth-graders each day read their books to her class before donating them to the second-grade classroom library.

This scenario shows you one way to use webs to help support your students' rehearsal and planning for writing. From this example, you can see how a visual display of the elements of a story and the important information from that story can be a springboard for retelling, rewriting, and creative writing. Your explorations with webbing and other genres of literature can be equally effective. By using literature as a model, you can help your students write better reports, information books, realistic fiction, and so on.

# I f You Give a Bear a Finger

If you give a bear a finger he'll
probly want a hand because a finger
isn't that filling for a bear.
Next he'll want a side order of ribs
just for the road. And seence he's
allready eating a sholder will be his
next meal. Next he'll want a neck becaus
a sholder is next to the neck and it is
easy to getto. Now a foot to freshen
his breth and seence a foot is next to the
leg a leg is what he'll have. Now for the
knee which he'll fill with cream.
Then your thigh will become a tooth
pick to him. Now he wants a glass
of milk to wash down the meal.
He'll go out run around burn of all
those callories. Now He's back
and he's hungry and he'll ask for
a finger, ....

**Figure 6.4** A story written by a fifth-grader from the web in Figure 6.3.

========================================= *Organizing with Webs*

As well as helping students identify what to include in their writing, webbing can help with organization. One of the things a writer does when she organizes information is to decide in what order and how to use ideas in her writing. Organizing is an important part of rehearsal and planning and a step that is often overlooked by teachers, however. We sometimes assume that children will intuitively know how to order their ideas in the most effective sequence, which isn't always the case.

We can show children how to include their ideas in webs and then sequence the ideas in an order that makes sense for what they will write. The following section shows you how this idea worked with a group of fourth-graders.

Some of the students in Lisa's fourth-grade classroom were reading biographies and asking questions about the authors. They wondered how the authors knew everything they included in the stories they wrote about other people's lives. Lisa thought this might be a good time to introduce biographical writing and the autobiography in particular. She read them *Broderick,* by Edward Ormondroyd, a short biographical fantasy about a mouse's life, and *A Weed Is a Flower: The Life of George Washington Carver,* by Aliki Brandenberg. She helped the students make webs of the important events and people in the lives of Broderick and Carver. Then the class as a whole made a web of the kinds of things they could include in their own autobiographies. They suggested topics such as birth, family, friends, future, hobbies, school, best memories, fears, and favorites. Throughout the creation of this web, there was discussion of how students might obtain some of the information they needed. Talking to parents, looking at birth certificates, thinking about major events in their lives, and their hopes for the future were all part of the planning.

By this time, the students were eager to make their own webs that would guide the writing of their own autobiographies. Tina was intrigued with the idea of a spider web and included such topics as "favorites," "birth," "family," and "future" in her web (see Figure 6.5).

Lisa encouraged her students to take their webs home and talk with family members to see what else they might want to include and to get any in-

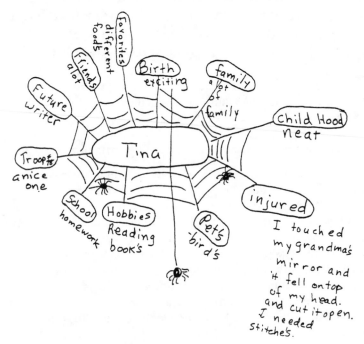

**Figure 6.5** Tina's web for her autobiography.

formation they needed. The next day the class talked about how sequence and order can affect a written piece. Lisa told her students that each strand on the web they had made the day before could be a separate paragraph or section in their autobiography. She then helped them sequence and number the strands on Broderick's and George Washington Carver's webs in the order the authors had used.

Next, Lisa read opening paragraphs of two biographies to the class. She chose two books by Jean Fritz, whose biography of Benjamin Franklin begins by describing the street on which he was born in Boston and doesn't really include details about his birth. In Fritz' biography of Christopher Columbus, the author begins with a description of Genoa as a city of ships and sailors and then talks about Columbus's birth. In this way, Lisa showed her students that they could rearrange the order of the strands or paragraphs in their autobiographies to add interest and to achieve a different effect.

After this look at order and form in four biographies and some discussion of ideas for organizing their own life stories, Lisa had her students tentatively number the strands in their webs to indicate the order in which they would include their ideas. She helped them understand that this order could be changed but that by having an overall organization in mind before writing, the composing would be easier and the finished product might be more interesting to read, as well as well-written. Her students then began using their webs to help them as they wrote their autobiographies.

Figure 6.6 shows the cover of Tina's book, which she describes as "fascinating." In Figure 6.7 Tina demonstrates the importance she places on her web by including it as the first chapter. Several children, like Tina, listed facts and ideas on their webs under each strand topic, so they wouldn't forget to include the information when they began writing.

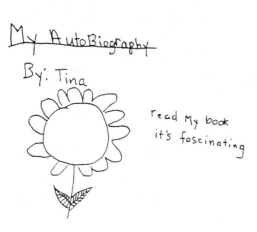

Context

page 1 My web
page 2 My birth
page 3 My childhood
page 4 My family
page 5 My injury
page 6 My pet
page 7 My future
page 8 My picture
page 9 My friends
page 10 My troop

My AutoBiography

By: Tina

read My book
it's fascinating

**Figure 6.6** The title page for Tina's book.

**Figure 6.7** The table of contents for Tina's book.

## Notetaking, Reporting, and Webbing

Webbing can be equally useful for students as they read and respond to information books. Webs can serve students as a method of notetaking and writing reports. One of the biggest problems with assigning written reports is that students often copy information directly from reference books, using words they cannot pronounce and do not know the meaning of. The resulting reports are disconnected bits of information copied from a number of sources, which the students themselves often do not understand. One way to alleviate this problem is to emphasize that a good report is a piece of writing that communicates the writer's ideas about a topic in a way that makes sense to an audience. To help students understand this, you need to give them a strategy for writing this kind of report, and webbing is an effective beginning strategy.

One third-grade teacher, Nancy, found that a good way to begin a report, once each student had a topic, was to have them brainstorm a web with strands for all the ideas they thought they might want to include in their report. By beginning with a web of possible ideas, her children then go about their reading and information gathering with a purpose. She shows them how to paraphrase and add specific information to their webs; she models for them how they can add strands and delete strands that don't seem important or are included in other strands.

Figure 6.8 shows the web Paulo created and Figure 6.9 shows the first draft of his report on Rosa Parks. In a conference with Nancy, Paulo realized that although he had included a rich fund of information from his reading on the web, he had not used it in his writing. She helped him see that each sentence in his report could be a topic sentence for its own paragraph and how the remaining information on his web would fit in each paragraph.

Later in the year, when her students had become familiar with story structure and could use webs to gather information and write reports, Nancy combined the two ideas to help them write their own original stories. Students first chose an animal to read about and gather information on (see Figure 6.10). Then Nancy had them use the structure of "problem, events, solution" in Figure 6.11 to establish a chain of events that would make up their story. Working from the web and the story-map outline, Shelly was able to write an excellent fact-based fantasy about "Katie Koala."

Webs can serve as a blueprint for first reports, by allowing children to construct a visual display of their topic. As students become more skillful writers and begin to deal with more information, you can show them how to use a heavy marker to brainstorm and a pencil to add information as they read from various information and reference books. You also will undoubtedly want to help them move to using such strategies as data charts, 3-inch by 5-inch notecards, and outlines to prepare their reports.

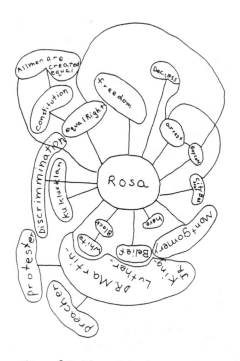

**Figure 6.8** The web Paulo created before writing his report.

Rosa Parks was a hero. She stared the bus boy- cot— She was a leader of her time. She was a freedom fighter.

**Figure 6.9** Paulo's first draft.

Keep in mind that webbing may not be necessary for all of your students, all of the time. But at first, it can provide a concrete way for them to re-hearse, plan, organize, and make decisions about their writing. Webs can act as a springboard to writing by providing the visual structure for what chil-dren will write. Using webs can not only help children improve the content of their writing but can also have an impact on the form and structure of what children write. Some children will use webs at first and quickly under-stand how to include or gather information so that they may move to another system of making notes or outlines for themselves. Other children will be comfortable with webs as a strategy for prewriting and use them consistently. Webbing does not need to become a ritual that everybody goes through each time they write; rather, it should be a strategy that children use until they find what works best for them.

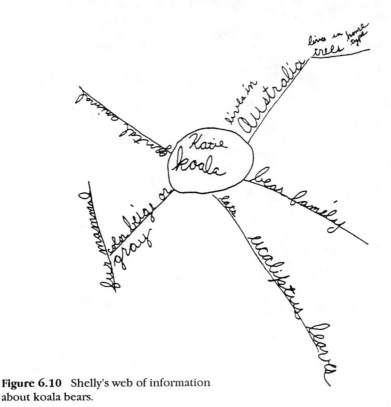

**Figure 6.10** Shelly's web of information about koala bears.

Problem    Events    Solutions →

can't climb
trees

1. Cary koala
calls Katie
Koala names
2. Casey Kanga-
roo says hop up
4. Joey Casey's
little boy
says to pull
herself up.
3. Kyle Koala
is born.
5. father and
mother Koala
have a talk
with Casey
two koala
sisters.

Cary koala
wises up
and insted
of making fun
of her sister
she helped her
sister Katie and
Cary tought
her sis to
climb trees.

**Figure 6.11** Shelly's story map outline.

## ========== *Responding to Literature with Webs*

As well as helping children plan and organize their writing, webbing can be an important vehicle for responding to literature and recording these responses. Writing is a more personal and private means of expression than participating in an open discussion, and so it can allow students a less risky forum for voicing a reaction or response than a class sharing session might.

Some teachers ask students to keep a reading response journal or literature log at the start of the school year. They sometimes ask children to make a web on one page in their journal for each book they read, and the journal then holds a record of all the reading they have done. These teachers encourage students to include a personal opinion or response to the book as part of their journal entry. In this way, students have a record of the title, author, setting, characters, plot, theme, and point of view of each book they have read, as well as their response to each book.

A journal of this kind gives students a sense of their progress in reading and allows them to look back at what they have read. Students can swap journals, look at each other's webs, and read the written response to see if they want to read a book someone else has read and written about. Students can also be paired with a "buddy" and write responses to each other's entries (Bromley, 1989). Response journals give students opportunities to practice writing that is meaningful to them. Response journals also provide important information about what kinds of books and which authors children seem to like, so that you can make suggestions to broaden the range of literature your children read.

Reading response journals can be a stepping stone to a deeper understanding and appreciation of literature. Calkins (1986) tells about a teacher who uses writing-reading response groups. In this classroom, small groups of children each read a different book, depending on the interests and ability of the group. A group uses multiple copies of the same book and each day they read for 30 minutes and then write responses in their journals. Following writing, they come together to share their responses and discuss questions the teacher provides. Calkins suggests that the most effective use of the responses is to have children voluntarily read them aloud to each other to begin the sharing time. In this way, children are encouraged to begin with and build on their own reactions to books. She says that as children hear how others respond and begin to interact and respond to each other, the ways in which they respond will change. They become more sensitive to a broader range of aspects that contribute to writing as well as reading, and their own opinions and feelings are confirmed. These response groups help children rethink books and stories from other's perspectives.

=============================================== *Summary*

Webbing can help link reading and writing for children. It supports a process approach to writing because webs are excellent tools to use to prepare for writing. This chapter has begun to show you how webbing can promote response to literature through several aspects of writing. The planning, organizing, notetaking, report writing, and sharing that children engage in as they read literature is enriched through webbing.

**REFERENCES** =================================================

Bromley, K. (1989). Buddy journals make the reading-writing connection. *The Reading Teacher, 43*(2), 122–129.

Calkins, L. M. (1986). *The Art of Teaching Writing.* Portsmouth, NH: Heinemann.

Cullinan, B. E. (Ed.). (1987). *Children's Literature in the Reading Program.* Newark, DE: International Reading Association.

Graves, D. (1983). *Writing: Teachers and Children at Work.* Portsmouth, NH: Heinemann.

Harste, J., Burke, C., & Short, K. (1988). *Creating Classrooms for Authors.* Portsmouth, NH: Heinemann.

Heald-Taylor, G. (1987). Predictable literature selections and activities for language arts instruction. *The Reading Teacher, 41*(1), 6–12.

Smith, F. (1982). *Writing and the Writer.* New York: Holt, Rinehart & Winston.

Stotsky, S. (1983). Research on reading/writing relationships: A synthesis and suggested directions. *Language Arts, 60*(5), 627–641.

*Children's Literature*

Bauer, C. F. (1981). *My Mom Travels a Lot.* New York: Warne.

Brandenberg, A. (1965). *A Weed Is a Flower: The Life of George Washington Carver.* Englewood Cliffs, NJ: Prentice-Hall.

Brown, R. (1985). *The Big Sneeze.* New York: Lothrop, Lee & Shepard.

Fritz, J. (1976). *What's the Big Idea, Benjamin Franklin?* New York: Coward-Mc-Cann.

_____. (1980). *Where Do You Think You're Going, Christopher Columbus?* New York: Putnam's.

Hogrogian, N. (1971). *One Fine Day.* New York: Collier.

Numeroff, L. (1986). *If You Give a Mouse a Cookie.* New York: Scholastic.

Ormondroyd, E. (1969). *Broderick.* Berkeley, CA: Parnassus.

Wood, A. (1984): *The Napping House.* New York: Harcourt Brace Jovanovitch.

# chapter 7

# Children's Literature Review Part I: Annotated Bibliography and Web Illustrations

This chapter contains annotations and webs for approximately 50 books, both picture books and books for older students that are primarily text. The bibliography includes Caldecott and Newbery Medal and Honor books, IRA Children's Choices books, books chosen by the Children's Book Council as outstanding science and trade books, and other examples of quality literature for K–8 children and youth. The selections reflect a diversity of subject matter and cultural heritages, including African, Asian, European, Hispanic, and native American.

Each annotation includes: a *Summary* of the story; a *Setting* that includes time and place; a list of *Characters;* a *Theme,* or underlying idea; a list of potentially difficult *Vocabulary* in the book; a brief description of the *Illustrations; Grade Level/Content Area,* which identifies grades for which the book is appropriate and themes or units in science, social studies, math, health, art, or physical education with which the book can be used; and suggestions for using the web with students in the classroom.

The books are categorized by genre: folktale, fantasy, realistic fiction, historical fiction, biography, poetry, and information books. Within each genre, books are in alphabetical order according to the author's last name.

## *Folktale* ════════════════════════════════════════

══ Aardema, Verna. *Why Mosquitoes Buzz in People's Ears.* (Leo and Diane Dillon, Illus.). New York: Dial, 1975.

**Summary:** A cumulative tale from West Africa that provides a rich explanation for the constant noise made by the tiny mosquito.

**Setting:** The jungle of West Africa.

**Characters:** Mosquito, Iguana, Python, Crow, Rabbit, Monkey, Mother Owl, King Lion, and other animals of the jungle.

**Theme:** Own up to your crimes or your guilt will haunt you; or, genuine intentions can be misinterpreted and cause disaster.

**Vocabulary:** Animal names and onomatopoetic sounds; yam, prowling, leaping, grumbling, slithering, scurried, burrow, council fire, glancing, startled, alarmed, timid, mischief, nonsense, uncertainty, plotting, demanded, annoyed, satisfied, guilty conscience, summons.

**Illustrations:** Vivid colors and cut-out shapes accentuate the geometric forms in these full-page pictures that imitate the artistic style of the West African people. Text appears white on a black background in nighttime scenes and black on a white background in daytime scenes. The story can be told from the pictures alone, but the rich language of the text should not be overlooked.

**Grade Level/Content Area:** In grades 3–6 social studies, this story supports a unit on communities around the world, or, specifically, the culture and traditions of West Africa. For children studying folktales, this story contains three traditional elements: it is a cumulative account, it explains a natural phenomenon, and animals possess human traits and characteristics. It can be compared with other folktales from other cultures.

**Sequence Web:** Because of its cumulative pattern, this story lends itself to introducing storytelling to children and involving them in retelling. After reading the story, present this web to the children and have them take turns retelling the sequence of events in the story.

You can also use the basic structure of this story to promote creative writing of the "porquoi" or "why" tale that answers a question or explains how animals, plants, or humans were created and why they have certain characteristics. Have children choose another natural phenomenon to explain, such as why lightning flashes or why rattlesnakes make a rattling sound. Have them identify a setting for their story, and then let them supply the names of animals from that setting for each ray of the sun. Then have the group generate an oral story to accompany their sequence web. Oral practice such as this gives children a good basis for writing their own cumulative tales.

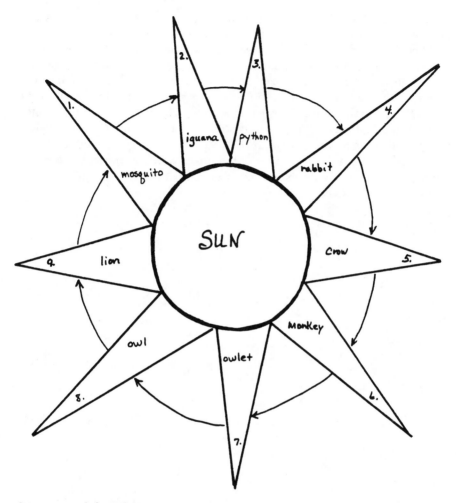

Sequence web for *Why Mosquitoes Buzz in People's Ears,* by Verna Aardema.

**Cause-Effect Map:** This story is effective in teaching the concepts of cause and effect. Make a chain of empty boxes, labeling every other one "cause" and "effect," beginning with the first box. To provide additional support in recognizing the pattern in the story, you can make all the "cause" boxes one color and all the "effect" boxes another color. Include arrows between boxes to designate direction. The first box represents the first event in the story—"Mosquito tells a lie"—which is a cause. The next box represents the effect of the first event, "Iguana puts sticks in ears." After reading the story aloud, give students this map with the first two boxes completed, and help them finish filling in the remainder of the boxes with appropriate causes and effects. Children can write a sentence in each box or draw a picture to represent the cause or effect.

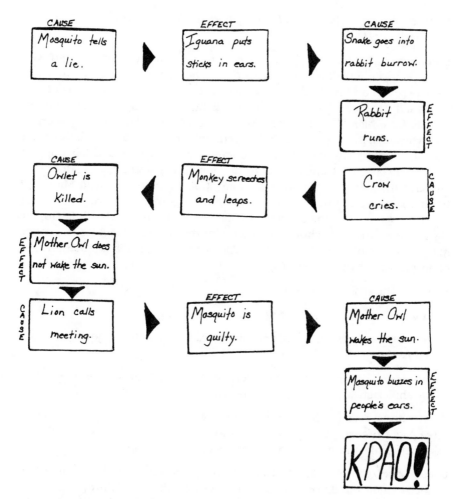

Cause-effect map for *Why Mosquitoes Buzz in People's Ears*, by Verna Aardema.

Bang, Molly. *The Goblins Giggle and Other Stories.* New York: Scribner's, 1973.

**Summary:** This book is a collection of folktales from Japan, Ireland, Germany, France, and China. The story "The Old Man's Wen" is about a man with a growth on his cheek who has learned to cope with it, although he remains sad. He meets goblins who consider his wen a sign of beauty and take it away from him. "The Boy Who Wanted to Learn to Shudder" concerns a boy whose family sees him as dull-witted and who sets out into the world to learn to shudder. He finds he has courage, determination, and ingenuity. In "A Soccer Game on Dung-ting Lake," a young boy's strength and father's talent save them from sea monsters. "Mary Culhane and the Dead Man" is a traditional graveyard story, with voices from the grave. It involves the acquisition of treasure after the successful completion of three trials. "The Goblins Giggle" is an Irish tale about a mother who rescues her daughter by rendering goblins helpless with laughter. (The remainder of this annotation concerns primarily "The Goblins Giggle.")

**Setting:** The Irish countryside.

**Characters:** Young girl, goblins, mother, nun, dogs.

**Theme:** Cleverness, strength, and humor can often achieve goals that seem unattainable.

**Vocabulary:** poker, goblins, shudder, ghost, lathe, hearth, nine-pins, blackthorn, shillelagh, sages, palanquin, abacus.

**Illustrations:** Full-page charcoal drawings, approximately one for every three pages of text, portray the old-world settings of these tales. The illustrations help make these wonderfully scary stories even more memorable.

**Grade Level/Content Area:** This collection lends itself well, in grades 5–8, to social studies units on various countries or cultures of Europe and Asia. These stories are also appropriate in a study of folktales from around the world.

**Story Map:** Either before or after reading "The Goblins Giggle" to students, you can present them with the basic structure of the story map, which includes the story title and the labels on the empty boxes and triangles. Discuss with students the common plot elements of problem, goal, events, and resolution, making sure that they understand these terms. After hearing or reading the story, help students fill in the appropriate information in each empty shape. When complete, this web can aid students in retelling the story or writing a synopsis of it.

This structure can also help students write their own stories. They can use either the characters from "The Goblins Giggle" or make up new characters and setting. If the latter, have students create a new set of plot elements, from which they can elaborate to create their own folktales.

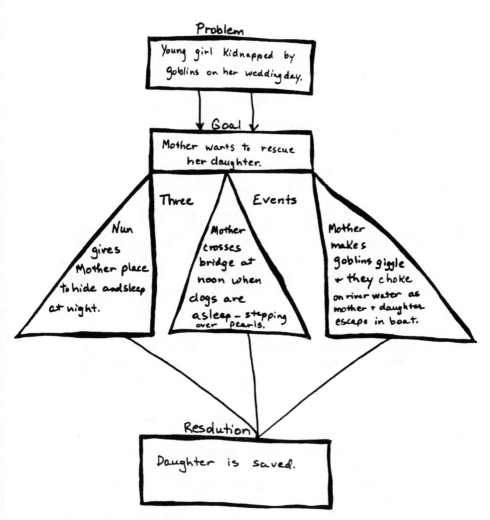

Story map for "The Goblins Giggle," by Molly Bang.

Goble, Paul. *Buffalo Woman.* New York: Macmillan, 1984.

**Summary:** A young Indian hunter marries a female buffalo in the form of a beautiful maiden. When his people reject her he must pass several tests before he is allowed to join the Buffalo Nation so that he can be with her.

**Setting:** The Great Plains of North America.

**Characters:** Young man, Buffalo woman, Calf-boy, Chief of the Buffalo Nation.

**Theme:** The buffalo and man share a common heritage.

**Vocabulary:** buffalo, Calf-boy, tipi, Straight-up-person.

**Illustrations:** The India ink and watercolor drawings are flat, one-dimensional representations similar to the tepee drawings of the Plains Indians, about whom the book is written. With shades of brown and black, Goble captures the massiveness of the shaggy buffalo. With bright colors and detailed drawings, Goble shares the authentic dress of these Indians and the expansiveness and beauty of the plains. Illustrations predominate across each double page; text is a secondary component.

**Grade Level/Content Area:** This native American legend is appropriate for students in grades 3–6. It could be used with a social studies unit on North American Indians, a geography lesson about the plains, a study of legends, or a lesson on character development, especially the traits of bravery and loyalty.

**Character Webs:** For the purposes of identifying and understanding character traits you can present these webs to students with only the characters' names supplied. Through group discussion, complete the webs with appropriate adjectives and descriptive words using students' responses.

Focus the discussion on how Goble develops the characters—through actions, pictures, or specifically stated descriptions—to help students gain a better understanding of how characterization is developed in this story. Students can use the character traits they identify, substitute new names for main characters, change the setting or theme of the story, and write their own stories. Using the structure of *Buffalo Woman* as a model can particularly help students who have trouble creating their own stories.

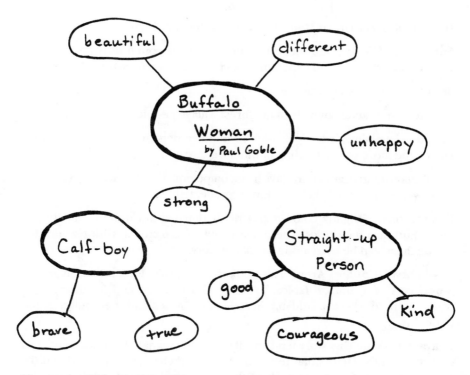

Character webs for *Buffalo Woman,* by Paul Goble.

Haley, Gail E. *The Green Man.* New York: Scribner's, 1979.

**Summary:** This is a European legend in which a young man becomes the Green Man for a year and experiences a character transformation.

**Setting:** The forests of Europe.

**Characters:** Claude, animals of the forest, village people.

**Theme:** Sometimes when we walk in another person's shoes, we become kinder and more understanding of others as a result.

**Vocabulary:** arrogant, vain, lavish, incompetent, beaters, leaner, defiantly, preserve, glean, hillock, lichen, mortar, pestle, tethered.

**Illustrations:** Brightly colored and richly detailed illustrations imitate medieval European tapestries. These nearly full-page pictures, with text printed beside them, can be used alone to tell the story.

**Grade Level/Content Area:** This book is appropriate for students in grades 3–6 as part of a unit on fables, folktales, and legends, and for students in grades 5 and 6 who are studying European countries and their cultures and traditions.

**Character Web:** This story lends itself nicely to an analysis of character and discussion of the factors that result in growth and change in an individual. To prepare students for the story, show them a blank character web first and/or discuss the idea of character growth and change that this legend is about.

After reading the story, divide your class into two groups, asking one group to brainstorm a list of words on chartpaper from the story or their own vocabularies that describe Claude's character; have the second group list words that describe the Green Man's character. Have students exchange lists to verify accuracy and add any other words they can. Then form one big group, and ask students to examine the lists for any descriptive words that fit both men's characters. Have students write these words or any other words they generate in the appropriate boxes. Then have them enter the best words that describe Claude and the Green Man in the appropriate boxes in the web. Then you can lead a discussion of how and why Claude changed, including students' experiences and feelings about positive character changes in their own lives. Explore the possibilities of the character change that might occur if the Green Man lived as the original Claude for a year, and discuss students' feelings about this negative character change.

The completed web can also provide a structure for writing descriptive paragraphs. Divide the class into three groups, asking one group to use words from the web to compose a paragraph describing the Green Man, but without using his name. Have a second group write about Claude in the same way and a third group describe the characteristics they share. Then read each paragraph to the class, asking the students to identify the character it describes.

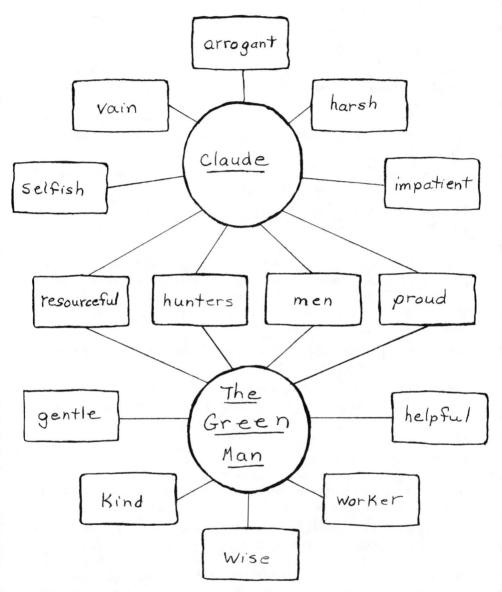

Character web for *The Green Man,* by Gail Haley.

Lofgren, Ulf. *The Boy Who Ate More Than the Giant and Other Swedish Folktales.* (S. LaFarge, Trans.). New York: William Collins & World Publishing Co. & U.S. Committee for UNICEF, 1978.

**Summaries:**  This book contains three folktales. *The Boy Who Ate More Than the Giant* is about a young goatherd who successfully outsmarts an angry giant, whose size does not necessarily match his intelligence. *The Master Tailor* is about a tailor who fools a client by seeming to work but actually accomplishing nothing. *The Three Billy Goats Bruse* is a tale of three billy goats troubled by a troll.

**Settings:**  For the three stories respectively:  the giant's mountain meadow and cabin, the tailor's shop, a stone bridge.

**Characters:**  A clever goatherd, his mother, an angry giant, and his ugly wife; a crafty tailor and a naive gentleman client; three billy goats and a wicked troll.

**Themes:**  *The Boy Who Ate* and *The Three Billy Goats* concern the outsmarting of creatures with great strength and powers by those who are smaller and less powerful, but clever. The theme of *The Master Tailor* is that show and fanfare often impress, but one should always look beyond that for what is real.

**Vocabulary:**  *(For The Boy Who Ate)* racket, commotion, goatherd, mere, rennet, curds and whey, wretch, flails of grain, threshing.

**Illustrations:**  Cartoon-style drawings are done in watercolor shades of brown and green, with heavily etched ink lines. The expressions on the faces of the giant, the little gentleman, and the troll suggest that they are vulnerable.

**Grade Level/Content Area:**  This book enriches a study of the Scandinavian countries in a grade 5 or 6 social studies unit on Eastern Europe, by helping students become familiar with other cultural traditions. The stories also are excellent for a study of folktales in grades 3–6, or as pure entertainment.

**Story Element Web:**  Either before or after reading *The Boy Who Ate* to students, you can present them with part of the story element web. Provide students with the story title and the words in the rectangles that represent the elements of a traditional folktale. Discuss these features, which are often found in folktales, and help students fill in the triangles with information from the story that corresponds to each element. When complete, this structure is useful for retelling or rewriting the story.

The story element web can help students creatively write other folktales. Give students the web with the elements in the rectangles and let them provide new information in each triangle, for example, "common people" might be a milkmaid, "conflict," a girl angers farmer, and so on. In this way, they can generate their own stories that contain the elements of a traditional folktale.

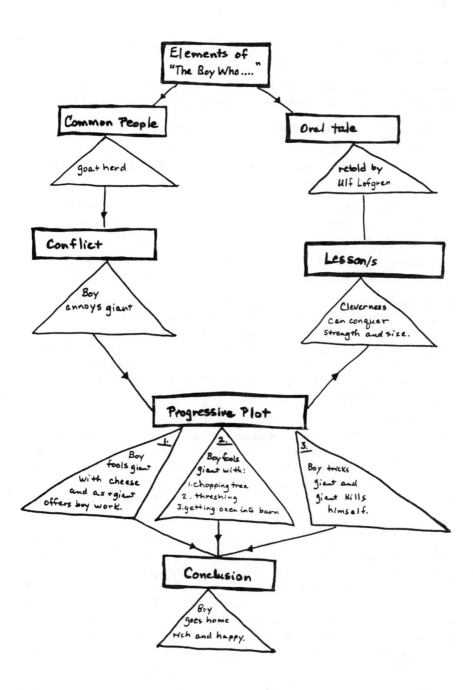

Story element web for *The Boy Who Ate More Than the Giant,* by Ulf Lofgren.

McDermott, Gerald. *Arrow to the Sun: A Pueblo Indian Tale.* New York: Puffin Books, Viking, 1986.

**Summary:** In this adaptation of a Pueblo Indian myth, a child searches for his father, and the story is told of how the sun comes to the world of man.

**Setting:** A Pueblo Indian village in southwestern United States and in the heavens.

**Characters:** Lord of the Sun, Young Maiden Boy, Pot Maker, Corn Planter, Arrow Maker, and other boys.

**Theme:** People can accomplish amazing things when they use their inner strength; or, with love, determination, and bravery, one can conquer the most powerful adversaries.

**Vocabulary:** pueblo, ceremony, kiva, endure, transformed, rejoiced, emerged, mocked, serpents.

**Illustrations:** Earth tones of orange, yellow, brown, and black dominate illustrations of the earth prior to the presence of the spirit of the Lord of the Sun. After the spirit world is introduced, colors become brighter and more vibrant, and the Boy brings these rainbow colors back to his people along with the spirit of the Lord of the Sun. Bright, rich colors and geometric shapes extend across full pages with text appearing as a minor part of each page in the open spaces of backgrounds.

**Grade Level/Content Area:** This folktale is appropriate for grades 1–3 and fits especially well with a social studies unit on communities around the world, since it is about the Pueblo culture. It would also be appropriate in a study of the history of the Southwest. For upper-grade students, it provides an example of the culturally universal theme of a deity and son sent to earth. The story can be used in a study of folktales, since it contains the common theme of a hero who must prove himself by overcoming adversity.

**Sequence Maps:** Maps like these, constructed after hearing or reading the story, make excellent models for student storytelling or writing. For younger children, a group story can be generated by having each child dictate or write a sentence to describe a different rebus picture. Older students enjoy retelling the story or writing descriptively and creatively about what happens to the boy as he passes through the four different Chambers of Ceremony; the Kivas of Lions, Serpents, Bees, and Lightning. This story can also be used as a springboard for creative thinking and writing. You might ask small

Sequence map for *Arrow to the Sun*, by Gerald McDermott.

groups of students to brainstorm and create original stories about a different main character and four different chambers of ceremonies. Or, students can rewrite the story by creating their own chambers and adversaries for the boy to conquer. Students enjoy using graph paper to draw geometric shapes and pictures to accompany their stories.

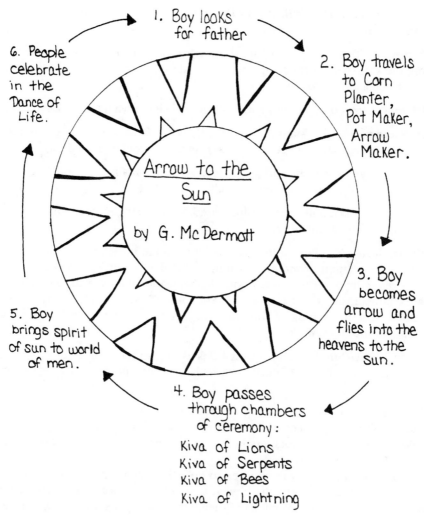

1. Boy looks for father

2. Boy travels to Corn Planter, Pot Maker, Arrow Maker.

3. Boy becomes arrow and flies into the heavens to the Sun.

4. Boy passes through chambers of ceremony:
Kiva of Lions
Kiva of Serpents
Kiva of Bees
Kiva of Lightning

5. Boy brings spirit of sun to world of men.

6. People celebrate in the Dance of Life.

Arrow to the Sun

by G. McDermott

Sequence map for *Arrow to the Sun*, by Gerald McDermott.

Steptoe, John. *Mufaro's Beautiful Daughters: An African Tale.* New York: Lothrop, Lee & Shepard, 1987.

**Summary:** This is an African tale about two beautiful girls who are called before the king, who is choosing a wife. The kindness of one of the girls results in her being chosen queen.

**Setting:** A long time ago in a small village and city in what is now Zimbabwe.

**Characters:** Mufaro, Manyara, Nyasha, Nyoka (character names are from the Shono language and reflect personality), small boy, old woman, King.

**Theme:** Vanity, deceit, and greed lead to a downfall; or, goodness is rewarded; or, "Pride goeth before a fall."

**Vocabulary:** bountiful, stole, silhouetted, acknowledges, commotion, destination, transfixed, chamber.

**Illustrations:** The illustrations are paintings done in rich colors that reflect the lush vegetation of the African jungle and the beauty of the people. Pictures generally cover two pages, with dialogue and actions used to communicate character traits. Illustrations are authentic (Steptoe studied actual ruins located near the setting of the story) and reflect respect and love for the people of southern Africa.

**Grade Level/Content Area:** This book is appropriate for grades K–3 and would enrich a study of folktales or social studies unit on Africa or foreign cultures.

**Character Web:** Before reading this story to children, show them the character web with the names of the daughters but no describing words. Tell the children that the two daughters in this story are the same in some ways and very different in other ways.

After reading, talk with children to help them explore their responses to the story, and ask them to share what they think the moral or theme of the story is. By accepting all versions of theme that they come up with, as long as they can support their idea, you help children understand that we all interpret things somewhat differently and that this diversity in ideas is good. Have children generate a list of words from the story that describes each daughter, adding their own descriptive adjectives. Discuss the ways that Steptoe develops his characters through action and dialogue.

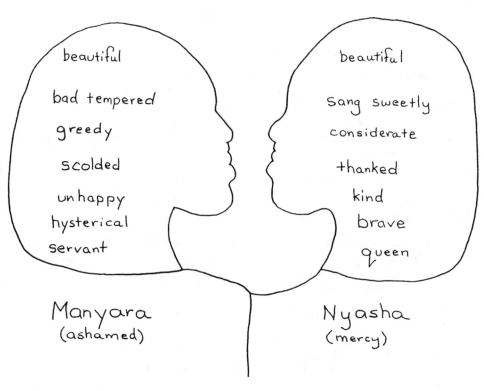

| beautiful | beautiful |
| bad tempered | sang sweetly |
| greedy | considerate |
| scolded | thanked |
| unhappy | kind |
| hysterical | brave |
| servant | queen |

Manyara
(ashamed)

Nyasha
(mercy)

Character web for *Mufaro's Beautiful Daughters,* by John Steptoe.

## *Fantasy* ====================================================

Babbitt, Natalie. *Tuck Everlasting.* New York: Trumpet, 1975.

**Summary:** Possessing eternal life after drinking from a magic spring, the Tuck family wanders about trying to live as inconspicuously as possible. When ten-year-old Winnie Foster stumbles onto their secret, the Tucks explain why living forever at one age is less a blessing than it might seem. Complications arise when Winnie is followed by a stranger who wants to market and sell the spring water.

**Setting:** Treegap, a rural community in Ohio, in the 1880s.

**Characters:** Winnie Foster, her mother, grandmother, and father; the Tucks—Angus, Mae, Jesse, and Miles; and the stranger.

**Theme:** The primary theme is that the cycle of life is inevitable and natural, or everlasting life is not necessarily a gift. Secondary themes involve growing from adolescence to adulthood, greed, and friendship that transcends time and accepts differences.

**Vocabulary:** eternity, melancholy, indomitable, petulance.

**Illustrations:** This American Library Association Notable Children's Book has no illustrations, except for the cover. On the paperback edition, the cover has a color drawing of a small red bungalow and a pond with two people in a rowboat.

**Grade Level/Content Area:** This book is suitable for students in grades 3–9. It works well with units on death and dying, the life cycle, or the novel. Younger students enjoy listening to it, and older students can read it themselves (it is written on about a fourth-grade level).

**Character Webs:** You can give students blank webs for the main characters, and as they hear or read the story, they can fill them in with adjectives that describe the characters. Completed webs can then be used as a basis for discussion of the story and its many themes.

If you use the book as a vehicle for studying the novel, Babbitt includes a variety of literary devices in her writing that students can easily identify: imagery, simile, metaphor, foreshadowing, and personification.

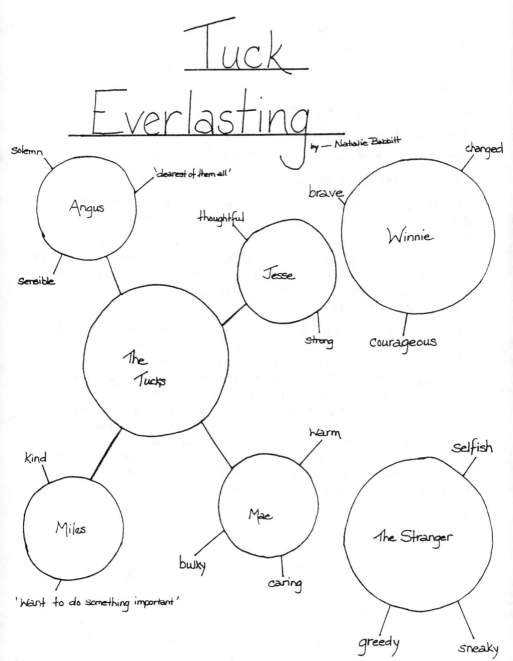

Character web for *Tuck Everlasting*, by Natalie Babbitt.

Barrett, J. *Cloudy with a Chance of Meatballs.* New York: Aladdin, 1978.

**Summary:** A tall tale about a community that receives its food from the sky, like the rain.

**Setting:** The land of Chewandswallow.

**Characters:** Mom, Grandpa, Henry, people of Chewandswallow.

**Theme:** What first appears to be marvelous can later be a disaster.

**Vocabulary:** prediction, sanitation, gorgonzola, mayonnaise.

**Illustrations:** Colored etchings of cartoon figures are done in bright pastels. Illustrations dominate each page, with text appearing in blocks in various locations on the pages.

**Grade Level/Content Area:** This book is suitable for grades 2-5 science studies of weather, weather forecasting and reporting, or food and nutrition. It is also a good example of a tall tale, or fantasy, for young students who are studying this category of literature.

**Story Map:** To provide a background for the story, discuss with students the definition of a tall tale and the characteristics of fantasy. Then, on the blackboard or chartpaper, present the cloud shapes labelled "setting," "characters," and "point of view" and the information listed as rain under each. Ask students to predict who they think the first-person narrator might be and what the plot and theme might be. Then read the story and, after encouraging students to discuss their reactions to it, have them decide what to add to the story map for "plot," "theme," and "point of view."

This book also lends itself well to creative writing. Students can create their own stories, using the elements of story on the story map, by changing the characters, setting, and plot before they begin writing.

Story map for *Cloudy with a Chance of Meatballs,* by J. Barrett.

= Carle, Eric. *The Very Hungry Caterpillar.* New York: Putnam's, 1970.

**Summary:** This story follows the life of a caterpillar as it grows, forms a cocoon, and emerges as a butterfly.

**Setting:** The green leaves of a shady tree.

**Character:** The hungry caterpillar.

**Theme:** The wonder and beauty of nature can be found in its simplest creatures.

**Vocabulary:** cocoon.

**Illustrations:** Full-page collage illustrations in vibrant colors are created with tissue paper, which is layered to create texture and shading. Cut-out circles on every other page allow the reader to glimpse what the caterpillar will devour next. Accompanying text is simple and has been translated into more than a dozen languages, so children around the world can enjoy this story.

**Grade Level/Content Area:** This book fits well with grades K–2 science units on life cycles and metamorphosis and K–1 math units on numbers and counting. The story contains sets of up to 10 objects and the names of the days of the week, so it can reinforce this vocabulary as well. It is also an example of the collage art form and serves as a good model for children who want to create their own collage illustrations.

**Story Map:** After the story is read to them, children enjoy taking turns and retelling it themselves. For children who have some reading skills, the story map shown here can be generated following the read-aloud. In addition, you can help them identify the progression of events in the story by adding the labels for the elements of story grammar and talking about them.

Story map for *The Very Hungry Caterpillar*, by Eric Carle.

**Setting**
In the light of the moon, an egg lay on a leaf.

**Beginning**
A caterpillar popped out of the egg. It was hungry.

**Reaction**
The caterpillar began to look for some food.

**Attempt**
He ate lots of food for one whole week.

**Outcome**
At the end of the week Caterpillar has a stomachache, so he builds a cocoon and goes to sleep.

**Ending**
When he came out of the cocoon, he was a beautiful butterfly.

Gerstein, Mordecai. *The Mountains of Tibet.* New York: Harper & Row, 1987.

**Summary:** After dying, a Tibetan woodcutter is given the choice of going to heaven or living another life anywhere in the universe.

**Setting:** A valley high in the mountains of Tibet.

**Characters:** The woodcutter, his family, the voice.

**Theme:** Most of us would make the same choices in our lives if we had them to make again; or, life is a series of choices.

**Vocabulary:** village, bright, universe, woodcutter, blazed, fireworks, frightened, pinwheel, sparkling.

**Illustrations:** The illustrations are of varied colors and intensities and have a slightly stylized quality, suggestive of miniature paintings from the East. Shape and arrangement of pictures and location of text change in relation to choices the woodcutter has.

**Grade Level/Content Area:** This book is useful in grades 3–6 social studies units on communities around the world or various cultural beliefs about death and dying, since it deals with a mountain community in Asia and reincarnation of the soul. It also is useful as a vehicle for strengthening prediction skills.

**Sequence Web:** Students need some background information on this story to best ensure their comprehension. You might begin by looking at a map of Asia with children, finding Tibet, and discussing the geography and life there. Children will profit from hearing about what *reincarnation* is and its importance to Eastern culture.

After hearing the story or reading it themselves, children can construct the story web shown, or one like it that includes the important events and choices the woodcutter had. From this web, lead a discussion of theme, being sure to accept any theme a child can support reasonably well from the story. If the idea of reincarnation is new to your children, encourage them to do further reading in the library to find out more about Eastern culture.

This story lends itself well to creative writing. You may want to ask children to think about and write accounts of what they think will happen when they die or what their choices might be if they were given the option of reincarnation.

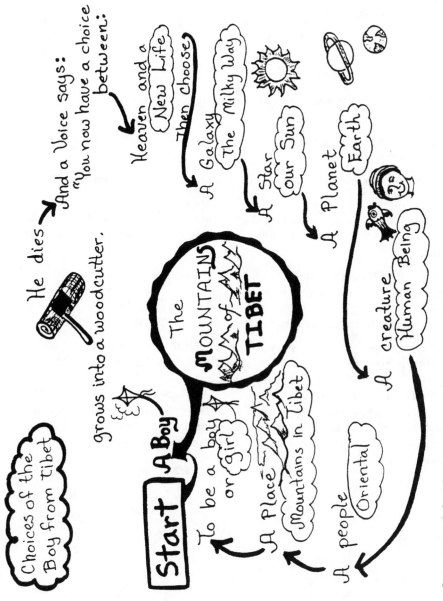

Sequence web for *The Mountains of Tibet*, by Mordecai Gerstein.

139

Kraus, Robert. *Another Mouse to Feed.* (Jose Aruego and Ariane Dewey, Illus.). New York: Prentice-Hall, 1980.

**Summary:** When Mr. and Mrs. Mouse become exhausted from overwork and caring for all their children, the little mice take over.

**Setting:** The Mouse's house.

**Characters:** Mr. Mouse, Mrs. Mouse, mouse children, Edgar (the oldest mouse child).

**Theme:** Many hands make light work when everyone in the family works to achieve one goal.

**Vocabulary:** instructor, wicker, employment, agency, scrubbing, necessities, extra, cashier.

**Illustrations:** Pictures of blue and green mice with pink ears dominate the pages of this book. The story is told in readable text that is subordinate to the pictures.

**Grade Level/Content Area:** This book fits well with a grades K–2 social studies unit on the family. It stresses the importance of the individual in the family, the interchangeability of roles, and that teamwork is needed to achieve goals. It can be used to explore adoption.

**Sequence Web:** After the story is read to children and discussed, you can help them construct a web that briefly tells the important events as they occurred. Transcribe these events on the web as children look at the pictures a second time and dictate them to you.

You might also present children with the events on the web out of their proper order and have children reorder them and number them as they happened. After young children have established the sequence of events, they enjoy dramatizing this story.

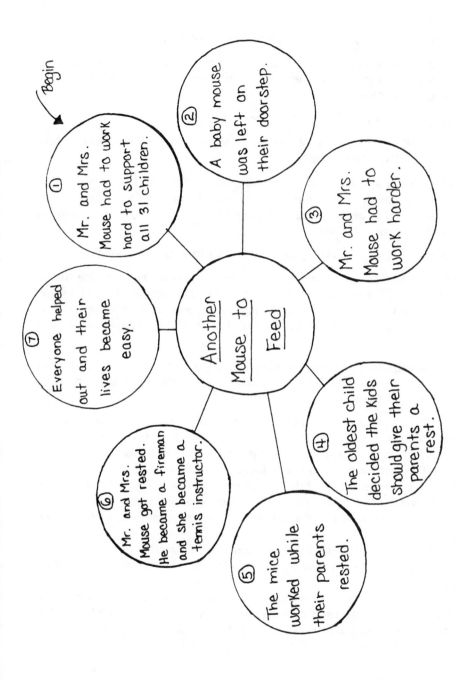

Begin

① Mr. and Mrs. Mouse had to work hard to support all 31 children.

② A baby mouse was left on their doorstep.

③ Mr. and Mrs. Mouse had to work harder.

Another Mouse to Feed

⑦ Everyone helped out and their lives became easy.

⑥ Mr. and Mrs. Mouse got rested. He became a fireman and she became a tennis instructor.

⑤ The mice worked while their parents rested.

④ The oldest child decided the kids should give their parents a rest.

Sequence map for *Another Mouse to Feed*, by Robert Kraus.

141

L'Engle, Madeleine. *A Wrinkle in Time.* New York: Dell, 1976.

**Summary:** Meg and Charles, with their friend Calvin, embark on an interplanetary mission to rescue their father, Mr. Murry, a scientist who has been missing for over a year.

**Setting:** Murry's home, Uriel, Camazotz.

**Characters:** Meg, Charles, Mr. and Mrs. Murry, Calvin, It, the Beasts, Mrs. Who, Mrs. Whatsit, Mrs. Which.

**Theme:** The major theme is that those who possess love and goodness can conquer the forces of evil. Minor themes include the need for perseverance, faith, and unity in time of danger; the need for love and acceptance; growing up; and children as heroes.

**Vocabulary:** tesseract, malignant, mental telepathy, extraterrestrial.

**Illustrations:** The only illustration is on the cover of the book, which shows two figures with a background of mountains and cloudy sky. One figure has the head and torso of a human, the legs, body, and tail of a horse, and the wings of a bird. The other figure is that of a head with red eye sockets in a blue circle.

**Grade Level/Content Area:** This book is suitable for students in grades 4–8 who are studying the solar system or astronomy, or fantasy or science fiction as a genre of literature.

**Story Map:** As an introduction to the story, first share with your students the "point of view," "main characters," and "setting" elements of the story map. Or, read the first chapter to them and then share this background information so they will have an understanding of what the book is about. Have students fill in the remainder of the map when the book is finished. A story map can be created that also includes problem, goal, attempts, and outcome, since there are a number of attempts that the children make to rescue Mr. Murry.

This book easily lends itself to discussion of a variety of topics. For example, the terms *protagonist* and *antagonist* can be explored and defined. The multiple themes, suspenseful action, and varied ages of the main character children make the story a high-interest one for almost any group of students, and so provoke lively discussions. It is especially appealing for adolescents because Meg matures and undergoes a character change that involves coming to terms with her weaknesses and making them her strengths.

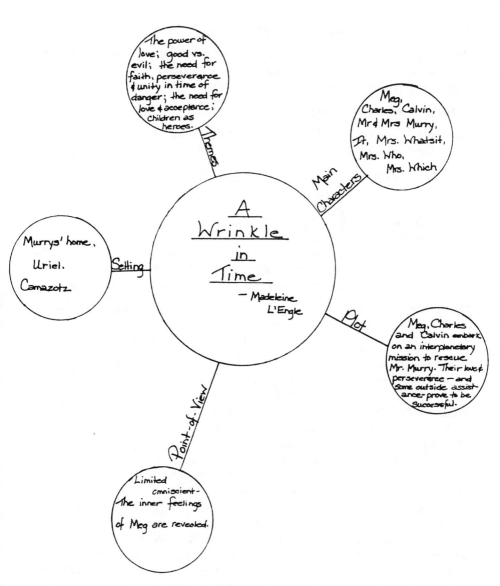

Story map for *A Wrinkle in Time,* by Madeleine L'Engle.

Shulevitz, Uri. *One Monday Morning.* New York: Macmillan, 1967.

**Summary:** This is a cumulative tale in which a king and queen and their growing entourage return each morning to a tenement house until the boy they have come to visit is at home to greet them.

**Setting:** A tenement apartment in a large city.

**Characters:** Little Boy, King, Queen, Little Prince, Knight, Royal Guard, Royal Cook, Royal Barber, Royal Jester, Little Dog.

**Theme:** There is no limit to the human imagination.

**Vocabulary:** Names of the days of the week and characters.

**Illustrations:** Illustrations become larger and more colorful as the story progresses and the Little Boy uses his imagination. Colors of the tenement buildings are dull and drab; in contrast, colors used to depict royalty are bright. Text and pictures are interwoven carefully so that the harder the Little Boy's imagination works, the more colorful become the illustrations.

**Grade Level/Content Area:** This book is suitable for grades K–2 as a purely enjoyable experience, as a vehicle for learning the names of the days of the week, or as a way of learning about the pattern of a cumulative tale.

**Story Map:** The cumulative nature of the story makes it good material for a directed listening-thinking activity, since students can make predictions about who they think will visit next and which day comes next. The story also lends itself to choral reading or individual retellings.

As a way of helping children recall events, construct the story map shown here after reading the story. For young children who are nonreaders, it may be enough to include only the names of the days of the week. For children who can read, add the names of the characters as they appear in the story and have children retell the story from the map.

The illustrations in this book are excellent to use in developing young children's visual literacy skills. While children examine the shapes, colors, and arrangement of the illustrations, you can help them learn about how Shulevitz manipulates these elements to enhance the story. Be sure to have children compare the first picture, in which the Little Boy sits at a window on a dreary, rainy day, with the last picture, in which he sits at the same window and the sun is shining. Have children note the objects in both pictures that as clues about the origin of the boy's imaginary royal friends.

| Weekly Appointment Book | | | | | | |
|---|---|---|---|---|---|---|
| Monday | Tuesday | Wednesday | Thursday | Friday | Saturday | Sunday |
| King, Queen and Little Prince | King, Queen, Little Prince and Knight | King, Queen, Little Prince, Knight and Royal Guard | King, Queen, Little Prince, Knight, Royal Guard and Royal Cook | King, Queen, Little Prince, Knight, Royal Guard, Royal Cook, and Royal Barber | King, Queen, Little Prince, Knight, Royal Guard, Royal Cook, Royal Barber and Royal Jester | King, Queen, Little Prince, Knight, Royal Guard, Royal Cook, Royal Barber, Royal Jester and a little dog |

Story map for *One Monday Morning,* by Uri Shulevitz.

Van Allsburg, Chris. *The Polar Express*. Boston: Houghton Mifflin, 1985.

**Summary:** A magical train ride on Christmas eve takes a boy to the North Pole to receive a special gift from Santa Claus.

**Setting:** The North Pole and a family's home.

**Characters:** Young boy, Santa Claus, Sarah, Mother, Father, Conductor.

**Theme:** The magic of Christmas is real for those who believe in it.

**Vocabulary:** Christmas, Santa, nougat, North Pole, harness.

**Illustrations:** Full-color pastel drawings create a sense of mystery, wonder, and magic throughout this book. Subdued colors and shapes give the pictures a softness of texture that is enhanced by snow and the semidarkness of evening. Each picture covers both facing pages, with text printed in a column on one side of a page.

**Grade Level/Content Area:** Use this story with K–6 children, who will enjoy it during the Christmas season. For children in grades 1 or 2, it enriches a study of the seasons; for students in grades 3–6, it is appropriate for the study of Christmas holiday celebrations around the world, variety in cultural beliefs, or fantasy as a literary genre.

**Concept Web:** Use the word *Christmas* as the organizing concept for a map of words to describe the concept. Using a concept map before reading the story helps assess and organize students' existing background knowledge and gives them a frame of reference for this story.

**Sequence Web:** Read the story to children and discuss the main actions of the plot. As children retell the story, you can transcribe what they dictate in the bubbles around the title, having them indicate where each action they relate fits in the sequence of events. To help children who might have trouble, write the first three or four words in each bubble and let the children supply the rest. Focus discussion on which actions in the story are based in fantasy and which in reality so that children learn to understand which elements of story are manipulated in this fantasy. You need to be sensitive both to children who hold beliefs in "the spirit" of Christmas and those who do not.

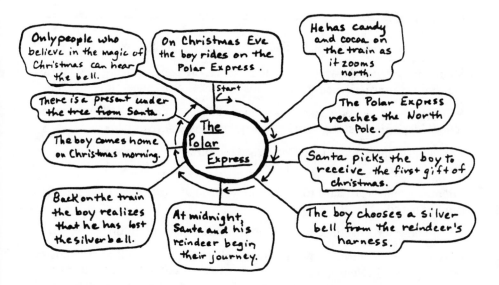

Sequence web for *The Polar Express,* by Chris Van Allsburg.

## *Realistic Fiction* ═══════════════════════════════════

Aliki (Brandenberg). *Feelings.* New York: Mulberry Books, 1984.

**Summary:** Vignettes, which include pictures, dialogues, poems, and stories, that portray universal emotions: jealousy, sadness, fear, anger, joy, love, etc.

**Setting:** Each vignette takes place in a different setting, such as a home, school, department store, birthday party, stage, grassy river bank.

**Characters:** A variety of children; readers, however, will see themselves as the main characters in this book.

**Theme:** Feelings are hard to explain in words, but we all have them and they can be shared.

**Vocabulary:** crocus, dialogue, outburst, chicken pox, attention.

**Illustrations:** Colorful drawings communicate feelings, such as the illustration entitled "Feeling Quiet," which is done in soft shades of lavenders, blues, greens, and yellows, showing a child with a teddy bear having a quiet picnic on the river bank. Arrangements of text and illustration convey meaning, such as in the illustration entitled "An Outburst in Many Words" that shows words bursting from the speaker's mouth in the direction of the child receiving the message.

**Grade Level/Content Area:** This book is suitable for use with children in grades K-3 in a health unit on awareness of the self or a language arts lesson on feelings. It can also be used to develop children's creative problem-solving skills.

**Story Starter Web:** After you read this book to children, help them develop a web with the title of the book in the center of the web and each feeling on one strand. In the bubble on the end of each strand, write a sentence starter. Have the group name all the things that make them feel happy, afraid, and so on, and discuss why each thing creates that particular feeling, listing them on the web. Do this for each of the feelings discussed in the book, and when you have written them on the web, use it as a springboard for making a book. Have each child make a five-page book (or more, depending on the number of feelings they want to include) called "My Feelings," with a cover and page for each section of the web. Be sure to have children give reasons for their feelings so that they learn to understand and verbalize these reasons.

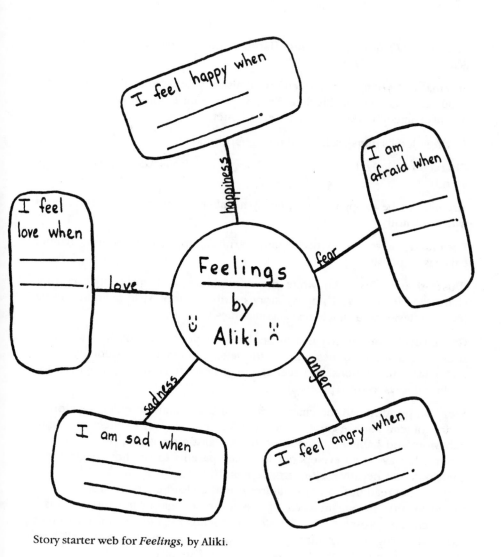

Story starter web for *Feelings*, by Aliki.

Blue, Rose. *Wishful Lying.* (Laura Hartman, Illus.). New York: Human Sciences Press, 1980.

**Summary:** A young boy feels left out of his busy family and fabricates stories about activities he and his family enjoy. When he is found out, he and his parents come to understand each other better.

**Setting:** Jody's home, school, and neighborhood.

**Characters:** Jody, his parents, Mrs. Marcus (the housekeeper), Pete (Jody's friend).

**Theme:** To be happy together, family members need to share their feelings with one another.

**Vocabulary:** recess, housekeeper, carnival, appreciate, punish, flannel pajamas, expensive.

**Illustrations:** Blue and white drawings done in blueprint style convey characters' feelings and portray story events. Cartoon-style balloons reveal Jody's fantasies, and simple text accompanies.

**Grade Level/Content Area:** This book is suitable for students in grades 1–5. It extends a social studies unit on the family and can help students better understand the actions and feelings of others. It is also appropriate for exploring ways to solve problems.

**Story Map:** Although the characters arrive at a somewhat quick solution to their problems and we know it actually takes much longer to effect change in behaviors and habits, this book portrays realistic emotions, problems, and actions. It may be an eye-opener for some parents to see how neglect can contribute to a negative self-image, depression, and aggression.

    You can read this story to children and then lead them in a discussion of the ideas that belong in each of the three triangles: "initiating events," "conflict," and "resolution." This story also lends itself to a character web of Jody's changing feelings throughout the story. Creating this web will help children better understand Jody's emotions and actions.

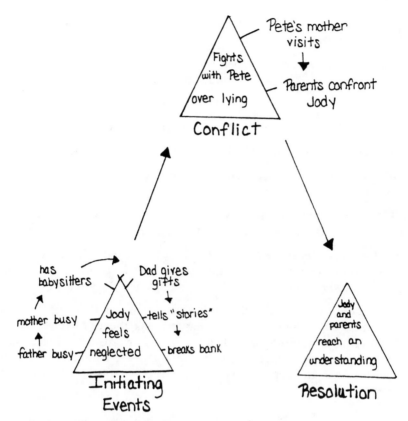

Story map for *Wishful Lying*, by Rose Blue.

=== Carrick, Carol. *The Foundling*. (Donald Carrick, Illus.). New York:
Seabury Press, 1977.

**Summary:** Christopher remembers his dog, who was killed in an accident,
and resists his parents' efforts to adopt a puppy.

**Setting:** A village on the seacoast.

**Characters:** Christopher, Mom, Dad, Tilton family, Ben.

**Theme:** Grief over a death includes many feelings that can change over time.

**Vocabulary:** nuzzle, animal shelter, abandon, cast, bait, cruised, furiously,
snapper, unfaithful, rummaged.

**Illustrations:** Pictures done in watercolor shades of brown and green are
usually full page and predominate over text. Illustrations often surround text.

**Grade Level/Content Area:** This book can be used in grades 1–4 in a
special lesson or unit on feelings and emotions or death and dying. It might
help children who have just lost a pet to understand their grief better.

**Feelings Web:** After reading this story to children, ask if any of them have
had a similar experience and how they felt. Ask them: What feelings did
Christopher have in the story? Write a list of these words on the blackboard.
Children may supply words like guilt, sadness, love, happiness, sympathy,
hope, excitement, and anger. Then draw the web with blank bubbles and ask
children:

- Which feelings did Christopher have at the beginning of the story?
- Which feelings did Christopher have at the end of the story?

Put these words onto the web, with feelings that occurred first in the
story entered into the top bubbles and feelings that came later in the story
entered into the bottom bubbles. Talk about the remaining words and decide
whether they came in the middle of the story, and if they did, put them in the
middle bubbles, or rearrange words as the group thinks is appropriate. Then,
for each feeling, ask children: What do you think caused Christopher to feel
this way? Write each response in the corresponding bubble.

With this finished web as a guide for discussion, ask children if they
recognize any feelings they may have had when their pet died. Talk with the
group about how feelings change over time and how natural this is.

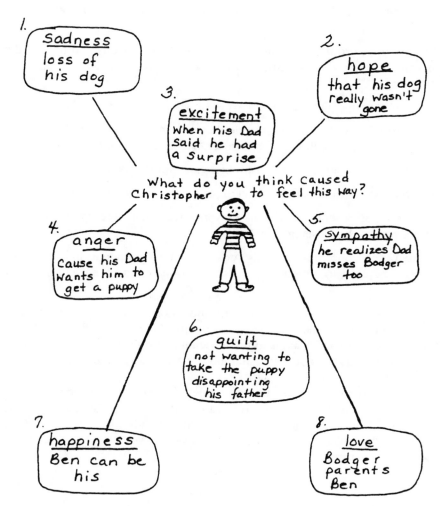

1. Sadness
   loss of
   his dog

2. hope
   that his dog
   really wasn't
   gone

3. excitement
   When his Dad
   said he had
   a surprise

What do you think caused
Christopher to feel this way?

4. anger
   Cause his Dad
   Wants him to
   get a puppy

5. sympathy
   he realizes Dad
   misses Bodger
   too

6. guilt
   not wanting to
   take the puppy
   disappointing
   his father

7. happiness
   Ben can be
   his

8. love
   Bodger
   parents
   Ben

Feelings web for *The Foundling*, by Carol Carrick.

Konigsburg, E. L. *From the Mixed-Up Files of Mrs. Basil E. Frankweiler.*
New York: Atheneum, 1968.

**Summary:** A brother and sister run away to New York City and hide in the Metropolitan Museum of Art, which leads them to make an interesting discovery.

**Setting:** Metropolitan Museum of Art in New York City.

**Characters:** Claudia Kincaid, Jamie Kincaid, Kevin, Steve, Mr. and Mrs. Kincaid, guards, Mrs. Basil E. Frankweiler, Saxonberg, Sheldon.

**Theme:** Perseverance and inquisitiveness are good traits to possess.

**Vocabulary:** Metropolitan Museum of Art, Michelangelo, pagan, statue.

**Illustrations:** Several pen-and-ink drawings accompany text. One of these is a floor plan of the museum.

**Grade Level/Content Area:** This book is suitable for students in grades 4–6. It might be used to enrich a social studies unit on cities, museums, or art history.

**Story Map:** Before reading the story to students or after you have read them the first chapter, make them a blow-up or copy of the museum's floor plan so they can see firsthand what is in the museum and how it is laid out. Then as you read the book, students can follow Claudia and Jamie as they hunt through the museum.

This story map includes the traditional elements of story grammar and can be generated or created together with children as they listen to the story. Before each episode, you can provide students with what the characters, setting, and problem are and have them dictate to you or fill in themselves the action and resolution.

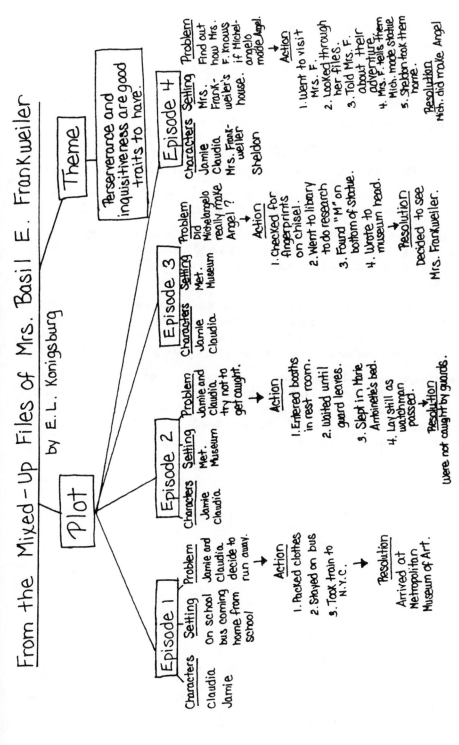

From the Mixed-Up Files of Mrs. Basil E. Frankweiler

by E.L. Konigsburg

**Plot**

**Theme**

Perseverance and inquisitiveness are good traits to have.

**Episode 1**

Characters
Claudia
Jamie

Setting
On school bus coming home from school

Problem
Jamie and Claudia decide to run away.

Action
1. Packed clothes
2. Stayed on bus
3. Took train to N.Y.C.

Resolution
Arrived at Metropolitan Museum of Art.

**Episode 2**

Characters
Jamie
Claudia

Setting
Met. Museum

Problem
Jamie and Claudia try not to get caught.

Action
1. Entered booths in rest room.
2. Waited until guard leaves.
3. Slept in Marie Antoinette's bed.
4. Lay still as watchman passed.

Resolution
were not caught by guards.

**Episode 3**

Characters
Jamie
Claudia

Setting
Met. Museum

Problem
Did Michelangelo really make Angel?

Action
1. Checked for fingerprints on chisel.
2. Went to library to do research
3. Found "M" on bottom of statue.
4. Wrote to museum head.

Resolution
Decided to see Mrs. Frankweiler.

**Episode 4**

Characters
Jamie
Claudia
Mrs. Frankweiler
Sheldon

Setting
Mrs. Frankweiler's house.

Problem
Find out how Mrs. F. knows if Michelangelo made Angel.

Action
1. Went to visit Mrs. F.
2. Looked through her files.
3. Told Mrs. F. about their adventure.
4. Mrs. F. tells them Mich. made statue.
5. Sheldon took them home.

Resolution
Mich. did make Angel

Story map for *From the Mixed-Up Files of Mrs. Basil E. Frankweiler*, by E. L. Konigsburg.

Lewin, Hugh. *Jafta's Father.* (Lisa Kopper, Illus.). Minneapolis, MN: Carolrhoda Books, 1981.

**Summary:** A young boy who believes that his father will someday return to his family recalls the things he enjoyed doing with his father, who works far away from home.

**Setting:** A village somewhere in present-day Africa.

**Characters:** Jafta, Jafta's father, Obed (Jafta's brother), Jafta's mother.

**Theme:** Hope and faith are sustained by the recollection of fond memories.

**Vocabulary:** poplars, swaying, bluegum (tree), baobab (tree), shoulders, stakes, snug, bundles, squeaking, sow, allowed, raft.

**Illustrations:** Simple, bold drawings done in shades of brown predominate over text, which is placed around the drawings. Illustrations are done from the perspective of a child and complement the text, which is written in first person.

**Grade Level/Content Area:** This book is suitable for use with children in grades 1-3 who are studying different kinds of families or communities in other countries. In a third-grade social studies curriculum, this book could be used to illustrate how economics and politics influence a family.

**Story Map:** Help children construct this story map of descriptive words and feelings after you have read the story to them. Supply children with the titles for each box, and let them decide what fits best in each box. You can write their suggestions in for them. The completed map now provides for a discussion of the story themes.

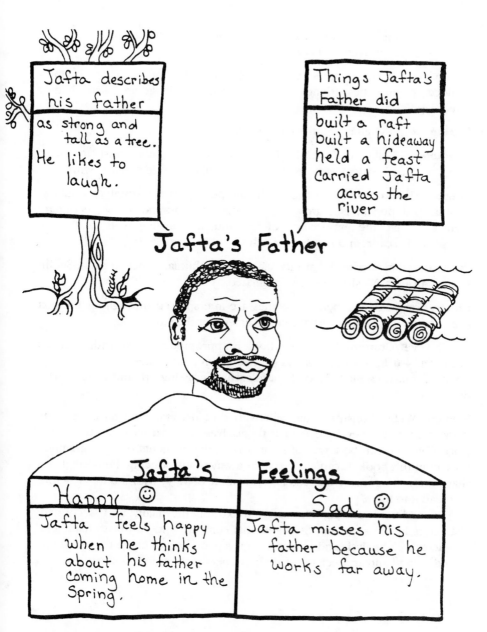

**Jafta describes his father** as strong and tall as a tree. He likes to laugh.

**Things Jafta's Father did**
built a raft
built a hideaway
held a feast
Carried Jafta across the river

## Jafta's Father

### Jafta's Feelings

| Happy ☺ | Sad ☹ |
|---|---|
| Jafta feels happy when he thinks about his father coming home in the Spring. | Jafta misses his father because he works far away. |

Story map for *Jafta's Father*, by Hugh Lewin.

══  Paterson, Katherine. *Bridge to Terabithia.* (Donna Diamond, Illus.).
New York: Harper & Row, 1977.

**Summary:**  Two fifth-graders, who are very different yet face common conflicts, become best friends and create a fantasy kingdom to which they can escape.

**Setting:**  Rural Virginia and the fantasy world of Terabithia.

**Characters:**  Leslie, Jess, their families, Miss Edmunds (Jess's music teacher), May Belle (Jess's sister), various students at Lark Creek Elementary School.

**Theme:**  The major theme is friendship and perhaps that through an unlikely friendship a person can grow and change in profound ways. Secondary themes involve the importance of individuality, dealing with death, the necessity of escape, and respect for nature.

**Vocabulary:**  hypocritical, baripity, clabber, Terabithia, Prince Terrien, Smithsonian Museum, Washington, DC, cremated.

**Illustrations:**  Twelve pencil sketches are interspersed throughout the text and provide just enough visual reinforcement for the story.

**Grade Level/Content Area:**  This book is appropriate for use with students in grades 4–6 in a social studies or health unit on issues of stereotyping, nonconformity, conflicts faced by adolescents growing up, and dealing with death.

**Element Web:**  Construct this web with students after you have read the story to them or they have read it themselves and you have discussed the story. The web can be a way of summarizing the elements of story grammar present in this book. It can also serve as a way of introducing the book if you share the setting, main characters, and point of view with students before you read it to them.

In addition, making character webs for the main and secondary characters in the story can help students compare and contrast characters. Character web analysis and comparison is a good way to encourage students to understand and appreciate the different personalities in this story.

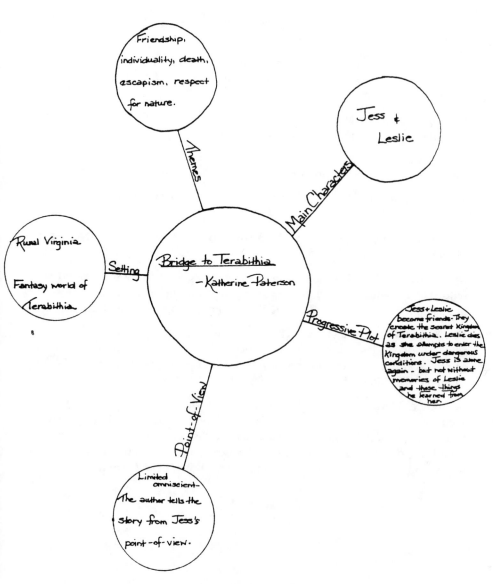

Element web for *Bridge to Terabithia*, by Katherine Paterson.

Surat, Michelle M. *Angel Child, Dragon Child.* (Vo-Dinh Mai, Illus.).
Milwaukee, WI: Raintree Publishers, 1983.

**Summary:** A Vietnamese girl attending school in the United States and
lonely for her mother who is still in Vietnam makes a friend whose idea en-
ables the mother to come to America.

**Setting:** The home and school environment of a young Vietnamese girl who
recently arrived in the United States.

**Characters:** Ut, her father, her mother, Little Quang (her brother), Chi Hai
(her older sister), Raymond (a boy at school), the principal.

**Theme:** Sometimes a person who at first seems unkind may turn into a
wonderful friend.

**Vocabulary:** tilted, jangled, rushing, twittered, screeched, gleamed, slung,
pinched.

**Illustrations:** Pastel-colored pencil drawings portray the sensitive and shy
nature of a young girl who misses her mother and give the trees and flowers
in some pictures an Oriental flavor. Text appears at the bottom of the pages.

**Grade Level/Content Area:** This book fits well into a social studies curriculum for grades 2 and 3. It introduces children to the variety of ethnic
groups living in a community and helps develop an understanding of how
foreign policy affects individual people.

**Sequence Web:** Introduce the book with a discussion of friendship, the
Vietnamese War, or a child's love for her mother before reading the story
aloud. Discussion following the story can focus on how Ut and Raymond's
friendship developed and its results. You can help children summarize this
discussion by constructing the sequence map shown or one like it.

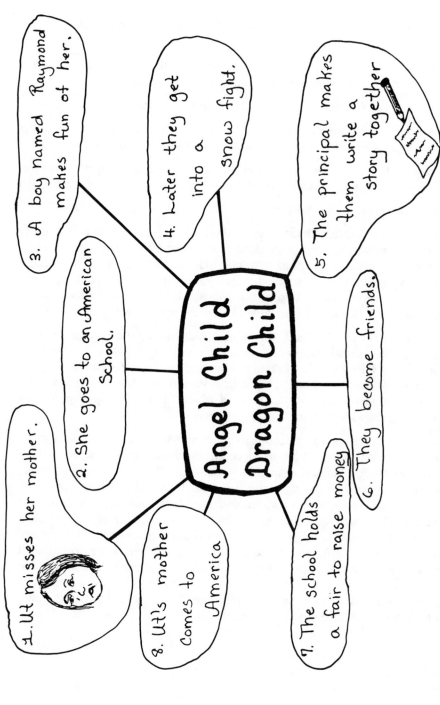

The central node reads:

**Angel Child
Dragon Child**

1. Ut misses her mother.

2. She goes to an American School.

3. A boy named Raymond makes fun of her.

4. Later they get into a snow fight.

5. The principal makes them write a story together.

6. They become friends.

7. The school holds a fair to raise money.

8. Ut's mother comes to America.

Sequence web for *Angel Child, Dragon Child,* by Michelle Surat.

Williams, Vera B. *A Chair for My Mother.* New York: Mulberry Books, 1982.

**Summary:** After all their furniture is lost in a fire, a child, her waitress mother, and her grandmother save dimes to buy a comfortable armchair.

**Setting:** An apartment in the city, a diner, and a furniture store.

**Characters:** A young girl, her waitress mother, the grandmother who lives with them, various other family members, and Josephine, the mother's boss.

**Theme:** When people work together they can make their dreams come true; or, cooperation and hard work yield happiness.

**Vocabulary:** diner, tips, bargain, tulips, block, "take a load off my feet."

**Illustrations:** The dominant color of the book is red, and on almost every page an important figure is painted the same red as the red roses on the chair shown at the end. Illustrations in bright, rich colors fill each left-hand page, while text appears on right-hand pages for the most part. Both text and picture are framed with a border that repeats the theme of the page, and a small picture of this theme is included below the text of each page.

**Grade Level/Content Area:** This book is suitable for use with children in grades K–3 in a social studies unit on families and communities. It focuses on a one-parent family with a working mother and no father figure and shows a diverse racial and ethnic mix in the neighborhood. The book emphasizes the necessity of saving to obtain a desired object. It is also appropriate for developing knowledge of the elements of story.

**Story Map:** After reading this book to children, have them help draw a story map like the one shown here to represent the plot. On the left, have them draw the wooden kitchen chair that Mom sits in after work, in the middle, the empty jar, and on the right, the armchair. These represent the problem, the action, and the solution respectively. Then have children talk about and describe what each drawing represents. The description of the problem should include what is the problem, why it is the problem, and how it came to be a problem. The action should include what each character does to lead the story further toward the solution. The solution should include why the armchair is the solution. Once children have verbalized each component of the story map, ask them to write the plot onto the story map. When the map is finished have children use it to retell the story.

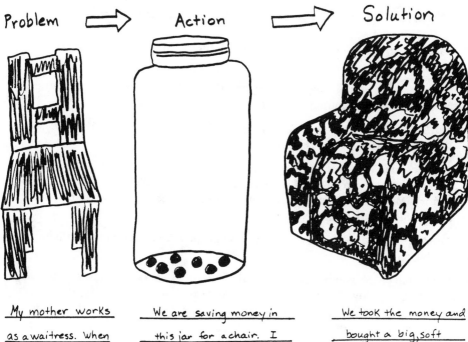

**Problem** ⟹ **Action** ⟹ **Solution**

| Problem | Action | Solution |
|---|---|---|
| My mother works as a waitress. When she comes home all she can rest her feet in this chair, because our furniture burned in a fire. | We are saving money in this jar for a chair. I put the money I earn in. My mom puts her extra tips in. Grandma puts her savings in. | We took the money and bought a big, soft chair. Now my mother has a comfortable place to sit after work. We sit in it with her. |

Story map for *A Chair for My Mother*, by Vera Williams.

## Historical Fiction ═══════════════════════════════════

Gardiner, John. *Stone Fox.* (Marcia Sewall, Illus.). New York: Harper & Row, 1960.

**Summary:** A young boy hopes to pay the back taxes on his grandfather's farm with the prize money from a dogsled race he enters.

**Setting:** Some time ago on a potato farm in Wyoming, and in Jackson, Wyoming, in view of the Teton Mountains.

**Characters:** Willy, his grandfather, Searchlight (Willy's dog), Doc Smith, Mr. Leeks (potato buyer), Miss Williams (Willy's teacher), Clifford Snyder (tax collector), Mr. Foster (bank president), Lester (general store owner), Mayor Smiley, Stone Fox, Samoyed dogs.

**Theme:** With determination, the small and powerless can successfully fight the big and powerful.

**Vocabulary:** Shoshone, Arapaho, Samoyed, dogsled race, taxes, savings account, crop, plow, harness, harvest, irrigation, acre, city slickers, derringer, authority, legal, ten dollar gold pieces, property, Wyoming, Teton Mountains, contestants, nine abreast.

**Illustrations:** Fifteen simple pencil drawings are interspersed throughout 80 pages of text. Each full-page illustration has a white border framing it, and each half-page illustration appears with text above or below.

**Grade Level/Content Area:** Appropriate for grades 3–8 social studies units on the history of the American West or the history of Wyoming specifically. It also is a good example of an American legend and fits well into a study of legends at any of those grade levels (Gardiner says this story was told to him by a friend).

**Character Web:** This is an excellent book to use for character analysis and to develop empathy with characters, since students immediately identify with Willy and his plight. Have students make a web of Willy's changing feelings throughout the story. Put a feeling on each line and the specific thoughts or quotes from the story that support the feeling in each bubble. Discuss Willy's character, the kind of person he is, whether or not he is admirable, and why.

Then divide your class into small groups and have each group choose another character to analyze in the same way. Give students a blank web and have them become that character, identifying feelings and support for these feelings as the story progresses. Have volunteers from each group share their character analysis with the class. Help students identify and understand the ways Gardiner develops character in this story.

This legend may spark student interest in reading more legends from the West. It may also encourage students to research and read some legends specific to the particular area of the country in which they live.

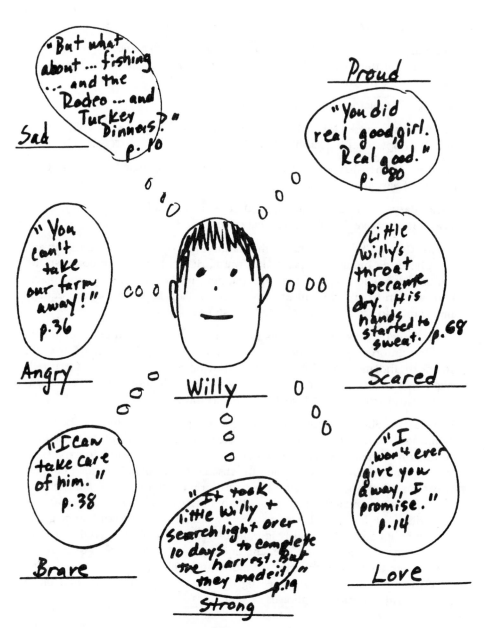

Character web for *Stone Fox*, by John Gardiner.

Goble, Paul. *Death of the Iron Horse.* New York: Bradbury, 1987.

**Summary:** In an act of bravery and defiance against the white men encroaching on their territory in 1867, a group of young Cheyenne braves derail and raid a freight train.

**Setting:** The plains of the American Northwest.

**Characters:** Sweet Medicine, Spotted Wolf, Porcupine, Red Wolf, Yellow Bull, Big Foot, Sleeping Rabbit, Wolf Tooth.

**Theme:** All men have the right to protect their lives, their liberty, and their pursuit of happiness.

**Vocabulary:** Character names (listed above), foretold, titi (the tree), tomahawks, locomotive, bewilderment, caboose.

**Illustrations:** Illustrations are in the traditional style of Cheyenne Indian art. The Cheyenne Indians are painted in warm, rich colors and, in contrast, the frontiersmen who are the antagonists appear in dark blue, grey, and black. Text, written from the point of view of the Indian, and pictures are equally important and are interwoven to tell this story.

**Grade Level/Content Area:** This story is appropriate for students in grades 2–6. It reinforces social studies units on western settlement, the lives of American Indians, and the growth of transportation in North America. It might also be used to introduce a study of discrimination, the effects of expansion and growth, or today's Indian reservations.

**Story Map:** Since it is told from the Indians' perspective and has been authenticated with Goble's research, this story is an excellent place to begin a discussion of the costs that were incurred in the development and expansion of our country. You might broaden the discussion to include other examples of expansion and growth that have had detrimental and devastating effects on both people and animals (e.g., acid rain in Canada and the Northeast).

This book lends itself well to helping students understand story grammar, since it contains the easily identifiable elements of story: setting, beginning, reaction, attempt, outcome, and ending. After children read or hear the story, show them the story map—a train with labels on each of the six cars. Have them retell the story discussing the important events and then fill in each car with appropriate phrases or sentences.

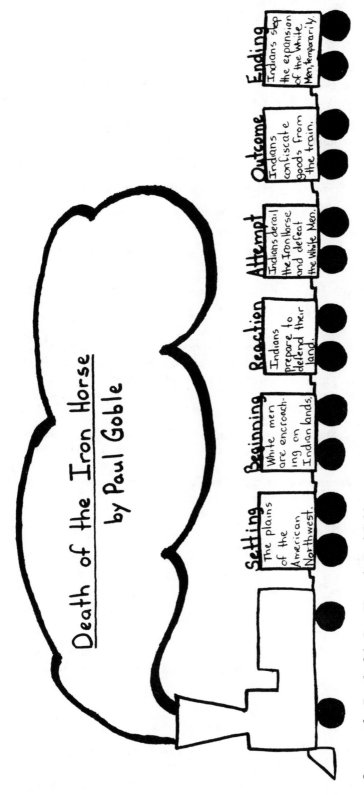

**Death of the Iron Horse**
by Paul Goble

Setting: The plains of the American Northwest.

Beginning: White men are encroaching on Indian lands.

Reaction: Indians prepare to defend their land.

Attempt: Indians derail the Iron Horse and defeat the White Men.

Outcome: Indians confiscate goods from the train.

Ending: Indians stop the expansion of the White Men, temporarily.

Story map for *Death of the Iron Horse*, by Paul Goble.

Grant, Anne. *Danbury's Burning: The Story of Sybil Luddington's Ride.* (Pat Howell, Illus.). New York: Henry Walck, 1976.

**Summary:** A sixteen-year-old girl aids the cause of the Revolution by riding 40 miles to round up her neighbors as a militia.

**Setting:** New York state near the Connecticut border in 1777.

**Characters:** Sybil, Rebecca, Archibald, Derick, Tertullus, Abigail.

**Theme:** Young people can make important contributions that change history.

**Vocabulary:** handsome, galloping, strangers, cinch, stirrups, Tories, muskets, ravines.

**Illustrations:** Large, double-page pencil drawings are done in black and white or pale pastels. Several illustrations depict the rhythmic cadence of the prose.

**Grade Level/Content Area:** This book is suitable for grades 2-5 social studies units on the American Revolution, colonial life, or important women of America. With the rhythmic cadence of its prose, this book is especially suitable for reading aloud. Students reading at third-grade level can read it independently.

**Story Map:** Show or give students a blank story map that contains only the various labeled shapes and directional arrows. As you read the story aloud, stop at appropriate points to ask them to paraphrase the text and supply the necessary information for the story map. The story can then be easily retold or rewritten from this simple visual display.

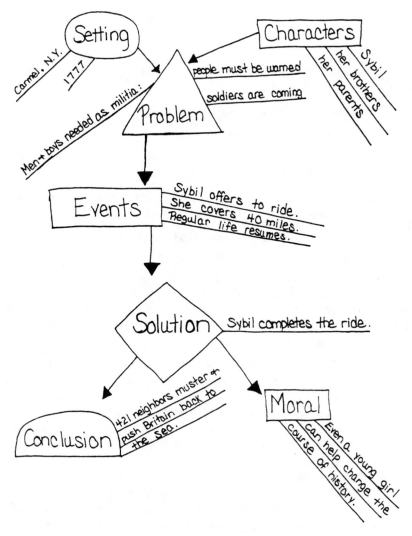

Story map for *Danbury's Burning: The Story of Sybil Luddington's Ride,* by Anne Grant.

Greene, Bette. *Summer of My German Soldier.* New York: Bantam, 1973.

**Summary:** In this ALA Notable Book of the Year, a twelve-year-old Jewish girl befriends and shelters one of the German prisoners of war in a camp in Arkansas.

**Setting:** Jenkinsville, Arkansas, during World War II.

**Characters:** Patty, her parents, Ruth (the family maid), Anton.

**Theme:** Courage is needed in times of adversity; or, because of friendship and love we often take huge risks and make personal sacrifices.

**Vocabulary:** discrimination, POW, concentration camp, patriotism, synagogue, Nigra, L'Chayim, der Spiegel, Nazi saboteurs.

**Illustrations:** There are no illustrations within the text. On the cover are several photographs taken from the movie.

**Grade Level/Content Area:** This book is suitable for use in grades 6–8 social studies units on World War II, prejudice and discrimination, and social awareness. It also may be helpful reading for students who feel the pressures society places on persons involved in relationships with others of different religions and/or race.

**Story Web:** Because the reader or listener is immediately confronted with characters, setting, and plot and may lose interest because there is so much new information to comprehend, it is a good idea to develop the background needed for the unsophisticated reader to understand the story. Prior to reading the book, discuss with students the time period, the countries involved in the war, the important social issues at that time, and the geographical setting of this story.

Students can create the simple story web shown here, which contains the elements of literature, after they read the story and discuss it. Or, you can provide the less sophisticated reader with this completed story map before they read. After reading the story, encourage students to discuss each of the "themes" concepts listed on the web. Also, be sure to talk about the conflicts among the characters and the reasons for them.

Make available to students other books about this time period after they have read and discussed this story. One recommendation is *Journey Home,* by Yoshiko Uchida, which is about Japanese prisoners of war and concentration camps in the West.

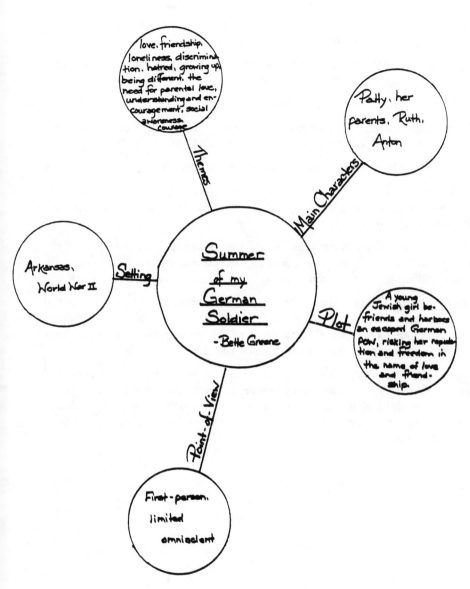

Story web for *Summer of My German Soldier*, by Bette Greene.

=== Griffin, Judith Berry. *Phoebe and the General.* (Margot Tomes, Illus.).
New York: Coward McCann & Geoghegan, 1977.

**Summary:** A thirteen-year-old black girl goes to work for George Washington with instructions to protect his life and unravel a mystery.

**Setting:** Fraunce's Tavern and Mortier House in New York City.

**Characters:** Phoebe Fraunce, Samuel (her father), Mary (the cook), Pompey (Mary's son), General Washington, Thomas Hickey (the villain).

**Theme:** The bravery and determination of a young girl changes the course of history.

**Vocabulary:** Commander-in-Chief, scoundrel, Mortier House, cobblestones, despair, compliments, salt cellar.

**Illustrations:** Pen-and-ink illustrations resemble the woodcut style of the time period the book portrays. Drawings occasionally feature browns, reds, blues, and whites and add authenticity and interest to details in the story.

**Grade Level/Content Area:** This book is suitable for grades 2–5 social studies units on the American Revolution, colonial American history, important American women, and black history. The progressive plot is readable and exciting and is a favorite with children and those who read to them.

**Story Map:** This story map with blank boxes can be given to students or put on the blackboard or chart paper before they read or hear the story. As the progressive plot unfolds, the boxes can be filled in with appropriate information. The completed map lends itself well to retelling or writing a brief account of the story.

Setting:
N. Y. C. in Revolutionary Times

Problem:
George Washington's life in danger

Goal:
Stop traitor and save the General

Events:
Phoebe becomes Washington's helper

Hickey befriends Phoebe

Hickey poisons Washington's food

Results:
Phoebe throws food out window
Chickens eat food and die
Phoebe is a heroine

Story map for *Phoebe and the General,* by J. B. Griffin.

Hall, Donald. *Ox-Cart Man* (Barbara Cooney, Illus.). Cedar Grove, NJ: Penguin, 1979.

**Summary:** This Caldecott Medal winner describes the day-to-day life of an early nineteenth-century New England family throughout the changing seasons.

**Setting:** Rural New England in the early nineteenth century.

**Characters:** the ox-cart man, his family, and the townspeople of Portsmouth market.

**Theme:** Each season of the year is filled with a special beauty; or, the life of a farmer follows the changing seasons.

**Vocabulary:** spinning wheel, flax, loom, linen, yoke, harness, honeycombs, embroidery, whittle, planks.

**Illustrations:** Reminiscent of the folk art popular during the nineteenth century, the illustrations are in rich colors, which change appropriately with the season. Pictures are one-dimensional, usually dominating an entire page with text found on the opposite page. The only double-page illustration with text below is of the long road the ox-cart man journeys to Portsmouth.

**Grade Level/Content Area:** This book is appropriate for children in grades K–3 who are studying colonial American life or the New England of long ago. It also fits a science unit on the cycle of the seasons. Since it is a circular story, it is a good model for a circle story.

**Circle Story:** Before reading this book to children, discuss the seasons and the order they follow. Put the four seasons in their proper sequence on a circle and have children add arrows. Then as children listen to the story, have them note in which season the ox-cart man and his family are depicted. After reading, ask children to think of all the things the family did during each of the seasons and enter these on the circle where each belongs. From the circle story children have generated, they can easily take turns retelling the story or even rewriting it. A discussion of the seasonal cycle can include:

- Which season is most important? Why?
- Could the seasons occur in a different order? Why or why not?
- Do our lives follow any kind of cycle? What is it?
- Are there other cycles of life that are important to us?

To relate the cycle of seasons to your students' lives, help children create a book of the four seasons. Divide your class into four groups, one for each season. Help each group think of things that occur during that season and have them draw pictures of those things. Transcribe captions that children dictate for you, or have children add their own descriptive captions. Children can share their picture and caption with the class before it becomes a part of the book.

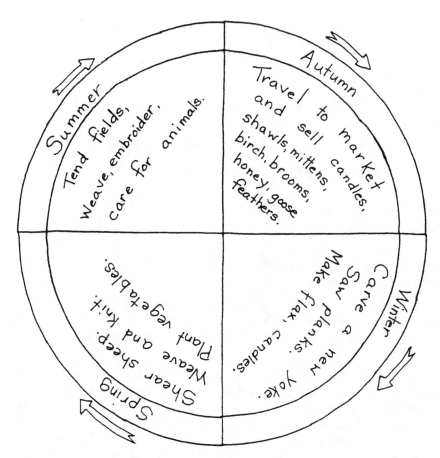

Circle story for *Ox-Cart Man*, by Donald Hall.

Levine, E. *If You Traveled on the Underground Railroad.* (Richard Williams, Illus.). New York: Scholastic, 1988.

**Summary:** This is the story of the Underground Railroad—how it worked, who rode it, and why it meant freedom.

**Setting:** In the Southern states and en route to the North and Canada, before the Civil War.

**Characters:** The courageous slaves and people who made the railroad work.

**Theme:** It took great courage to escape and to help people escape from slavery.

**Vocabulary:** abolition, fugitives, railroad workers, conductors, station masters, stations.

**Illustrations:** Drawings done in muted brown tones are found on every page and supplement the text, which is primary. Neither illustrations nor text dramatize nor idealize this period of history.

**Grade Level/Content Area:** This book fits well with social studies units in grades 3–6 on slavery and its abolition, black history, or the Underground Railroad. It is also appropriate for developing an understanding of courage and bravery.

**Concept Web:** Introduce and use this concept web before students read the book. Use of the web helps organize and develop background information students already possess about slavery and prepares them to appreciate and understand the Railroad better. Have students think about and discuss each of the eight topics on the web, adding any topics they think of, and enter at least two of their opinions about each topic on the web itself.

To summarize what they learned after finishing the book, students can create their own web with "Underground Railroad" as the organizing concept. This activity may result in the generation of topics that the book did not explore and can encourage further research and reading by helping to focus students on areas for further investigation.

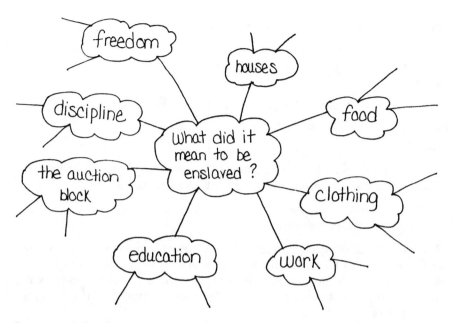

Concept web for *If You Traveled on the Underground Railroad,* by E. Levine.

Lewis, Thomas. *Hill of Fire*. New York: Harper & Row, 1971.

**Summary:** A Mexican farmer discovers a hole in his field that begins to emit smoke and finally becomes a volcano, which forces the people in his village to move.

**Setting:** A century ago on a small farm and village in Mexico (Paricutin).

**Characters:** The farmer, Pablo (his son), people from the village, government officials.

**Theme:** The unexpected may happen when you least expect it; or, natural phenomena have a profound effect on the lives of people.

**Vocabulary:** village, foolish, market, cinnamon, plowing, lava, burros, uniform, amigo, fiesta, el Monstruo.

**Illustrations:** Drawings with watercolor washes of browns and grays portray the farmer and his life in the fields. Reds and yellows are added to the pictures when the volcano begins to emerge, and these colors intensify as the volcano's eruptions increase. Text and illustrations complement each other well and are arranged in no set pattern.

**Grade Level/Content Area:** In grades 1-3, this book fits science units on the ecosystem and energy transfer in the physical environment, and the formation of volcanoes specifically. It is also appropriate for grades 2-5 social studies units on communities around the world, the geography of Latin America and Mexico, and how geographical and geological changes affect people's lives.

**Sequence Map:** Since this book has a progressive story line, there are several passages that lend themselves well to the promotion of comprehension through the prediction of outcomes. As you read this story to students, stop occasionally at points where the next event is uncertain and ask students to guess or predict what they think will happen. Be sure to have students support their predictions, using either information from the text or their own background knowledge. In this way, students learn to think about and verbalize reasons for their opinions.

After reading the story, have students create a simple sequence of events as they occurred in the story, like the one shown in the map on the facing page. The map can be entirely written as students dictate, or it can contain simple drawings to make it easier for young children to "read." Encourage students to use the map to retell the events of the story.

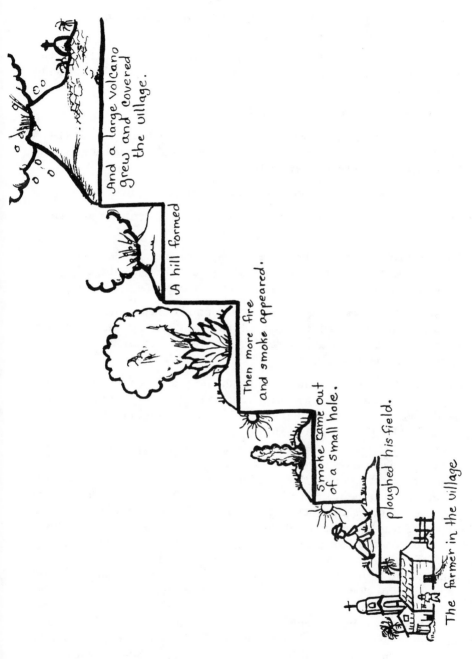

And a large volcano grew and covered the village.

A hill formed

Then more fire and smoke appeared.

Smoke came out of a small hole.

ploughed his field.

The farmer in the village

Sequence map for *Hill of Fire*, by Thomas Lewis.

Provenson, Alice and Martin. *The Glorious Flight Across the Channel with Louis Blériot.* New York: Viking, 1984.

**Summary:** This Caldecott Medal winner tells the story of a Frenchman who builds his own flying machines and finally flies across the English Channel to win a prize.

**Setting:** 1901–1909 in Cambrai, France.

**Characters:** Louis Blériot, Alceste, Charmaine, Suzette, Jeannot, Alice, Gabrielle, Alphonse Juvet and his son Cesar, Achille Duval (policeman), Gabriel Voisin (pilot), Alfred Le Blanc (friend).

**Theme:** Perseverance, ingenuity, and courage will help us attain our goals.

**Vocabulary:** Character names (listed above), valiant, aeronaut, inevitable, prospect.

**Illustrations:** Full-page pictures are in rich colors and include many details of French life. Pictures cover both facing pages and dominate the text, which is written in a few sentences across the bottom of pages.

**Grade Level/Content Area:** This book supports social studies units in grades 3–5 on transportation, specifically airplane history, pilots, and the design and construction of airplanes. It also enriches a unit on European studies or French culture in the 1900s.

**Sequence Map:** After reading or hearing the story, ask each student what he or she thinks is the theme or message or lesson of this story. Students should give reasons for their choice of theme and any statements of theme should be accepted as long as they can be substantiated. In discussing the variety of responses, use the words *perseverance, ingenuity,* and *courage,* and make sure that students know the meanings of these words.

After discussing theme, help students make a sequence map of the important events in the story that support a theme. The map might look something like the one shown here, with clouds for each event and a line connecting each in sequence to the airplane. The elements of story are easily identified from this sequence map. The problem or goal is found in the first cloud, the attempts or events are evident in the next six clouds, with the resolution found in the seventh cloud. As students identify these, label them on the map so that they see how the elements of story grammar appear in this story.

These story elements lend themselves easily to creative writing for students who need a basic structure. Have students use the same theme they identified from the story and brainstorm some other possible problems and events or attempts and resolutions. Have the group orally compose a story from one of these scenarios before having the students write individual stories, using the products of their brainstorming and the story elements as a structure.

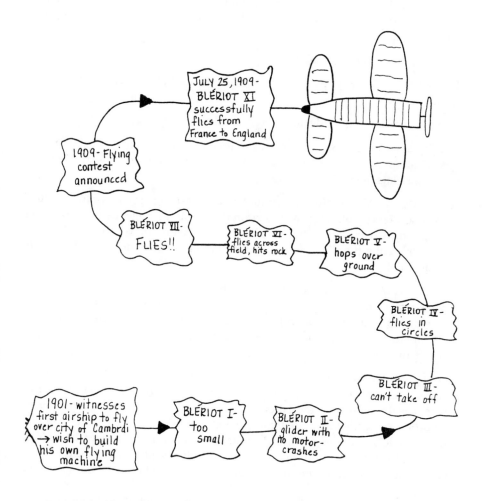

JULY 25, 1909-
BLÉRIOT XI
successfully
flies from
France to England

1909- Flying
contest
announced

BLÉRIOT VII-
FLIES!!

BLÉRIOT VI-
flies across
field, hits rock

BLÉRIOT V-
hops over
ground

BLÉRIOT IV-
flies in
circles

BLÉRIOT III-
can't take off

1901- witnesses
first airship to fly
over city of Cambrai
→ wish to build
his own flying
machine

BLÉRIOT I-
too
small

BLÉRIOT II-
glider with
no motor-
crashes

Sequence map for *The Glorious Flight across the Channel with Louis Blériot,* by
Alice and Martin Provenson.

Sewall, Marcia. *The Pilgrims of Plymouth*. New York: Atheneum, 1976.

**Summary:** This book recreates the coming of the Pilgrims to the New World. The daily flow of their lives and the demanding roles of women, men, and children are explored.

**Setting:** America in the 1620s.

**Characters:** The Pilgrims, Governor William Bradford, Squanto, Massasoit, Samoset.

**Theme:** The strong, hardy, and determined survive.

**Vocabulary:** breeches, boulter, sheate bread, cow cumber pickles, doublet, jerkin, juniper, lug pole, pottage, sachem, vergi, wattle, whortle berries, spinage, sallats, mug wort.

**Illustrations:** Watercolor illustrations emphasizing reds, oranges, and browns are either full-page, with text on the adjoining page, or on two facing pages, with text either at the top or bottom. Pictures have a rough look to them, portraying the life-style of the early colonials, and they include a great deal of detail.

**Grade Level/Content Area:** This book is appropriate for grades 3–5 social studies units on American history, life in the colonies, and the growth of communities. This book provides an in-depth study of colonial history and government and provides great detail about how an early community was organized and settled.

**Concept Webs:** Before reading the story or after reading the first few pages, discuss the roles of various people in a community. Then show children the concept webs with only the labels: "men's duties," "women's duties," and "children's duties." Ask students to predict what they think some of the different people's duties in a colonial community might be, and write their ideas on the webs. After reading the book, have students fill in all the duties that were not mentioned, adding or changing any of their first predictions if it is appropriate.

Students can supply other duties that they can think of, and these can be added to the webs, sparking further reading on topics that were not covered in the book. In fact, if you divide your class into three groups, menfolk, womenfolk, and youngfolk, you can have each group read and report back to the class on other aspects of these people's lives such as what each did for entertainment.

An interesting comparison can also be made between the duties of these three groups in the students' community today and those listed for the colonists. Just make another set of webs and have students supply modern-day duties. Then compare the webs and talk about some of the differences between them.

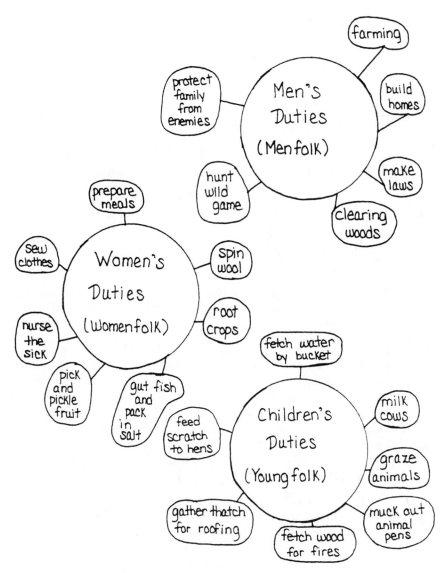

Concept web for *The Pilgrims of Plymouth,* by Marcia Sewall.

*Biography* ═══════════════════════════════════════════════════

═══  Faber, Doris. *Eleanor Roosevelt: First Lady of the World.* New York:
     Viking, 1985.

**Summary:** This book tells the story of Eleanor Roosevelt's life, showing her
as a real person with strengths and weaknesses who struggles through her
youth to become a strong and effective adult.

**Setting:** New York City, England, Albany, and Washington, DC.

**Characters:** Eleanor, her parents, her grandmother, Franklin Roosevelt, her
children.

**Theme:** Even those who are confident and influential as adults may have
been shy and awkward as youths.

**Vocabulary:** homely, shy, alcoholic, governor, Olympics, polio, First Lady,
Declaration of Human Rights, peace.

**Illustrations:** One or two pencil drawings highlight important moments in
each chapter of the book. Each chapter contains about five pages of text, including famous quotes, conversations with friends, and evidence found at the
Roosevelt's home in Hyde Park.

**Grade Level/Content Area:** This book complements a study of United
States history in grade 5 and/or Western European history in grade 6. The
text helps develop an understanding of one woman's contribution to our national politics and gives a human flavor to study of the depression and World
War II. Since the book describes Eleanor's transformation from a shy and
awkward girl into a self-confident and influential woman, it also lends itself
well, in grades 3 through 6, to a unit on women as leaders or a study of personal growth and change related to careers.

**Event Web:** Draw a circle on the blackboard or chart paper, divide it into 16
segments, and write in only the years from the inner wedges on the event
web. Then as you read the story to students or they read it themselves, they
can fill in the important things that Eleanor did or roles she played in those
years. Students may find other accomplishments they wish to record, and so
you may need to expand the web. Focus discussion on Eleanor's personality
as a young person and the changes and reasons for them that resulted in the
personality that characterized her as an adult. You might ask students what
they think motivated her in her adult years to do what she did and what they
think her dreams for the future were.

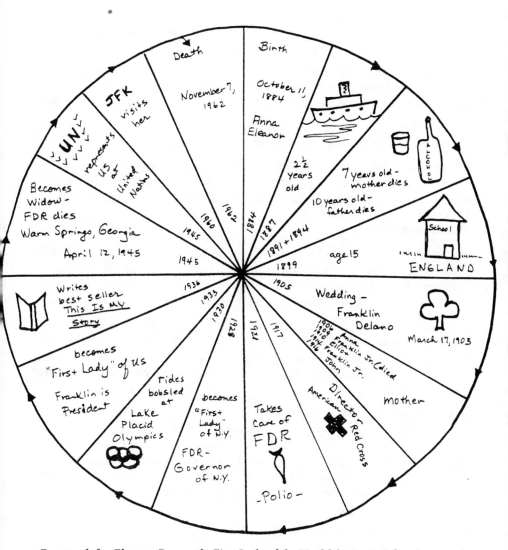

Event web for *Eleanor Roosevelt: First Lady of the World,* by Doris Faber

Fritz, Jean. *The Double Life of Pocahontas.* New York: Puffin Books, 1987.

**Summary:** This is the story of the famous American Indian woman, told from her perspective, who married Englishman John Rolfe and played two very different roles, one in the white culture and one in her native Indian culture.

**Setting:** Chesapeake Bay area, Jamestown, and England.

**Characters:** Pocahontas, Powhatan (her father), Rawhunt (her brother), Opechancanough (brother of Powhatan), Japizaws and his wife (who betrayed Pocahontas), Tomocomo (Indian ambassador who accompanied her to England), John Smith, Captain Newport, John Rolfe (her husband), Thomas Rolfe (her son).

**Theme:** People of one culture can choose to follow the values and life-style of another culture, but they always retain a basic loyalty to the values and life-style of the first; or, understanding another culture requires an open mind, information, and respect, which are often difficult to achieve.

**Vocabulary:** Names of main characters, Chesapeake Bay, Okee, Christian, longhouse, Jamestown project, West Indies, Potomac River, charter, colony, Bermuda Islands, dysentery, gout, scurvy, convicts, hostage, heathen, musket, widower, conversion, royal savage, London, civilize, tuberculosis, Thames River.

**Illustrations:** The only picture is on the cover of the book: Pocahontas is shown standing on the edge of the Potomac River looking over her shoulder at the English ships sailing up the river. This color illustration shows her as a beautiful Indian girl, and it captures the idea of the ensuing conflict between the two cultures. A map within the five-chapter text shows the Chesapeake Bay area at the time of the story, including the location of important villages, rivers, and some story events.

**Grade Level/Content Area:** This book strengthens grades 4 and 5 social studies units on the history of exploration and colonization in the United States, native American Indian cultures, and/or the clash of the white man's and Indian's cultures. Since it is the story of a famous young woman's life, it can be an inspiring way to learn history for young girls as well as boys. The book is also important for its documented and authentic account of history and can be used comparatively with *Pocahontas*, written by Ingri and Edgar D'Aulaire in 1946. The D'Aulaires' account is narrower in scope than Fritz's and depicts Pocahontas and John Smith as much more virtuous and less human than does Fritz's.

**Character Webs:** The two titles discussed above contain very different accounts of Pocahontas's life and provide excellent vehicles for comparing and

Character web for *The Double Life of Pocahontas*, by Jean Fritz.

The web contains the central node "Pocahontas" connected to:

- Wanting to be released from her English captors
- Impressed with John Smith's courage
- becoming sick with tuberculosis after a year in England
- converted to Christianity
- proud
- married to an Indian at 14
- troubled by the double nature of her life
- happy to come to London
- missing her people
- well received by English society
- Strong
- straight
- a wild dancer
- uncomfortable in the English-style clothes
- the one who saved John Smith's life twice
- happy
- emotional
- overwhelmed by London
- loyal to her tribe
- a worshipper of the sun
- happy in both Indian and English worlds for a long time
- unhappy because her husband didn't understand Indian ways
- afraid to go back to America
- angry at John Smith for foresaking her and her people
- Still a strong believer in Okee
- Married to an English man
- Sympathetic to the English settlers
- Sometimes like her name, which meant "lively, frolicsome"
- not happy with her first husband
- afraid for her people in America because of England's plan to convert them
- reluctant to join the Christian way of life

187

contrasting the way history is viewed at different times and by different people. Read both accounts to your students, probably beginning with the D'Aulaires' story first since it was written first and is less inclusive than Fritz's version. As you read each story have students construct a character web of Pocahontas's feelings, actions, and relationships to others. The lists shown here include major points made by the authors, many of which students will suggest for inclusion on their webs as they listen to the stories.

Have students make comparisons, based on the two finished character webs, between the scopes of the two stories, the different ways in which Pocahontas and John Smith in particular are portrayed, possible author bias, documentation and authentication, and the resulting knowledge we have of history. Help students see that writers of both historical fiction and biography should use actual historical accounts, letters, and documents as much as possible so that history is related according to facts and the reader can then make his or her own judgments about it.

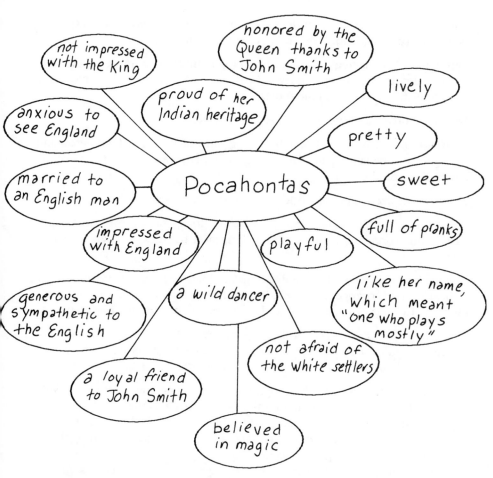

Character web for *Pocahontas,* by Ingri and Edgar D'Aulaire.

Fritz, Jean. *Where Do You Think You're Going, Christopher Columbus?* (Margaret Tomes, Illus.). New York: Putnam's, 1980.

**Summary:** This factual, but amusing, biographical account of Columbus's life includes accounts of his many sea voyages and focuses on his determination to be the first to reach the Indies.

**Setting:** Europe and the New World in the fifteenth century.

**Characters:** Christopher Columbus, King John of Portugal, King Ferdinand and Queen Isabella of Spain, various explorers, crew members, natives of the newly discovered islands.

**Theme:** The secrets of the world are waiting to be discovered.

**Vocabulary:** philosopher, nautical mile, griffons, Moors, Mohammedans, viceroy, interpreter, reckoning, delegation, monstrosities, rampaged, peninsula.

**Illustrations:** Black and white drawings alternate with color drawings done in brown, gold, orange, and pink. These illustrations on every page mirror the accurate facts of a text that is authenticated by the author's research.

**Grade Level/Content Area:** This biography is well suited to a 4th-grade social studies unit about explorers, or a 5th-grade unit in American history, or a 6th-grade unit on the exploration of the New World.

**Time Line:** Before reading this biography, draw a time line for students with the dates 1450 and 1506 at either ends. Ask students why they think these are important dates and then add the words "born" and "died" or "birth" and "death." Then figure out Columbus's age at his death (56), and roughly divide the time line into quarter segments by writing in the years 1465, 1480, and 1495, which gives students a guide to use as they include events. As you read, have students fill in important events in Columbus's life and the years in which these things happened. A completed time line allows students to see at a glance that Fritz has highlighted Columbus's explorations as his major accomplishments.

To help students understand and appreciate the vision and goal that drove Columbus to accomplish what he did, add "goal" on the time line prior to 1470 and "resolution" at about 1520 (the year Magellan completed the trip around the world that Columbus had planned to do himself). Label the happenings between these two as "events." Help students verbalize Columbus's long-range goal, his short-range goals, and their resolutions. Then relate these aspects of Columbus's life to other leaders and great figures they have studied, helping students see how they all held some type of vision or goal and the determination to obtain it.

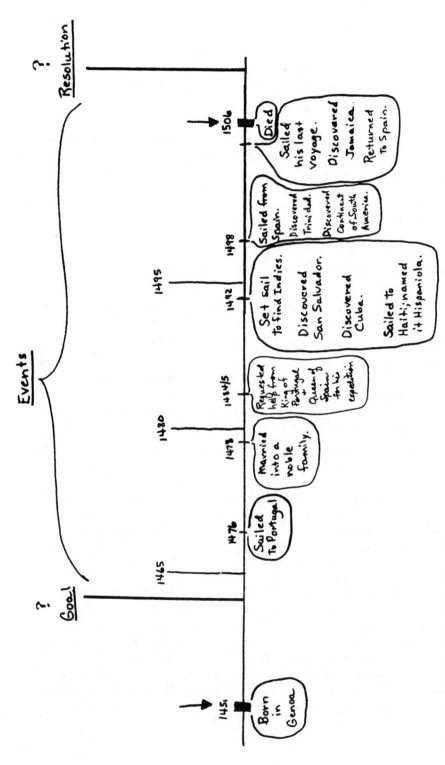

Time line of Christopher Columbus's life.

Haskins, Jim, and Kathleen Benson. *Space Challenger: The Story of Guion Bluford.* Minneapolis: Carolrhoda Books, 1984.

**Summary:** This 1984 Outstanding Science Tradebook is about Guion (Guy) Bluford, the first black American in space, who was part of the crew of the space shuttle "Challenger." The story depicts his struggle through school and his family's support in helping him achieve his goals.

**Setting:** Guy at home and at school.

**Characters:** Guy, his mother and father, brothers—Eugene and Kenneth, wife—Linda, and children, Guion III and James T.

**Theme:** Determination and work can make a dream come true.

**Vocabulary:** aerospace, technical, simulator, satellite, pharmaceutical, McDonnell Douglas.

**Illustrations:** Both color and black and white photographs are interspersed with text and show Guy at different stages in his life. Direct quotes from conversations among family members add realism to the pictures.

**Grade Level/Content Area:** This book fits well in grades 3–6 social studies units on careers or explorers, or in a science unit on rocketry or space travel. It is also a good book to use with students who have learning disabilities or reading difficulties because Guy had trouble in school with reading but overcame his problems with family help.

**Character Web:** You can introduce this character web to students before they read or listen to the story so that they have a purpose for their reading. As you discuss the vocabulary in the rocket, tell students that each arrow stands for potential problems or obstacles for which Guy had to find solutions in order to overcome them and become successful. After reading the book, have students discuss the problems and solutions the text identifies, as well as any they can think of that he may have had but were not discussed and ways that he might have solved them. Write these under "problems" and "solutions" on the web.

Use the completed web as a springboard for discussion of possible problems your students might have in achieving their own dreams and some plans of action they might employ to overcome these problems. This story of a real person's life is an excellent one for helping students begin to identify and explore their own aspirations. Students might write their own biographies based on the structure of the character web, using vocabulary that describes their own projected growth and predicting possible problems and solutions that their own futures might hold.

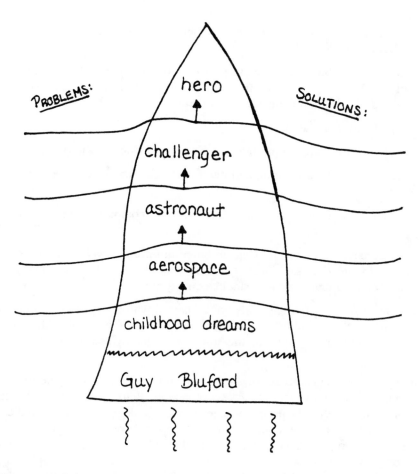

Character web for *Space Challenger: The Story of Guion Bluford,* by J. Haskins and K. Benson.

Koch, Charlotte. *Florence Nightingale.* (Michele Chessare, Illus.). New York: Dandelion Press, 1979.

**Summary:** This book tells the story of Florence Nightingale's life from the age of 10 when she cared for stray animals, to the year 1860, when she became head of the first nursing school in London.

**Setting:** London in the 1800s.

**Characters:** Florence, her mother, her father, and sister Parthe (Parthenon).

**Theme:** Those who are caring and determined can make a difference in the world.

**Vocabulary:** homeless, ill, vulnerable, society, compassionate, disfigurement.

**Illustrations:** Watercolor drawings in blues and purples with white borders are found in the centers of pages. The shapes and hues of these striking illustrations contain humor and a dream-like quality as well.

**Grade Level/Content Area:** This book fits well with social studies units in grades 4–6 on the Constitution and equal rights, careers, or English life in the 1800s. It is also appropriate for the study of biography as a genre of literature.

**Concept Web:** This web activity develops student awareness of the variety of careers available to them regardless of gender. Before reading this book, draw a flower with a heart in the center and blank petals, with "medical care" inscribed on one petal. Show students the book and talk about Florence Nightingale's fame as it relates to the web you have started. Discuss her compassion and love for others as central to what she accomplished. After reading the book, help students fill in their basic human needs on the other petals. Ask questions like: What is meaningful work? What are people's needs?

Then have small groups of students brainstorm lists of the careers these needs suggest by answering the question: Who provides these needs? Write the careers or jobs that fit each need on the web near the corresponding petal, using the jobs shown on the web as examples.

A discussion of the completed web might center on these questions:

- Are there jobs that overlap to fill different needs?
- Which jobs are for women? Men? Why?
- What happens when men do "women's jobs"? When women do "men's jobs"?

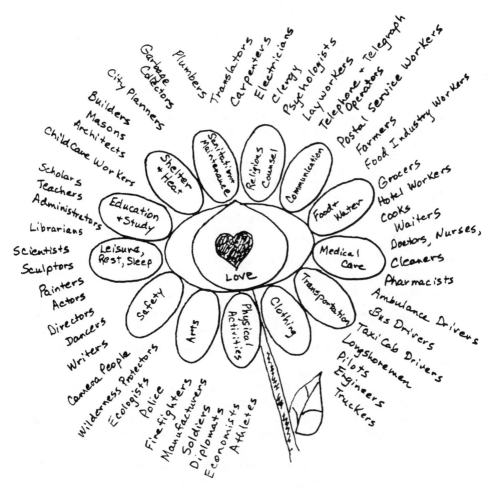

Concept web for *Florence Nightingale*, by Charlotte Koch.

The content and illustrations of this book can be compared with other books on Florence Nightingale's life. For example, *Lonely Crusader: The Life of Florence Nightingale 1820–1910*, written by Cecil Woodham-Smith in 1951 contains realistic drawings and photographs, which are in contrast to Chessare's cartoon-style drawings. Help students see that illustrators make choices in the art they include and discuss possible reasons for these choices. Have students read or listen to both books to decide which pictures and story idealize Florence more and which show her as more human, with both strengths and flaws of character. Be sure to discuss with students the implications of the lack of footnotes or references in the Koch book and the inclusion of six pages of sources in the Woodham-Smith book.

Lepsky, Ibi. *Albert Einstein.* (Paolo Cardoni, Illus.). Woodbury, NY: Barron's Educational Series, 1982.

**Summary:**  A young boy fails in school but triumphs over this adversity to become one of the greatest scientists of our time.

**Setting:**  Germany, almost a century ago.

**Characters:**  Albert, Mama, Papa, Maja (Albert's sister), Albert's teacher and classmates.

**Theme:**  A person should not be judged solely on the basis of his or her outward appearance.

**Vocabulary:**  absentminded, ignored, company, colony, history, geography, memorize, incapable, gymnastics, granite, improvise, compass, curtly, anguish, genius, theories, distracted, precise.

**Illustrations:**  Pastel colors and cartoon-like illustrations accompany text. The style of characters' clothing appears authentic for the time period in which Albert lived, and the simple, yet distinctive illustrations support the text well.

**Grade Level/Content Area:**  This book supports grades 2–4 units of study in the physical sciences on energy, matter, the atmosphere, and the universe. It also provides a personal introduction to the life of a scientist for students in grades 3–7 who are studying careers. Since Albert experienced difficulties in school, yet overcame them, this story also is excellent to share with children who have problems with learning. Albert's life can inspire a student who has a negative self-concept and thus serve as a positive model.

**Character Web:**  As students listen to this story or read it themselves, have them fill in either the words that describe Einstein (on the strands of the web) or sentences from the story that describe his habits or actions (in the bubbles at the ends of the strands). After the story is read, have students fill in unfinished parts of the web.

If students can benefit from a vocabulary extension activity, ask them to supply synonyms for the descriptors on the strands. Have them use a dictionary or thesaurus to identify new words that mean the same thing as the words they have on the web.

With an individual student or small group that experiences learning difficulties, lead a discussion of how students feel they may or may not be similar to Einstein. Be sure to focus on Einstein's triumph over adversity and his tremendous contribution to science and technology today.

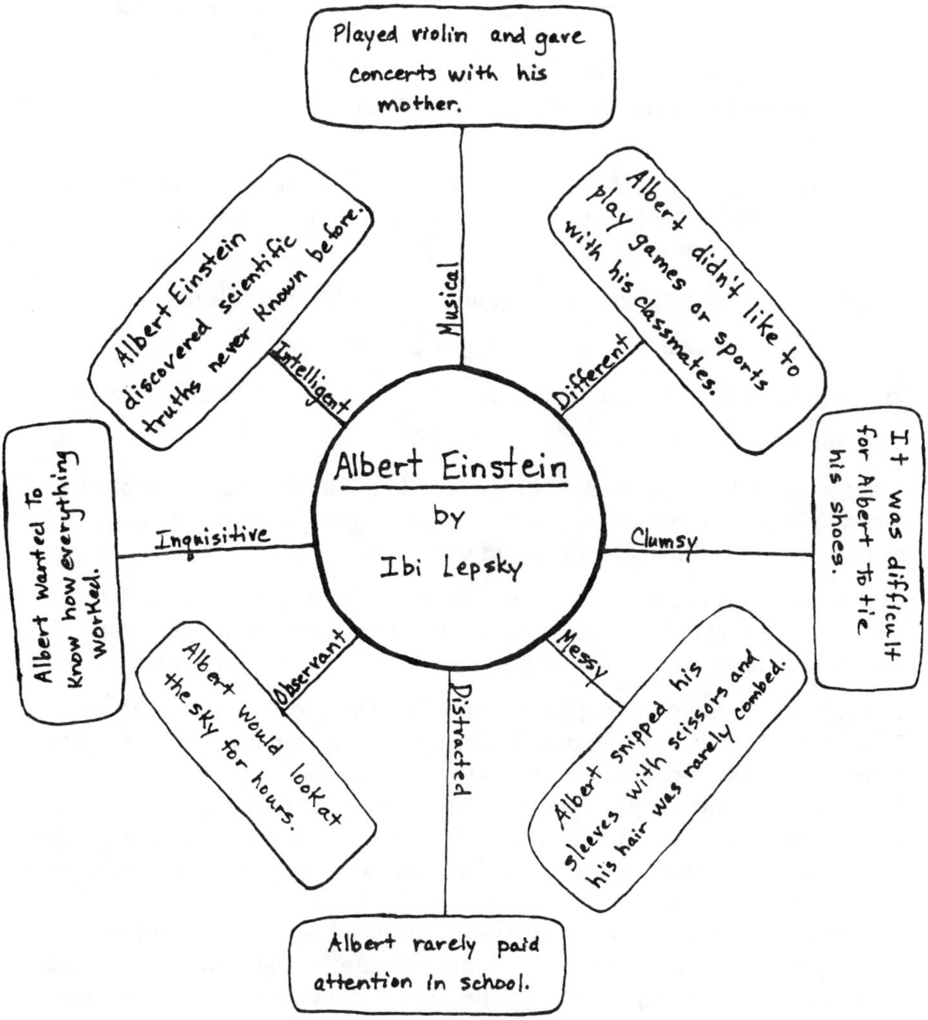
Albert Einstein
by
Ibi Lepsky
Musical
Played violin and gave concerts with his mother.
Different
Albert didn't like to play games or sports with his classmates.
Clumsy
It was difficult for Albert to tie his shoes.
Messy
Albert snipped his sleeves with scissors and his hair was rarely combed.
Distracted
Albert rarely paid attention in school.
Observant
Albert would lookat the sky for hours.
Inquisitive
Albert wanted to know how everything worked.
Intelligent
Albert Einstein discovered scientific truths never known before.

Character web for *Albert Einstein,* by Ibi Lepsky.

*Poetry* ══════════════════════════════════════════════

══  de Regniers, Beatrice Schenk. *A Week in the Life of Best Friends and Other Poems on Friendship.* (Nancy Doyle, Illus.). New York: Atheneum, 1986.

**Summary:** A collection of poems describing some of the joys and sorrows of friendship between children, between parent and child, between child and pet.

**Setting:** Everyday settings, including home, school, and neighborhood.

**Characters:** All kinds of parents, children, and a few pets.

**Theme:** In friendships there are both happy and sad times between people.

**Vocabulary:** No difficult words.

**Illustrations:** Pictures are delicately colored line drawings that complement the simple poetry selections. Half-page drawings appear on almost every page, with poems filling the remainder of the page.

**Grade Level/Content Area:** These poems are appropriate for students in grades 2-5 for lessons in listening appreciation, or a health unit on self-understanding, or a unit on poetry as a genre of literature and writing poetry.

**Concept Web:** After reading the poems to students, lead a discussion about what makes friendships special relationships. Ask students to define the similarities and differences between friend and acquaintance, friend and enemy. Then have students supply words that describe a special friendship they have with someone and put these words in the arrows of the web, similar to the one shown here. Students can then use these words to write their own poems.

Encourage students to illustrate their original poems. The simple nature of the pictures in this book should promote the feeling that students can draw their own accompanying pictures. Some students in your class might want to write and illustrate their own book of poems.

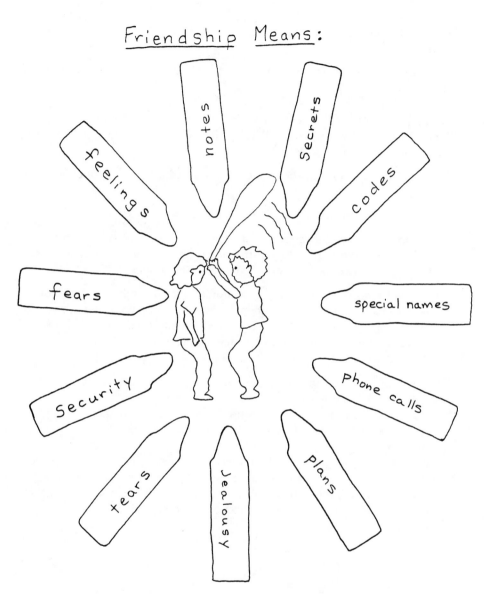

Concept web for *A Week in the Life . . .* , by B. S. de Regniers.

Hopkins, Lee Bennett. *More Surprises.* (Megan Lloyd, Illus.). New York: Harper & Row, 1987.

**Summary:** This is an easy-to-read collection of the poetry of many authors.

**Setting:** Varied settings.

**Characters:** Subjects for the poems vary, but they are divided into six topics: "Some People," "Body Parts," "Living Things," "How Funny," "Hot and Cold," and "In School and After."

**Theme:** Themes vary, but the innocence and carefree nature of childhood are clearly evident.

**Vocabulary:** inventing, somersault, stalk, lingers, wren, luscious, dapples.

**Illustrations:** Detailed illustrations appear in a range of colors—from bright and bold to soft and pastel—to suit the mood or topic of the poem they accompany. One or two illustrations appear with each poem.

**Grade Level/Content Area:** This collection of poems is suitable for children in grades K–3 and can be read to them for pure listening enjoyment. The poetry on "Living Things," "Body Parts," and "Hot and Cold" fit well with science units for these grades. These poems can also serve as models for student-created poetry.

**Topic Web:** You can introduce the poems in this book to children with a simple topic web like the one shown. From the web, children can predict what they think the poems will be about before you read them, and after hearing the poems children can identify their favorites, sharing their reasons with the class.

If children want to write their own poems, they can use the topics shown in the web that Hopkins has identified and write poems that fit in these areas. Or, children can create new topics and write poems for these new areas, making their own class collection of poetry using Hopkins' topics as a model.

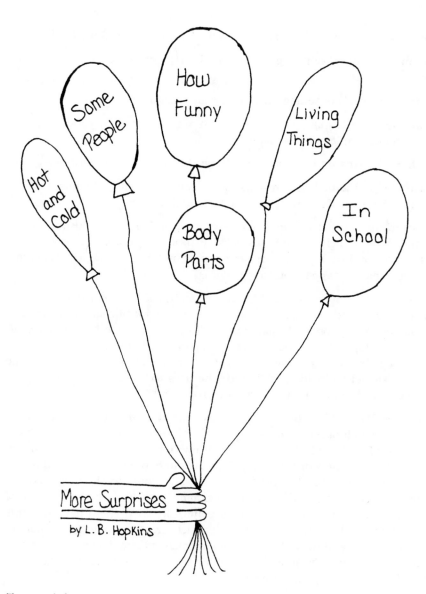

Topic web for *More Surprises,* by L. B. Hopkins.

Lobel, Arnold. *The Book of Pigericks.* New York: Harper & Row, 1983.

**Summary:** Thirty-eight original limericks, or pigericks, created by Old Pig about all manner of pigs.

**Setting:** A variety of settings in Old Pig's imagination.

**Characters:** Old pigs, young pigs, rich pigs, poor pigs, rude pigs, shy pigs—and all suspiciously human-like.

**Theme:** Humans are funny and should be able to laugh at themselves.

**Vocabulary:** Nantucket, Van Nuys, Schenectady, Duluth, Chanuts, Cohoes, Decatur, Spokane, Savannah, Woonsocket, Moline.

**Illustrations:** Lobel's subtle, pastel-colored, and detailed illustrations accompany these lighthearted pigericks. Elaborate yet delicate straight-line borders around each picture give the appearance of a formal, old-fashioned portrait. Limericks appear on facing pages.

**Grade Level/Content Area:** Children in grades K–6 enjoy listening to this book as pure entertainment, and it fits well with a specific language arts unit on poetry writing, or bookmaking in grades 2–4. Visual/verbal literacy skills can be developed by having children compare these illustrations with other works by Lobel, such as *Frog and Toad Are Friends,* in which Lobel uses the same detail but limits the pastel colors he uses to green and brown, which complement the content of the Frog and Toad series.

**Key Word Web:** After you have read this collection of limericks to children, you might help them construct a key word web (like the one shown) with the vocabulary Lobel used to describe his variety of pigs. Encourage students to add any appropriate words they feel Lobel could have used that he did not.

You can use one of Lobel's limericks as a model for helping students write their own limericks. Help them examine each line for the number of syllables and the lines for the rhyming pattern he used. Then have students choose an animal as a subject for their limerick, create a key word web of descriptive words, and write their own limerick using them. Some students may enjoy working together on a limerick since it is not as easy to do as it looks, and collaboration may bring success.

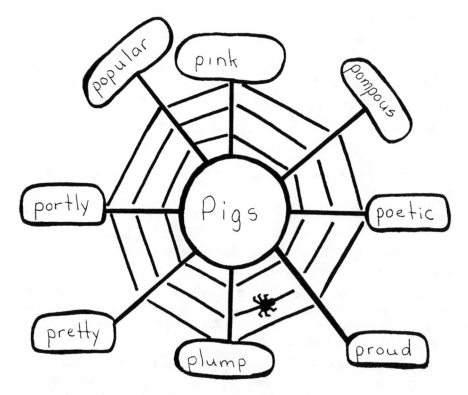

Key word web for *The Book of Pigericks,* by Arnold Lobel.

Silverstein, Shel. *A Light in the Attic.* New York: Harper & Row, 1981.

**Summary:**  These poems are about improbable characters and situations, with some realistic topics, but most humorous and silly. Topics range from the mundane ("Hiccup Cure," "Messy Room," "Eight Balloons") to those of a more serious nature ("Deaf Donald" about the lack of communication between a deaf boy and a girl who likes him).

**Setting:**  Varied.

**Characters:**  See web.

**Theme:**  Humor is present even in the smallest object, uneventful happening, or unlikely situation.

**Vocabulary:**  Most of the language is comprehensible to young readers, who love the imaginative nonsense words that Silverstein uses.

**Illustrations:**  Black ink drawings accompany nearly every poem and complement the content of the poetry.

**Grade Level/Content Area:**  Children in grades K–6 enjoy these poems for their lighthearted and humorous treatment of everyday topics. This collection is appropriate for students in grades 3–6 who are studying characterization in writing, or who are writing their own poetry.

**Character Web:**  Introduce this book of poems with the web of the names of Silverstein's created characters. Just the preposterous names intrigue and tantalize students to read the poems themselves or listen to them read.

If these poems are used to initiate creative writing, you can ask students to brainstorm some of their own preposterous characters and use them as topics for their poems. The rhyme and repetition of some of Silverstein's poems can serve as models that children who have trouble writing can directly imitate.

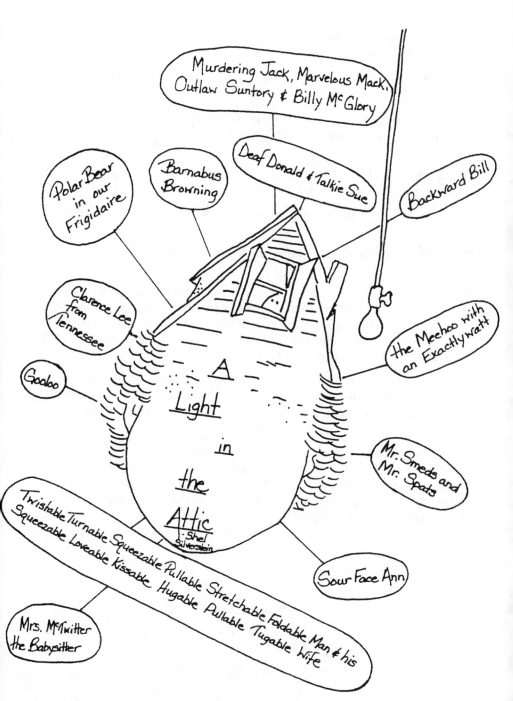

Murdering Jack, Marvelous Mack, Outlaw Suntory & Billy McGlory

Polar Bear in our Frigidaire

Barnabus Browning

Deaf Donald & Talkie Sue

Backward Bill

Clarence Lee from Tennessee

the Mechoo with an Exactlywatt

Gooloo

A Light in the Attic
Shel Silverstein

Mr. Smeds and Mr. Spats

Twistable Turnable Squeezable Pullable Stretchable Foldable Man & his Squeezable Loveable Kissable Hugable Pullable Tugable Wife

Sour Face Ann

Mrs. McTwitter the Babysitter

Character web for *A Light in the Attic,* by Shel Silverstein.

Streich, Corrine (Ed.). *Grandparents' Houses*. (Lillian Hoban, Illus.). New York: Greenwillow, 1984.

**Summary:** A collection of poems about grandparents from many different countries and cultures around the world.

**Setting:** Present-day ranches, kitchens, mountain tops, bedrooms, pastures in many different cultures (e.g., Zuni, Japanese, Chinese, Hebrew, American, German, etc.).

**Characters:** Poems are written from the point of view of grandchildren telling about their grandparents.

**Theme:** The love and reverence we have for our parents' parents is universal.

**Vocabulary:** legacy, dignity, innumerable, staff, snuff box, sturdiness, bliss, serenity, tradition.

**Illustrations:** Full-color pastel illustrations contain colors, textures, backgrounds, settings, or objects native to the particular culture from which the poem originated. Illustrations convey feelings about a particular people's attitudes concerning grandchildren and grandparents. All illustrations are full-page and framed by the white border of the page.

**Grade Level/Content Area:** This collection of poems is suitable for social studies units in grades 3–6 on families and communities from around the world. It also fits well with a unit on listening appreciation, poetry as a genre of literature, and writing poetry.

**Character Web:** Create this character web with students after they have read the poems or you have read them aloud. Create the web as a visual representation of your discussion with students about the universal feelings people have about grandparents or the common traits they possess regardless of culture. Students can use the completed web to write a poem about grandparents the world over or about their own grandparent/s.

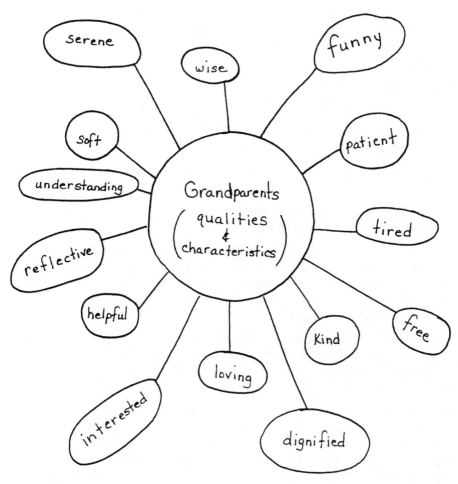

Character web for *Grandparents' Houses,* by Corrine Streich.

== Willard, Nancy. *The Voyage of the Ludgate Hall: Travels with Robert Louis Stevenson.* (Alice and Martin Provenson, Illus.). San Diego: Harcourt Brace Jovanovitch, 1987.

**Summary:** This is a poem based on the letters Robert Louis Stevenson wrote describing an adventurous ocean voyage.

**Setting:** On board a cargo steamer from London to New York in the 1800s.

**Characters:** Robert Louis Stevenson, his family, various animals, such as apes, baboons, monkeys, and eels, and a few passengers.

**Theme:** Even a difficult ocean crossing can be a delight and pleasure to the senses.

**Vocabulary:** voyage, journey, squall, mutton, buttermilk, gabardine, confirming, hearty embrace, retractable.

**Illustrations:** Done in a primitive style, these flat, one-dimensional acrylic paintings effectively portray the people and buildings of a hundred years ago. These award-winning illustrations, the inclusion of part of an actual letter written by Stevenson on his voyage, and Willard's introduction confirm the authenticity of this lovely book.

**Grade Level/Content Area:** Suitable for students in grades 3–6 to promote appreciative listening or to learn about the characteristics of poetry. It also can enrich social studies units on types of transportation or the England and America of the 1800s.

**Element Web:** Use this web to reinforce the characteristics of poetry only after students have heard the story read orally at least twice. Then give students the web with the characteristics printed on each strand and have them supply examples of each characteristic from the text of the poem itself. This poem provides many fine examples of the characteristics of good poetry.

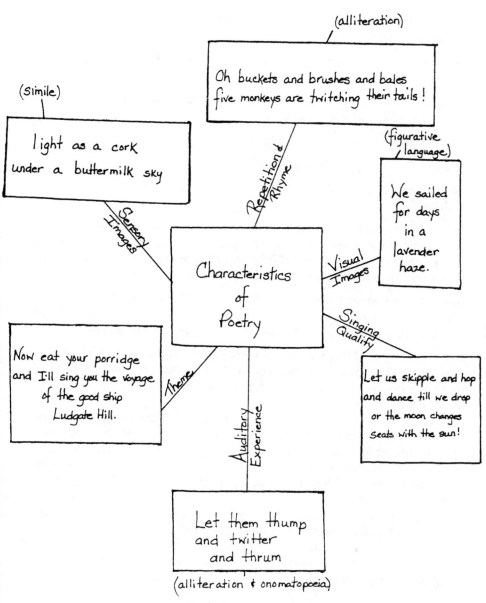

(alliteration)

Oh buckets and brushes and bales five monkeys are twitching their tails!

(simile)

light as a cork under a buttermilk sky

(figurative language)

We sailed for days in a lavender haze.

Repetition & Rhyme

Sensory Images

Characteristics of Poetry

Visual Images

Singing Quality

Now eat your porridge and I'll sing you the voyage of the good ship Ludgate Hill.

Theme

Let us skipple and hop and dance till we drop or the moon changes seats with the sun!

Auditory Experience

Let them thump and twitter and thrum

(alliteration & onomatopoeia)

Element web for *The Voyage of the Ludgate . . .*, by Nancy Willard.

Worth, Valerie. *Small Poems*. (Natalie Babbitt, Illus.). New York: Farrar, Straus and Giroux, 1972.

**Summary:** This is a collection of unrhymed poetry about a variety of ordinary objects, from chairs to cows to carrots.

**Setting:** Poems are set in the here and now in places like the front porch or with a dog lying under a maple tree.

**Characters:** Ordinary, everyday objects.

**Theme:** Beauty is present in the simplest of objects.

**Vocabulary:** zinnias, fringed, amethysts, emerald, topaz, sapphire, opal, hollyhocks.

**Illustrations:** Simple illustrations drawn in black ink show detail and texture of objects. Pictures are sometimes full-page, with the poem found on the facing page, and sometimes half-page, with poem and picture arranged together on a page to complement each other's content.

**Grade Level/Content Area:** Children in grades 2–4 enjoy this collection of poems, which provides a good introduction to unrhymed poetry in a unit on listening appreciation, poetry as a genre of literature, or writing poetry.

**Key Word Web:** First, tell children what *Small Poems* is about and then read the poems aloud. You can help children visualize the images conjured up by the poems by describing in detail an image brought to your mind by one of the poems.

As a way of examining the kinds of words that best evoke images, you can help children create a key word web like the one shown here. Ask children for the objects in the poems that they most enjoyed, and place these objects on the strands of the webs. Then reread the poems so that students can identify the special high-image words that Worth uses, and include these in the bubbles on the web.

If you are going to involve children in writing their own poems, particularly those who lack confidence in their ability, you can use the same type of key word web. Have children identify the objects they want to write poems about, putting these on a new web. Then have them brainstorm special, high-image words, which they can use to write their own poems.

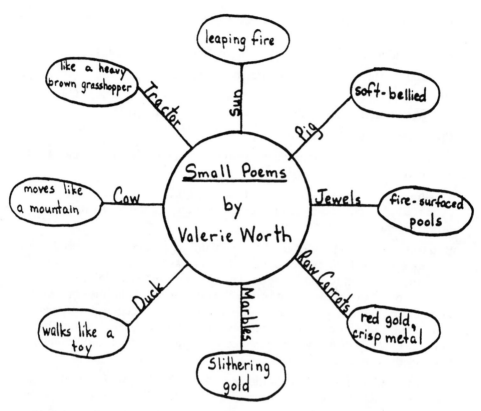

Key word web for *Small Poems*, by Valerie Worth.

## Information Books

Aliki (Brandenberg). *How a Book Is Made.* New York: Crowell, 1986.

**Summary:** This book provides a detailed explanation of writing, illustrating, editing, and publishing a picture book.

**Setting:** From the author's home to the publishing company.

**Characters:** Cats and the manuscript.

**Theme:** The cooperation of many people over a long period of time is necessary to create a work of art.

**Vocabulary:** manuscript, contract, typeface, galley, copy editor, typesetter, proofreader, production editor, designer, color separator, stripper, plate, proof, blueprint.

**Illustrations:** Each page of the book contains small, detailed, colored, pen-and-ink cartoon-like drawings of cats, with diagrams of the various machines and processes used to make a book. The narrative text provides an objective explanation of the bookmaking process, while cartoon balloons contain the more casual and humorous conversations of the cats. Technical information and complex ideas are made more accessible with boxed, handwritten definitions, mechanical diagrams accompanied by sequenced steps, and statements made by the ever-present cats.

**Grade Level/Content Area:** Students in grades 2–6 enjoy this book about the commercial aspects of bookmaking. It reinforces appreciation for the writer/author, books and writing in general, and extends a project on personal bookmaking. With older students, the book is useful in a unit on careers since so many different people and jobs are involved in the process.

**Concept Web:** If you use the book to explore with your students the many jobs in the publishing world, you can develop a Job Web together, or have a small group of students create it and share it with the rest of the class after they have read and studied the book. You can also provide students with an opportunity for creative thinking that extends beyond the scope of this book. For example, there are many other jobs created for people after the book is actually published, such as warehouse operator, packager, truck driver, sales clerk, library shelver, bookstore owner, and book vendor. Students can create a second web for these or add them to their first web.

**Sequence Map:** Before students read this book or you read it to them, show them only the first and last balloons in the sequence map of events that occur in the life of a book. After reading, help students fill in the remaining balloons, by working from the beginning to the end of the process. Or, provide students with every other balloon entry and help them fill in the missing steps. If students have made or are making their own personal books, they can create a sequence map to show the steps in the process they use.

# HOW A BOOK IS MADE by Aliki

- AUTHOR WRITES STORY
- EDITOR + PUBLISHER READ IT.
- CONTRACT IS SENT TO AUTHOR + ILLUSTRATOR
- ARTIST MAKES HANDMADE BOOK
- EDITOR CHANGES TEXT. DESIGNER CHANGES ART
- TYPEFACE CHOSEN
- COPY-EDITOR CHECKS SPELLING, GRAMMAR, + PUNCTUATION
- TYPE-SETTER SETS TYPE ON GALLEYS
- PROOF-READER CHECKS GALLEYS
- ARTIST PREPARES FINISHED ARTWORK IN FULL COLOR
- ART CHECKED FOR MISTAKES
- PRODUCTION EDITOR MAKES COST ESTIMATES + PRODUCTION SCHEDULES, ORDERS PAPER
- DESIGNER MAKES MECHANICALS- FITS TEXT + ART TOGETHER
- COLOR SEPARATOR MAKES FILMS
- FILMS PUT TOGETHER BY STRIPPER
- PRINTING PLATES ARE MADE FROM THE FILMS
- PLATES MAKE COLOR PROOFS
- FILMS + TEXT TOGETHER MAKE BLUEPRINT
- PLATES PUT ON BIG CYLINDERS OF FOUR COLOR PRINTING PRESS
- PRINTING ONLY TAKES 1 DAY
- PAPER SHEETS ARE BOUND, HARD COVER IS MADE + DUST JACKET WRAPPED AROUND
- SALES CONFERENCE
- BOOK REVIEWED BY LIBRARIANS + NEWSPAPERS.
- SALESPEOPLE SELL BOOK TO BOOKSTORES
- LIBRARIES BUY COPIES
- YOU BUY IT

Sequence map for *How a Book Is Made*, by Aliki.

213

Aliki (Brandenberg). *Dinosaurs Are Different.* New York: Harper &
Row, 1985.

**Summary:** This book explains how the various orders and suborders of dinosaurs were similar and different to each other in structure and appearance.

**Setting:** A museum.

**Characters:** Dinosaur models and the children who visit the museum.

**Theme:** Similarities and differences determine classifications.

**Vocabulary:** Various dinosaur names, which even young children delight in
learning (contained in concept web).

**Illustrations:** Black line drawings filled with bright colors depict scenes inside a dinosaur museum that show dinosaur models and skeletons and children with mothers, fathers, friends, teachers, and a child in a wheelchair. Dialogue balloons contain the observations and conversations of children actively learning in this exciting setting. Text is separate from illustrations and
provides an objective account of pictures.

**Grade Level/Content Area:** This book is appropriate for life science units
on survival, dependency, and extinct animals. Children in grades K–4 who are
studying reptiles, dinosaurs, museums, or the process of classifying will enjoy
this book.

**Concept Web:** Read this book to children, discussing its content with them
as you read. Before creating a concept web for the content of this book, fa-
miliarize them with the idea of a concept web based on animals they already
know. Help children make a concept web for pets with two classes—dogs
and cats. The classes of dogs might be *large* and *small* and the classes of cats
might be *long-haired* and *short-haired* or *tame* and *wild*, with specific
names of each type included under these categories.

When children see how to classify familiar animals according to likenesses and differences, then you can help them create the concept web for
this book. Initially, provide them with the first two levels (ruling reptiles,
lizards and birds). Then supply children with the next six vertical lines that
represent categories or classes within the subgroups, and have them supply
vocabulary for the rest of the web. Names of dinosaurs and words that describe their most distinguishing characteristics will determine where each fits
in the web.

Children can go on to independently constructing their own webs on a
variety of topics. These webs make good starting points for writing reports,
too, since they contain information that is organized and classified into categories that can be described.

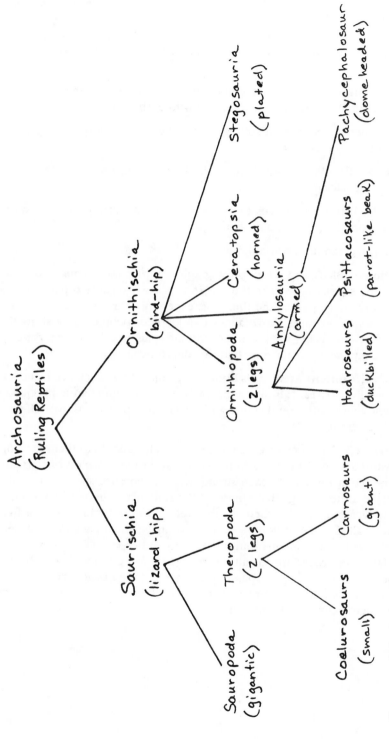

Concept web for *Dinosaurs Are Different*, by Aliki.

Brenner, Barbara. *Faces*. (George Ancona, Illus.). New York: Dutton, 1970.

**Summary:** In words and photographs, this book describes the five senses and gives examples of what we experience with each sense.

**Setting:** There is no special setting, rather the pictures are of people and things in our everyday world.

**Characters:** People who are young, old, large, small, male, female, and of various ethnic backgrounds.

**Theme:** Each of us possesses the same five senses, yet each of us experiences the world in our own different way.

**Vocabulary:** geraniums, sousaphone.

**Illustrations:** Black and white photographs capture the theme of uniqueness and the special powers of the five senses. Each sensory organ is introduced in a full-page photo, and things we experience through our senses are pictured as well. Pictures show faces of all kinds of people. They show the texture of a woodpecker's soft feathers and the roughness of a hemp rope, as well as a dripping ice cream cone that can almost be tasted.

**Grade Level/Content Area:** This book complements a K–2 science or health unit on the five senses. It is also appropriate for developing an appreciation of the uniqueness of the individual and for encouraging a positive self-concept at these grade levels.

**Story Starter Web:** After you read this story to children, help them develop a web with the title of the book in the center and each sense on one strand. In the bubble at the end of each strand, write a sentence starter. Have the group name all the things that complete the sentences, discuss why each is especially pleasing, and list them on the web. Have each child make a five-page book called "All About Me," with a cover page and a page for each section of the web that contains things that the child especially likes. You can follow the same procedure for all the senses by using the sentence starter "We don't like to . . . " and expanding the books to ten pages. You need to be sure to have children give reasons for their choices so that they learn to verbalize their feelings and preferences.

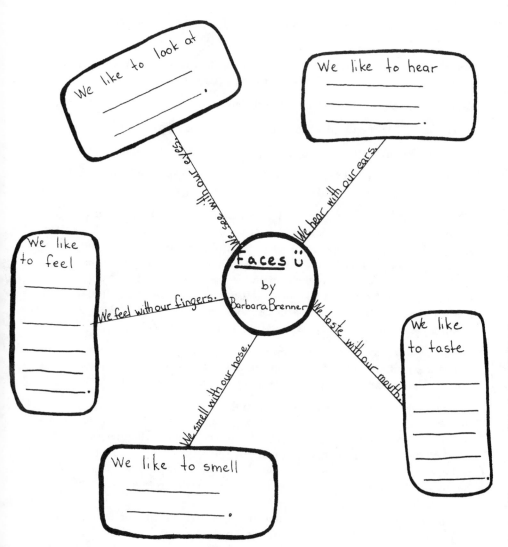

Story starter web for *Faces*, by Barbara Brenner.

de Paola, Tomie. *Charlie Needs a Cloak.* Englewood Cliffs, NJ: Prentice-Hall, 1973.

**Summary:** A shepherd shears his sheep, cards and spins the wool, weaves and dyes the cloth, and sews a beautiful new red cloak.

**Setting:** The story takes place on Charlie's sheep ranch.

**Characters:** Charlie the shepherd, Charlie's sheep, a small mouse.

**Theme:** Men and animals enjoy an interdependent relationship.

**Vocabulary:** shear, card, spin, weave, sew, cloak (these words are listed in a mini-glossary at the end of the book).

**Illustrations:** Pictures are pencil drawings with muted colors, except the bright red of Charlie's cloak, which is the most important element in the story. A small mouse appears in every picture. Text is printed at the top of each page, and it documents the process Charlie uses to make a new cloak for himself. Pictures occupy the remainder of the page, and they depict a series of hilarious errors that take place in the process. One sheep in particular is not pleased with the way Charlie uses the wool and uses trickery that has comical results to try to keep Charlie from finishing his project.

**Grade Level/Content Area:** Appropriate for K–2 children, this book enriches a social studies unit on the interdependence of man and animals, a unit on textile manufacturing, or a lesson on sequence of events.

**Sequence Map:** Have children listen to this story, look at the pictures, and discuss and enjoy the process of making a cloak and Charlie's humorous problems. Then help children establish the sequence of factual events that resulted in a finished cloak, and transcribe the steps they identify. Discussion will result in a sequence map like the one on the next page. Or you can jumble the five steps in the process and help children rearrange them until they are in order.

Don't overlook the possibilities of exploring the humor in this book. Since the pictures tell a different story than the text and children enjoy finding these humorous differences, help them find the hilarious errors Charlie makes and transcribe them onto the map at the appropriate point in the cloak-making process.

The illustrations can also serve as the basis for composing a story from a different point of view. Children can orally tell or rewrite the story from the perspective of the sheep that used trickery on Charlie. This story lends itself to roleplaying as well as storytelling, since children can invent their own dialogue between Charlie and his sheep.

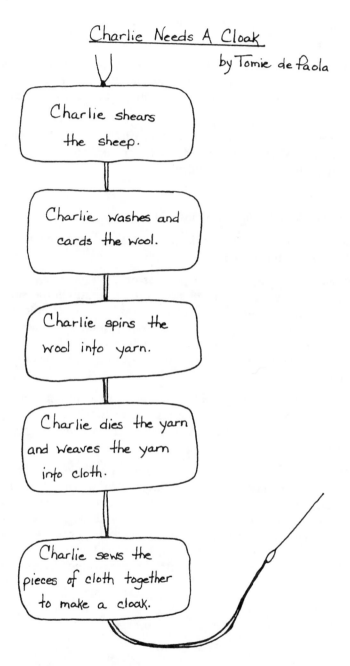

Charlie Needs A Cloak
by Tomie de Paola

Charlie shears the sheep.

Charlie washes and cards the wool.

Charlie spins the wool into yarn.

Charlie dies the yarn and weaves the yarn into cloth.

Charlie sews the pieces of cloth together to make a cloak.

Sequence map for *Charlie Needs a Cloak,* by Tomie de Paola.

Lewis, Naomi. *Puffin.* (Deborah King, Illus.). New York: Lothrop, Lee, & Shepard, 1984.

**Summary:** This story traces the life of a young sea bird born on an island off the northern coast of Scotland. It discusses the bird's birth, care by mother and father, growth, independence, migration, and return to begin its own family.

**Setting:** The setting ranges from a north coastal Scottish island, across the Atlantic Ocean, to Newfoundland and Nova Scotia in Canada, and back again to where the puffin was born in Scotland.

**Characters:** The puffin.

**Theme:** The cycle of life for a sea bird ends where it begins.

**Vocabulary:** fledgling, shallows, tide, prey, breakers, breeding, murk, skuas, secluded, boulders, burrows, nestling, oil slick.

**Illustrations:** Full-page watercolor pictures on the right side of every page supplement the narrative on the left side of the page to tell the story of the puffin's life. As the puffin grows and develops, so do his colors. Vibrant shades of blue and green capture the ocean, while pictures at sunset and the first light of morning show varying intensities of color. The picture of the puffin encountering the oil slick is dark and communicates the deadly nature of these accidents.

**Grade Level/Content Area:** This book is appropriate for children in grades 2 and 3 in a study of the life cycles of birds and animals or ecology in general. It fits well with units in grades 4–6 on migration, the oceans, ecology, and environmental hazards.

**Factual Web:** Before reading the story, solicit any prior knowledge students have about puffins by making a list of what they know. Then help them classify their facts into categories (physical appearances, food, home, etc.), and start a factual web that includes each category and the facts students supplied. After students read or hear the story you (or they) can add information (both categories and facts) to the partially completed web. The finished web gives students a guide for retelling the story or for writing a report about the puffin.

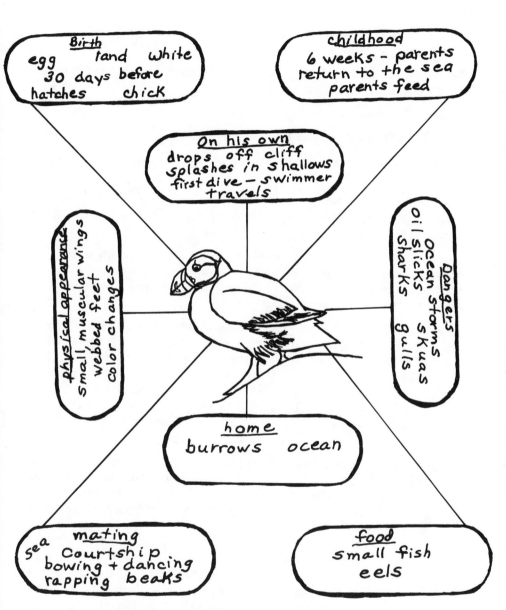

**Birth**
egg ~~land~~ white
30 days before
hatches     chick

**childhood**
6 weeks - parents
return to the sea
parents feed

**On his own**
drops off cliff
splashes in shallows
first dive — swimmer
travels

**physical appearance**
small muscular wings
webbed feet
color changes

**Dangers**
Ocean storms
oil slicks  skuas
sharks  gulls

**home**
burrows   ocean

**mating**
sea  Courtship
bowing + dancing
rapping beaks

**food**
small fish
eels

Factual web for *Puffin*, by Naomi Lewis.

Michel, Anna. *Little Wild Lion Cub.* (Tony Chen, Illus.). New York: Random House, 1980.

**Summary:** This book relates the life and development of a lion cub from his birth to age six, when he will be a full-grown lion.

**Setting:** The woodlands of Africa.

**Characters:** lion cub, mother lion, and other lions.

**Theme:** Helpless and newborn young grow to be self-reliant and independent.

**Vocabulary:** woodlands, thicket, guarded, prowling, wiggled, trotted, grunted, growl, dashed, kicked, whirled, wrestled, leapt, sharpened, grazing, pounce, chase, dodge.

**Illustrations:** Illustrations in this book are black with a variety of gray watercolor washes of differing intensities. Text generally appears across the tops of pages, leaving the remainder of the page for expressive illustrations with real texture, depth, and perspective.

**Grade Level/Content Area:** This book is of interest to children in grades K-2 who are learning about the natural world and the growth and development of different kinds of animals. In grades 2-4, when children study survival and stages of the life cycle, this book shows how a young animal lives, thrives, and becomes independent. The book also provides an excellent introduction to careers and life planning for students in grades 3 and 4. In a language arts or writing lesson, the vocabulary in this book lends itself well to learning and using words that refer to movement.

**Sequence Map:** As preparation, you can show children the five boxes in this sequence map before they read or hear the story, or children can generate the map after reading the story. The five boxes out of sequence can be shared with children, and they can arrange them in the proper order after hearing the story.

If this book is used in conjunction with a career or life-planning lesson there are many possibilities. Children can generate a web for their own growth and development in five or more boxes that parallel the lion cub's. Or they can make webs for what they imagine to be the sequence of events that leads to a person becoming a doctor, dentist, teacher, and so on.

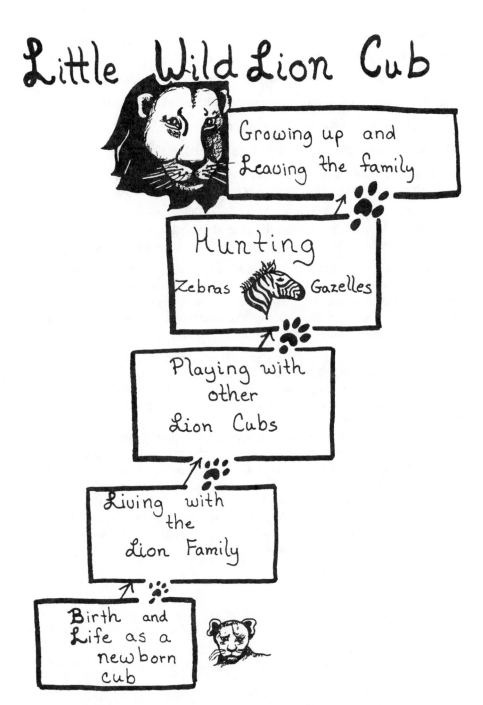

# Little Wild Lion Cub

Growing up and Leaving the family

Hunting

Zebras Gazelles

Playing with other Lion Cubs

Living with the Lion Family

Birth and Life as a newborn cub

Sequence map for *Little Wild Lion Cub*, by Anna Michel.

Wandro, Mark, and Joani Blank. *My Daddy Is a Nurse.* (Irene Trivas, Illus.). Boston: Addison-Wesley, 1981.

**Summary:** This book presents fathers in some nontraditional careers.

**Setting:** A variety of environments where different careers are found.

**Characters:** Fathers shown performing different jobs.

**Theme:** Career choice is not necessarily defined by gender.

**Vocabulary:** nurse, flight attendant, preschool teacher, telephone operator, ballet dancer, weaver, office worker, homemaker, librarian, dental hygienist.

**Illustrations:** Pencil drawings on the right side of every page show fathers in a variety of jobs. Text on the left side of every page is in paragraph form and describes what the father does in that particular work setting.

**Grade Level/Content Area:** In grades K–3 social studies, children learn about their community and its members, the family and its structure, and often are introduced to careers. This book provides a good starting point from which to begin to learn about careers. You can read this book to young children, while most second- and third-graders can read it themselves.

**Concept Web:** You can create this web with children after you read the book to them or after they read it themselves. Ask children to identify the theme of the book and begin with that in the center of the web, filling in the ten careers that the book includes. Children can add vocabulary that describe each job.

This web needs to be extended beyond the scope of this book, however, since fathers have many other careers that are not included. So, begin an outer circle of other careers that fathers have, such as lawyer, carpenter, plumber, salesman, professor, doctor, truck driver, gas station attendant, computer programmer, and so on, being careful to include jobs that are both white-collar and blue-collar. Help children see that women also can hold any of these jobs and that the organizing concept "Daddies can be anything" can be changed to "People can do anything."

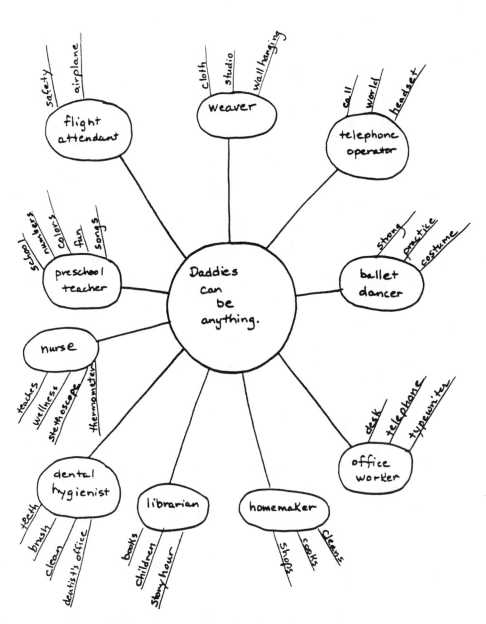

Concept web for *My Daddy Is a Nurse,* by Mark Wandro and Joani Blank.

# chapter 8

# Children's Literature Review Part II: Annotated Bibliography

These 145 annotations include both picture books and books for older students that are primarily text. Webbing can be used with these books as you integrate them with the content areas of science, social studies, math, language arts, health, music, or art. They include Caldecott and Newbery Medal and Honor books, IRA Children's Choices books, titles chosen by the Children's Book Council as outstanding science and trade books, and other examples of quality literature for grades K–8. These annotations include examples of books about children and youth with handicaps and children and youth with various heritages, including African, Asian, European, Hispanic, and native American.

Each annotation includes a bibliographic reference with a section called *Summary* and a section called *Grade Level/Content Area Use*. With the information provided, you can decide whether and how to use webs with these books to promote children's enjoyment and appreciation of a certain topic and/or teach, reinforce, or enrich certain ideas or information included in your curriculum.

The books are categorized by genre: folktale, fantasy, realistic fiction, historical fiction, biography, poetry, and information books. Within each genre, books are in alphabetical order according to the author's last name.

## *Folktale* ═══════════════════════════════════════════

Clement, Claude. *The Painter and the Wild Swans.* (Frederick Clement,
Illus.). New York: Dale Books, 1986.

**Summary:** A famous painter in rural Japan of the past sees wild swans and
must capture their beauty. His quest causes him to forfeit everything else,
and in doing so he learns the nature of true beauty and becomes a swan.

**Grade Level/Content Area Use:** In a K–5 art class, this book can be used to
introduce a discussion of beauty. In social studies, it supports a unit on other
cultures and a discussion of how death is viewed in other cultures.

Cole, Brock. *The Winter Wren.* New York: Farrar, Straus & Giroux,
1984.

**Summary:** In this folktale set in a Europe of long ago, Simon and his little
sister Meg go in search of Spring, who would not come to their village. They
go to Winter's farm, where Meg turns into a wren and Simon follows the
wren's directions three times before he finds Meg and brings Spring back to
their village.

**Grade Level/Content Area Use:** Children in grades 2–3 who are learning
about seasonal changes enjoy this story. It also complements a unit on folktales and fairy tales, since it possesses the traditional folktale elements.

de Paola, Tomie. *The Mysterious Giant of Barletta.* San Diego:
Harcourt Brace Jovanovitch, 1984.

**Summary:** This is a folktale from Italy with full-page, soft color illustrations.
The giant statue that has always stood in front of the Church of San Sepolcro
in Barletta is called upon to save the town from an army of a thousand men
that is destroying all the towns and cities along the lower Adriatic coast.

**Grade Level/Content Area Use:** Appropriate for students in grades 2–4
studying folktales of different countries or exploring our Italian heritage.

Fleischman, Sid. *The Whipping Boy.* (Peter Sis, Illus.). Mahwah, NJ:
Troll, 1987.

**Summary:** This Newbery Medal book is a fairy tale based on an actual practice in many royal households of the past. Prince Brat misbehaves but cannot
be spanked because he is heir to the throne. So a poor street boy named
Jemmy is forced to suffer the Prince's punishments and be his whipping boy.
The two of them run away together and have an adventure that changes both
their lives.

**Grade Level/Content Area Use:** For students in grades 3–6, this story enriches units on European history, friendship and responsibility, and writing
adventure stories based on historical facts.

Hall, Amanda. *The Gossipy Wife.* New York: Bedrick-Blackie,1981.

**Summary:** Ivan finds a chest of old coins and, afraid that his wife will tell the landlord and he will lose them, he decides to trick her and the landlord. He is finally tricked himself and the landlord prevails.

**Grade Level/Content Area Use:** In grades 2–4, this story can be used in a unit on folktales as an example of a Russian tale. In language arts, it presents a message about gossip.

Hamilton, Virginia. *The People Could Fly: American Black Folktales.* (Leo and Diane Dillon, Illus.). New York: Knopf, 1987.

**Summary:** This collection of 24 stories and 40 illustrations represents the main body of black folklore. There are trickster tales, in which Bruh Rabbit outwits stronger animals, frightening devil tales, tales full of riddles and humor, and moving tales of freedom. It is written so that both readers and storytellers can capture the rhythms of the language.

**Grade Level/Content Area Use:** In grades 1–6, this book fits social studies units on folklore or African American heritage. It provides a variety of tales that might be read and discussed during Black History Month or to complement a study of the Civil War, slavery, or storytelling.

Kamen, Gloria. *The Ringdoves.* New York: Atheneum, 1988.

**Summary:** This story is an adaptation of a tale from the Fables of Bidpai, classic fables from India first told in 300 B.C. By uniting, several loyal animal friends work together to outwit and elude a hunter.

**Grade Level/Content Area Use:** In grades 2–6, where folktales of the world are the focus of a reading or language arts unit, this book fits well. It also enriches a science unit on animals and a social studies unit on the concept of unity and community as necessary for survival.

Lobel, Arnold. *Fables.* New York: Harper & Row, 1980.

**Summary:** In this Caldecott Medal Book, there are 20 one-page, modern-day fables, each accompanied by a one-line moral and a full-page drawing done in soft pastel colors. Humorous stories are told about a crocodile, duck, lion, hen, baboon, ostrich, camel, kangaroo, pig, elephant, and other animals that are personified with clearly identifiable human traits.

**Grade Level/Content Area Use:** Students in grades 2–9 enjoy and understand these short stories, which can motivate the writing of original fables or enrich a unit on living things.

Lobel, Arnold. *A Treeful of Pigs*. (Anita Lobel, Illus.). New York: Scholastic, 1979.

**Summary:** This is a European folktale about the lazy farmer who makes promises to help his wife with the farm work "on the day that pigs grow in trees like apples," "on the day that pigs fall out of the sky like rain," etc. She finally outsmarts him and he learns to keep his promises.

**Grade Level/Content Area Use:** Children in grades 1–3 enjoy this tale, and it supports a language arts unit on folktales, a social studies unit on European history and culture, or a science unit on animals or pigs.

Mosel, Arlene. *Tikki Tikki Tembo*. (Blair Lent, Illus.). New York: Holt, 1968.

**Summary:** This old tale explains why the Chinese "give all their children little, short names instead of great long names." It is a charming story about a little boy with a long name who falls into a well and almost drowns because his name is so long that his brother has a difficult time reporting the accident.

**Grade Level/Content Area Use:** Appropriate for grades 1–3, this story fits a unit on folktales from around the world. It also enriches a unit on the Orient or China and a unit on the origins and meanings of names.

Polacco, Patricia. *Rechenka's Eggs*. New York: Philomel, 1988.

**Summary:** Babushka is making colored eggs for the Easter Festival in Moskva. She finds an injured goose and nurses it back to health only to have it break all her eggs. The next day Rechenka, the goose, lays a decorated egg and continues to do so until there are 13 eggs for Babushka. When the goose leaves for the wild, it lays one exquisitely decorated egg, which hatches into a gosling that stays with Babushka forever.

**Grade Level/Content Area Use:** This book, set in Eastern Europe or Russia of the past, can be used in grades K–3 where traditions in other cultures are being studied in social studies.

Ransome, Arthur. *The Fool of the World and the Flying Ship*. (Uri Shulevitz, Illus.). New York: Farrar, Straus & Giroux, 1986.

**Summary:** A Russian peasant boy, who is looked down upon by his parents, wins the hand of the Czar's daughter. He has the help of a wise old man and seven other men with unique talents.

**Grade Level/Content Area Use:** In grades 2–5, this folktale supports a unit on folktales from other countries and a study of discrimination, as it is a springboard for discussions about the treatment of peasants and retarded people.

Schwartz, Alvin. *Scary Stories to Tell in the Dark.* (Stephen Gammell, Illus.). New York: Harper & Row, 1986.

**Summary:** This is a collection of American folklore first told by the pioneers and now retold by the author. It includes tales of horror about ghosts, skeletons, witches, "jump" stories, scary songs, and modern-day tales of fright that bring "shivers of pleasure." Schwartz provides notes and sources to validate and explain the origin of his tales.

**Grade Level/Content Area Use:** This collection enriches a social studies unit in grades 3–9 on western settlement or a unit on American folklore and storytelling.

Siberell, Anne. *Whale in the Sky.* New York: Dutton, 1982.

**Summary:** This Northwest Indian tale, the retelling of an authentic legend, is illustrated with woodcuts and tells the story of totem-pole carvings. Thunderbird (a golden eagle), Whale, Frog, Raven, and Salmon are the characters in this tale about why whales live in the ocean and not in rivers.

**Grade Level/Content Area Use:** Children in grades 1–3 studying animals, the Northwest Indians, legends, or folktales enjoy this simple tale of the weak and strong.

Singer, Isaac Bashevis. *Why Noah Chose the Dove.* (Eric Carle, Illus.). New York: Farrar, Straus & Giroux, 1973.

**Summary:** In this retold story, each of the animals of the world boasts about his own important virtues and differences so that he will be chosen to enter the arc. The dove finally tells Noah that "I don't think of myself as better or wiser or more attractive than the other animals" and "Each one of us has something the other doesn't have." So Noah takes all the animals onto the arc and they forget their grudges against each other.

**Grade Level/Content Area Use:** In grades K–3 social studies, this book develops children's awareness and appreciation of differences and diversities.

Stevens, Janet. *The Town Mouse and the Country Mouse.* New York: Holiday House, 1987.

**Summary:** In this adaptation of an Aesop's fable, a town mouse and a county mouse are cousins and visit each other. The town mouse finds the country too boring and the country mouse finds the town too hectic.

**Grade Level/Content Area Use:** For children in grades K–4, this story supplements a science unit on animals, a social studies unit on different lifestyles and communities, or a language arts unit on fables.

== Wilde, Oscar. *The Selfish Giant.* (Lisbeth Zwerger, Illus.). Natick, MA: Picture Book Studio, 1984.

**Summary:** A selfish giant refuses to allow the children of the village to play in his garden, which makes Spring mad enough to keep Winter there all year long. One day, the children creep back in and Spring returns, with the giant helping one small boy into a tree. When the giant dies, the small boy returns to take him to paradise.

**Grade Level/Content Area Use:** Students in grades 2–5 learn the traditional folktale components from this story of selfishness versus selflessness.

== Winter, Jeanette. *Follow the Drinking Gourd.* New York: Knopf, 1988.

**Summary:** Based on a folk song of the same name, the story tells about an old sailor who traveled to the plantations teaching the slaves the song that contained a secret message about how to escape to freedom in Canada by following the big dipper, which points north. It describes the journey of a brave group of runaway slaves who listened to the song and made their escape.

**Grade Level/Content Area Use:** Students in grades 4–7 studying slavery and the Underground Railroad in social studies enjoy this story, which can be enriched with the actual song and music.

== Wolkstein, Diane. *The Banza: A Haitian Story.* (Marc Brown, Illus.). New York: Dial, 1981.

**Summary:** Tiger and Goat become friends, and Tiger gives timid Goat a banza—or banjo—for her protection. When Goat finds herself up against 10 hungry tigers, she plays a ferocious song that frightens the tigers away. Textured drawings are done in bright, Caribbean colors.

**Grade Level/Content Area Use:** This book can be used with children in grades 2–3 who are learning about other cultures. The flora, fauna, and symbols of Haiti and the Caribbean are found in this book.

== Zelinsky, Paul O. *Rumpelstiltskin.* New York: Dutton, 1986.

**Summary:** This is a Caldecott Honor book with colorfully striking pictures. It is a retold version of the story of a strange little man who forces the miller's daughter to give him all she has, including the promise of her firstborn child, in exchange for his help in spinning straw into gold for the king. When she becomes queen and her child is born, the little man comes back to collect. But she guesses his name, and so her debt is forgiven and the little man rides off in a wooden spoon.

**Grade Level/Content Area Use:** Children in grades K–4 enjoy this story as an example of the traditional fairy tale, in which the pattern of three is found. It complements a language arts unit on fairy tales and contains sexism in the form of women portrayed as good and men as evil, which should be discussed with children as appropriate to the time period.

Zemach, Harve. *Duffy and the Devil.* (Margot Zemach, Illus.). New York: Farrar, Straus & Giroux, 1973.

**Summary:** This is the story of Squire Lovel's servant girl, Duffy, who bargains with the devil to do her knitting for her. She marries the squire, and the housekeeper helps her find a way to settle her bargain with the devil. An unexpectedly humorous ending and pictures that have a soft color wash give this Caldecott Medal book added charm.

**Grade Level/Content Area Use:** For grades 2–4, this story complements a language arts unit on fairy tales. It is a humorous Cornish version of Rumpelstiltskin that can be compared to the original.

## *Fantasy*

Bang, Molly. *The Paper Crane.* New York: Greenwillow, 1985.

**Summary:** In this story with a Japanese flavor, a kindly restaurant owner's slacking business is restored when a gentle old man lends him a magic paper crane. Even after the old man returns for the crane, people continue to frequent the restaurant, proving that goodness and kindness are rewarded.

**Grade Level/Content Area Use:** This story fits an art unit on origami or collage and a social studies unit on economics for grades PreK–3.

Banks, Lynn Reid. *The Indian in the Cupboard.* New York: Avon, 1982.

**Summary:** A nine-year-old English boy, Omri, receives a magic cupboard for his birthday that makes a small plastic Indian toy come alive. The escapades he and his friend Patrick have with Little Bear, the tiny Iroquois Indian, help Omri understand that with power comes responsibility, and that friendship means trust and keeping promises. The story includes an Indian who lived during the time of the French and Indian Wars, a cowboy who lived in Texas in the 1880s, and a doctor from Civil War days.

**Grade Level/Content Area Use:** This book enriches grades 3–6 social studies units on several periods of our history. It explores the realities of power, the requirements of human beings, and friendship.

═══ Banks, Lynn Reid. *The Return of the Indian.* New York: Avon, 1986.

**Summary:** In this sequel to *The Indian in the Cupboard,* Omri brings Little Bear back to life with the magic cupboard and discovers that the Indian has been critically injured in the French and Indian Wars and needs his help. The book explores issues surrounding war, peace, power, and responsibility.

**Grade Level/Content Area Use:** Students in grades 3–6 like this sequel, which has similar uses to the first volume.

═══ Conly, Jane L. *Racso and the Rats of NIMH.* (Leonard Lubin, Illus.). New York: Harper & Row, 1986.

**Summary:** This is a sequel to *Mrs. Frisby and the Rats of NIMH* in which Racso, a city rat who is the son of one of the rats who left the original farm, brings all sorts of new inventions and ideas to the country. Racso can read and shares with the other rats his knowledge of dancing, candy, the lyrics to rock songs, and his ideas about reprogramming computers. He and the other rats stop their river valley from being developed into communities in which people can live.

**Grade Level/Content Area Use:** This book reinforces a grades 3–6 social studies unit on the impact of technological change on a community. Students experience the emotions of those whose future is threatened and are involved in their problem-solving methods.

═══ Holabird, Katherine. *Angeline and Alice.* (Helen Craig, Illus.). New York: Clarkson Potter, 1987.

**Summary:** Two mice discover the importance of teamwork when their acrobatics are the hit of the gymnastics show at the village fair.

**Grade Level/Content Area Use:** For children in grades K–2 who are learning about cooperation in social studies or animals in science.

═══ Howe, James. *The Celery Stalks at Midnight.* (Leslie Morill, Illus.). New York: Avon, 1983.

**Summary:** This humorous story about Chester the cat, Harold the dog, Howie the dachshund puppy, and Bunniculla, a bunny, takes the reader along for some adventure when Bunniculla is missing from his cage and the other animals try to find this supposed vampire bunny.

**Grade Level/Content Area Use:** In grades 4–6, this book fits a science unit on animals and complements the writing of fiction using animal personification.

Lewis, C. S. *The Lion, the Witch, and the Wardrobe.* New York: Macmillan, 1950.

**Summary:** This story is about four children who enter the magical kingdom of Narnia, through the back of a wardrobe in an old mansion in England. In Narnia, winter always prevails until the children break the wicked Snow Queen's spell.

**Grade Level/Content Area Use:** In grades 5–8, this fantasy is enjoyed for its adventure and the victory of the forces of good over evil.

Lionni, Leo. *Six Crows.* New York: Knopf, 1988.

**Summary:** A farmer erects a scarecrow to be rid of the crows in his wheat field. The crows try to scare it away with a kite, which frightens the farmer. This escalates until the owl acts as mediator amd convinces them all to talk it over.

**Grade Level/Content Area Use:** This book fits in a K–3 social studies unit on cooperation and living harmoniously with others, or in a science unit on living things.

Lobel, Arnold. *Frog and Toad Are Friends.* New York: Harper & Row, 1970.

**Summary:** This book has five short stories in which Frog and Toad help each other, as only caring friends can, to solve each other's problems, such as a lost button, never getting any mail, and being embarrassed about one's looks in a bathing suit.

**Grade Level/Content Area Use:** In grades K–3, this book fits a social studies unit on friendship and a science unit on amphibians or animals.

Marshall, James. *What's the Matter With Carruthers? A Bedtime Story.* Boston: Houghton Mifflin, 1972.

**Summary:** A bear named Carruthers is grumpy and unpleasant, and two pigs named Emily and Eugene are worried about him and set out to cheer him up. After many attempts, they finally discover that it is time for the bear to hibernate and that is why he is out of sorts.

**Grade Level/Content Area Use:** For children in grades K–3, this book supplements a science unit on the seasons or hibernation, and a social studies unit on friendship.

O'Brien, Robert. *Mrs. Frisby and the Rats of NIMH.* (Zena Bernstein, Illus.). New York: Atheneum, 1971.

**Summary:** Experimental rats who received steroids escape from a laboratory and come to a farm outside Washington, D.C., where Mrs. Frisby and her children live. The rats can read and they build their own community on the farm but finally leave to establish a society free of dependence on humans.

**Grade Level/Content Area Use:** This book fits in grades 3–6 social studies units on communities and their cultural, political, economic, and geographic aspects.

Ryder, Joanne. *The Snail's Spell.* (Lynne Cherry, Illus.). New York: Viking, 1988.

**Summary:** An imaginative young boy in a garden full of lush plants and numerous animals feels himself becoming smaller and smaller. He thinks he is the soft gray snail and he glides through the garden as the snail does, its feelers charting its course.

**Grade Level/Content Area Use:** K–3 children studying the environment or the interdependence of plants and animals in science enjoy this story that can initiate dramatic movement and improvisation.

Sandford, John. *The Gravity Company.* Nashville: Abingdon Press, 1988.

**Summary:** This is a story about how the automatic switch at the Gravity Company is accidentally turned off and everything in town becomes weightless until Mortimer realizes what is happening and turns the gravity back on slowly.

**Grade Level/Content Area Use:** Students in grades 1–3 studying the force of gravity or weightlessness in space enjoy this story. It generates creative discussion and can be a model for storytelling or story writing (e.g., The Cat Machine).

Steig, William. *Brave Irene.* New York: Farrar, Straus & Giroux, 1986.

**Summary:** This is a modern fairy tale of love and courage set in England, where a dressmaker falls ill and has just finished a gown for the duchess to wear to a ball that evening. The dressmaker's daughter, Irene, fights a snowstorm and freezing weather to deliver the gown.

**Grade Level/Content Area Use:** In grades 1–3, this story fits a unit on folktales, English or European history, or members of olden-day communities.

Van Allsburg, Chris. *The Garden of Abdul Gasazi.* Boston: Houghton Mifflin, 1979.

**Summary:** A boy left alone and in charge of a disobedient dog gets into trouble when he chases the dog into a retired magician's garden where a sign warns them not to go. The magician turns the dog into a duck, who steals the boy's hat and flies away. When the dog's master returns and the boy tells her about the magician's trick, suddenly the dog and hat reappear.

**Grade Level/Content Area Use:** In grades 1–4, this book is a springboard for a discussion of magic and responsibility, and of art appreciation.

═══ Williams, Margery. *The Velveteen Rabbit.* (William Nicholson, Illus.). New York: Doubleday, 1970.

**Summary:** A stuffed rabbit discovers that becoming real happens when you are loved for a long time at the expense of your looks. Having served his master well, the rabbit is thrown out after the boy recovers from scarlet fever. With the help of a fairy, he eventually becomes a real rabbit in reward for his love and faithfulness.

**Grade Level/Content Area Use:** Students in grades 3–6 may better understand what is important to them and who they are as they discuss vanity, love, faithfulness, and inner versus outer selves.

═══ Winthrop, Elizabeth. *Sloppy Kisses.* (Anne Burgess, Illus.). New York: Penguin, 1983.

**Summary:** Emmy Lou, a young pig, goes to school and learns from a classmate that "kissing is for babies," and so doesn't allow her father to kiss her anymore. But she soon misses her parents' kisses and affection and questions the wisdom of her friend's advice.

**Grade Level/Content Area Use:** This book fits a grades K–2 science unit on animals or a social studies unit on the family.

═══ Yolen, Jane. *Commander Toad and the Dis-Asteroid.* (Bruce Degen, Illus.). New York: Coward-McCann, 1985.

**Summary:** Commander Toad and his crew of frogs on the space ship Star Warts answer a mysterious call for help from a flooded asteroid. Helping pigeon inhabitants means overcoming a language barrier and using Toad's amphibious skills to unplug the asteroid drains.

**Grade Level/Content Area Use:** This book fits in grades 1–3 science units on the solar system, space, or amphibians.

## *Realistic Fiction* ══════════════════════════════════════

═══ Ackerman, Karen. *Song and Dance Man.* (Stephen Gammell, Illus.). New York: Knopf, 1988

**Summary:** Three children go to visit their grandpa, who takes them on a nostalgic visit to the attic where he finds his old banjo and puts on a song and dance show from his vaudeville days. Bright colored illustrations communicate the gaudy glamor of the vaudeville stage.

**Grade Level/Content Area Use:**  In K-3 social studies, this book fits a unit on the family. Respect for what our elders have experienced and have to offer is also portrayed, as well as some of the history of drama in the United States.

=== Blume, Judy. *Tiger Eyes*. Scarsdale, NY: Bradbury, 1985.

**Summary:**  When her father is killed, a fifteen-year-old girl named Davey, her mother, and younger brother move from Atlantic City to New Mexico to stay with relatives. This is the story of how each of them progresses through the grieving process, and how Davey matures as well.

**Grade Level/Content Area Use:**  For students in grades 8–12, this book provides background for a social studies unit on nuclear war and disarmament, since Davey gets herself involved in this issue.

=== Cleary, Beverly. *Dear Mr. Henshaw*. (Paul O. Zelinsky, Illus.). New York: Dell, 1983.

**Summary:**  In this Newbery Medal book, sixth-grader Leigh Botts moves to a new school and experiences the separation and divorce of his parents. The text is a series of letters he writes to his favorite author and journal entries in which his life is humorously described.

**Grade Level/Content Area Use:**  This book reinforces journal and letter writing in language arts and shows how a young boy deals with problems and makes friends in a new community.

=== Clifton, Lucille. *Everett Anderson's Goodbye*. (Ann Grifalconi, Illus.). New York: Holt, 1983.

**Summary:**  A young black boy has a difficult time coming to terms with his grief after his father dies. The story takes him through the grieving process, from denial, anger, bargaining, and depression to acceptance. It is written as rhymed poetry that expresses the boy's emotions and his mother's quiet support.

**Grade Level/Content Area Use:**  In grades K-3, this story supports a unit on the family or death and dying.

=== Drescher, Joan. *My Mother's Getting Married*. New York: Dial, 1986.

**Summary:**  This is the story of Katy's reservations and uncertainty about her mother's remarriage and her acceptance of her new stepfather, who indeed does not take all her mother's love.

**Grade Level/Content Area Use:**  Children in grades K-1 learning about different types of families in social studies enjoy this story of a successful blended family.

 Foster, Doris Van Liew. *Feather in the Wind.* (Ati Forberg, Illus.). New York: Lothrop, Lee & Shepard, 1972.

**Summary:** In this account of experiencing a hurricane, a boy finds a young bird that he shelters until the storm passes.

**Grade Level/Content Area Use:** Students in grades 2–4 who are studying the forces of weather in science appreciate this story that contains much information.

 Girard, Linda. *At Daddy's on Saturdays.* (Judith Friedman, Illus.). Niles, IL: Albert Whitman, 1987.

**Summary:** A young girl named Katie learns to deal with the anger, concern, and sadness surrounding her parents' divorce. She discovers that she still has a close relationship with her father.

**Grade Level/Content Area Use:** This book fits a social studies unit in grades PreK–3 on the family.

 Greene, Betty. *Philip Hall Likes Me. I Reckon Maybe.* (Charles Lilly, Illus.). New York: Dell, 1974.

**Summary:** A black sixth-grade girl named Beth Lambert of Pocahontas, Arkansas, has a crush on her class rival, Philip Hall. She gets involved in such adventures as catching turkey thieves, winning calf-raising contests, and making mountain-top rescues as well as capturing Philip's affections.

**Grade Level/Content Area Use:** This book is appropriate for students in grades 4–6 as a complement to a social studies unit on communities, the South, or Black History Month.

 Greenwald, Sheila. *The Mariah Delany Lending Library Disaster.* New York: Dell, 1986.

**Summary:** An eleven-year-old sets up her own library and lends her father's books in competition with the New York Public Library. She has problems when her borrowers do not return their books or pay their fines.

**Grade Level/Content Area Use:** Students in grades 3–6 enjoy this humorous story that fits with a social studies unit on economics and starting a business.

 Herman, Charlotte. *Millie Cooper, 3B.* (Helen Cogancherry, Illus.). New York: Puffin, 1987.

**Summary:** This story is about a third-grader in 1946 who has never written with anything but a pencil and desperately wishes for a newly invented Reynolds Rocket ballpoint pen so she can do well in her spelling tests and discover who she is by writing an autobiography.

**Grade Level/Content Area Use:** This story supports a language arts unit in grades 2-4 on writing, handwriting, or the autobiography.

= Lord, Bette Bao. *In the Year of the Boar and Jackie Robinson.* (Marc Simont, Illus.). New York: Trumpet, 1987.

**Summary:** Set in Brooklyn in the 1950s, this episodic story tells about a Chinese immigrant, Bandit, and her family's immersion in a culture that is foreign to them. Baseball finally becomes Bandit's passion and helps her make the link between dragons and New York City.

**Grade Level/Content Area Use:** This book fits grades 3-4 social studies units on the nature of cities, immigration, Asiatic cultures, and the problems of being new and different.

= Pearson, Susan. *Happy Birthday, Grampie.* (Ronald Himler, Illus.). New York: Dial, 1987.

**Summary:** Martha gives her 89-year-old Swedish grandfather, who is blind and in a home for the aged, a special birthday gift. She makes him a card that he can read with his fingers—with raised letters, doily, and felt heart—to which he responds warmly.

**Grade Level/Content Area Use:** In grades 2-3 social studies, this book supports the study of cultural diversity and promotes understanding of the aged and blindness.

= Peterson, Jeanne Whitehouse. *I Have a Sister, My Sister Is Deaf.* (Deborah Ray, Illus.). New York: Harper & Row, 1977.

**Summary:** A sister shares positive experiences about her deaf sister and explains how deafness itself does not hurt but how her sister's feelings are hurt when people do not understand her disability.

**Grade Level/Content Area Use:** In PreK-2, this book increases understanding of the hearing impaired. It builds knowledge of finger spelling and lip reading and promotes an appreciation of how people with disabilities have many similarities to others.

= Polushkin, Maria. *Kitten in Trouble.* (Betty Lewin, Illus.). New York: Bradbury, 1988.

**Summary:** A story for beginning readers, told with repetitive prose and humor, about all the typical things a kitten can do to get into trouble.

**Grade Level/Content Area Use:** The story fits a PreK-1 social studies unit on the family or a science unit on animals.

═ Rylant, Cynthia. *Night in the Country.* (Mary Szilagyi, Illus.). New York: Bradbury, 1986.

**Summary:** This book takes a close look at the goings-on of a variety of animals at night in the country when it should be quiet. Softly colored illustrations invite the reader to explore the sights and sounds of the night.

**Grade Level/Content Area Use:** This book is appropriate for K-2 children involved in a science or health unit on the senses or sound.

═ Schwartz, Amy. *Annabelle Swift.* New York: Orchard Books, 1988.

**Summary:** Annabelle Swift's first day of kindergarten is rough because of advice and coaxing from her older third-grade sister. All ends well, and Annabelle's first day at school is a success.

**Grade Level/Content Area Use:** In PreK-K social studies, this book fits units on the family and the community, where school fears and confidence in oneself are topics for discussion.

═ Udry, Janice May. *How I Faded Away.* (Monica De Bruyn, Illus.). Niles, IL: Albert Whitman, 1976.

**Summary:** A boy experiences a lack of self-esteem at school due to his mistakes, insecurity, and lack of recognition (invisibility). At home he experiences security, love, and recognition (visibility). Finally, through his musical ability he gains approval at school.

**Grade Level/Content Area Use:** Appropriate for children in grades K-3, this book helps children understand feelings and the importance of pride in accomplishment.

═ Vigna, Judith. *Nobody Wants a Nuclear War.* Niles, IL: Albert Whitman, 1986.

**Summary:** Two siblings who are worried about nuclear war set up their own shelter. When their mother discovers this, she discusses with them the things that people have done and are doing to make the world safe from nuclear weapons.

**Grade Level/Content Area Use:** For children in grades 1-3, this book supports a study of current issues and world peace in social studies.

═ Viorst, Judith. *The Tenth Good Thing about Barney.* (Eric Blegvad, Illus.). New York: Macmillan, 1988.

**Summary:** When his cat Barney dies, a boy tries to think of the ten best things about his pet in an attempt to overcome his grief. His parents help him in gentle ways to accept the death.

**Grade Level/Content Area Use:**  In grades 1–3, this book complements a social studies unit on the family or death and dying.

===  Williams, Vera B. *Cherries and Cherry Pits.* New York: Greenwillow, 1986.

**Summary:**  This is a story about Bidemmi, a young black girl, who tells and colorfully illustrates four stories, each of which contains a main character who leaves the subway carrying cherries home to eat and share with his or her loved ones. In the last story she tells about herself and what she does with the pits left from her cherries. She plants and tends them until they grow and become trees loaded with fruit that she shares with her neighbors.

**Grade Level/Content Area Use:**  Children in K–2 enjoy this story as an enrichment to a social studies unit on the family or urban communities, or a science unit on plants.

===  Yolen, Jane. *Owl Moon.* (John Schoenherr, Illus.). New York: Scholastic, 1987.

**Summary:**  This Caldecott Medal book tells the story, in text and picture, of a father who takes his young child out into the woods on a still, cold night to look for owls. The special relationship between a father and child, who is finally old enough for this long-awaited adventure, and a message of hope are found in this quiet story.

**Grade Level/Content Area Use:**  This book supports grades 2–4 science units on the natural world, nature appreciation, or birds, and a social studies unit on the family, self-identity, or rural life in winter time.

===  Zolotow, Charlotte. *William's Doll.* (William Pene DuBois, Illus.). New York: Harper & Row, 1972.

**Summary:**  This is the story of a boy named William who wants a doll but is discouraged by his brother, the boy next door, and his father. His grandmother's realistic handling of the problem helps break old stereotypes and provides a sensible and caring solution.

**Grade Level/Content Area Use:**  Children in grades 1–2 enjoy this book that complements a social studies unit on the family, becoming an individual, and changing roles of family members.

## *Historical Fiction* ═══════════════════════════════════════

===  Benchley, Nathaniel. *Sam the Minuteman.* New York: Harper & Row, 1969.

**Summary:**  A young boy living on a farm in Lexington, Massachusetts becomes a minuteman and, with his father, responds to Paul Revere's message.

About 80 minutemen defend their land and people against 1,000 British soldiers, and Sam's friend is wounded. Its theme is the bravery and courage of even the youngest citizen in the colonies in helping to establish a free country.

**Grade Level/Content Area Use:** In grades 1-3 social studies, this book fits a unit on the American Revolution or colonial life.

== Brenner, Barbara. *Wagon Wheels.* (Don Bolognese, Illus.). New York: Harper & Row, 1978.

**Summary:** The Muldie brothers, two young black boys, spend three months traveling and following a map that leads them to where their father has settled in the West. This story depicts the hardships of life in the wilds and portrays the Indians as helping the settlers.

**Grade Level/Content Area Use:** In grades 1-3, this easy-to-read book complements a social studies unit on Western settlement by the pioneers or a unit on black history.

== De Angeli, Marguerite. *The Door in the Wall.* New York: Doubleday, 1949.

**Summary:** A young boy named Robin, recently crippled by a strange disease, goes to live with some monks when the plague strikes London. With perseverance and the monks' help, he becomes independent and skilled and saves the town where his parents live.

**Grade Level/Content Area Use:** This book fits in grades 3-7 social studies units on the history of western Europe and England, and in developing awareness of the abilities of persons with disabilities.

== Fife, Dale. *North of Danger.* New York: Dutton, 1978.

**Summary:** Based on a true story about a twelve-year-old boy, Arne must warn his father, who is a leader of the resistance in hiding, of the German occupation of Spitsbergen. With the help of a fur trapper, he risks his life traveling 200 miles to his father's camp and successfully warns him.

**Grade Level/Content Area Use:** In grades 3-7, this book fits with a social studies unit on World War II or, specifically, with a study of Scandinavia.

== Fritz, Jean. *Shh! We're Writing the Constitution.* (Tomie de Paola, Illus.). New York: Scholastic, 1987.

**Summary:** This is a story of the Constitutional Convention, based on careful research that includes amusing and relevant anecdotes about the people involved in its writing. Both black and white and color illustrations accompany the text, which also includes the text of the Constitution.

**Grade Level/Content Area Use:** Students in grades 3–7 who study the history of the United States and a participatory form of government in social studies enjoy this accurate look at how the Constitution was drawn up.

Haley, Gail E. *Jack Jouett's Ride.* New York: Viking, 1973.

**Summary:** Based on historical records, this is the story of a young boy who rode 40 miles through the woods at night to warn the Virginia legislators, who were meeting in Charlottesville, that the British were coming. The legislators were able to hide their political documents and escape.

**Grade Level/Content Area Use:** In grades 4–5 where the American Revolution is studied, this personal story complements the social studies text.

Harvey, Brett. *My Prairie Year.* (Deborah Kogan Ray, Illus.). New York: Holiday House, 1986.

**Summary:** This story is based on the diary of the author's grandmother and is about a family who left their home in Maine to become homesteaders in the West. The book describes the details of pioneer life, including everyday chores and threats to survival.

**Grade Level/Content Area Use:** For children in grades 3–5 studying the early West and the Dakotas, especially, in social studies, this book is appropriate.

Hunt, Irene. *Across Five Aprils.* Chicago, IL: Follett, 1964.

**Summary:** This is the story of the Creightons, a southern Illinois family, who are torn between their loyalty to their southern background and loyalty to their country during the five years of the Civil War. The main character is a young boy named Jethro.

**Grade Level/Content Area Use:** Students in grades 5–8 studying the Civil War in social studies enjoy this personal look at how a war can divide family loyalties. The war is examined from both the North and South points of view.

Jackson, Louise A. *Grandpa Had a Windmill, Grandma Had a Churn.* (George Ancona, Illus.). New York: Parents' Magazine Press, 1977.

**Summary:** The reader is taken back to the author's childhood home in the 1940s in rural Texas and memories of grandpa and grandma are recounted. Photographs accompany the text.

**Grade Level/Content Area Use:** In grades 2–4, this book can be used with children who are studying farm life or rural life in the South 50 years ago, or animals in science.

MacLachlan, Patricia. *Sarah, Plain and Tall.* New York: Harper & Row, 1985.

**Summary:** Anna and Caleb's father places a newspaper ad for a wife and mother and receives a letter from Sarah in Maine. Sarah brings her cat and comes for a month's visit to their prairie home, which is very much different from her home by the sea. This is a gentle story about love and the changes it brings to the lives of two lonely children and their father.

**Grade Level/Content Area Use:** This book is appropriate for children grades 3–6 and complements a study of early family life in the colonies and pioneer settlement, or a unit on death.

Melville, Herman. *Moby Dick* (Adap. by Joanne Fink). (Hieronimus Fromm, Illus.). Morristown, NJ: Silver Burdett, 1985.

**Summary:** A classic retold in an understandable format, this is the story of Ishmael and Queequeg, who sail out of Nantucket Harbor on a whaling ship with Captain Ahab, who is intent on finding and killing Moby Dick, the largest white whale in the world. Each page of text, in large print, is accompanied by a brightly colored picture.

**Grade Level/Content Area Use:** For students in grades 2–6, this book fits a social studies unit on colonial America or a science unit on mammals or ocean dwelling animals.

Paterson, Katherine. *Jacob Have I Loved.* New York: Crowell, 1984.

**Summary:** This is the story of twin 13-year-old girls growing up on a tiny Chesapeake island in the early 1940s. The story centers around the life of Louise, who befriends a mysterious sea captain, experiences a hurricane, becomes a waterman as she works with her father, and wishes for an education. She finally sets herself apart from her pampered sister, Caroline, and discovers what her values are.

**Grade Level/Content Area Use:** For students in grades 6–9, this book enriches a social studies unit on various cultures within the United States, or the eastern shore specifically.

Rappaport, Doreen. *The Boston Coffee Party.* (Eileen Arnold McCully, Illus.). New York: Harper & Row, 1988.

**Summary:** Based on a true incident, this is the story of Sarah and Emma, sisters who become involved with their mother and other angry women of Boston in an attempt to hold down the prices of sugar and coffee in the American colonies during the revolutionary war.

**Grade Level/Content Area Use:** In grades 2–4, this book coincides with a social studies unit on the revolutionary war or a study of women in our history.

═══ Rawls, Wilson. *Where the Red Fern Grows.* New York: Bantam, 1985.

**Summary:** This story is about the life of a 10-year-old boy who lived with his family in a log cabin in the foothills of the Ozarks in northeastern Oklahoma and his adventures with his two coon hounds, Old Dan and Little Ann. It is based on a local legend about the sacred red fern planted by an angel.

**Grade Level/Content Area Use:** Students in grades 4–7 enjoy this story that complements a social studies unit on life in the mountains or the Midwest 50 years ago.

═══ Speare, Elizabeth George. *The Witch of Blackbird Pond.* Boston: Houghton Mifflin, 1958.

**Summary:** In this Newbery Medal book, Kit Tyler's parents die and she leaves Barbados in the 1770s to live in Connecticut with Puritan relatives. She can read and write, is quite emancipated in comparison with her female relatives, and is tried as a witch.

**Grade Level/Content Area Use:** Students in grades 4–7 enjoy this account of the life of a young girl who is different and ahead of the times in which she lives. It fits a social studies unit on pre-revolutionary United States.

═══ Taylor, Theodore. *The Cay.* New York: Avon, 1969.

**Summary:** Just before World War II, 11-year-old Phillip is on a ship bound from Curaçao, a Dutch island in the Caribbean, back to Virginia when the ship goes down. He finds himself blind from a head injury and shipwrecked on a barren island with a West Indian named Timothy. Taught by his mother not to befriend or trust blacks, Phillip struggles for survival, adjusts to his blindness, and comes to rely on and love the old man.

**Grade Level/Content Area Use:** This book fits a grade 5–9 social studies or science unit on the Caribbean and life in a temperate climate, or a unit on racial and ethnic diversity or black history, since it helps children appreciate human goodness and wisdom independent of race.

═══ Turkle, Brinton. *Obadiah the Bold.* New York: Viking, 1965.

**Summary:** Obadiah, a young Quaker boy, receives a spyglass for his birthday, and this sparks his desire to become a pirate, until a conversation with his father helps him realize that being a pirate is not a harmless adventure.

**Grade Level/Content Area Use:** In grades 2–4, this book fits a social studies unit on life in early Massachusetts. Geography, life-styles, language, and the advisability of choosing a reputable role model can also be explored.

═══ Uchida, Yoshiko. *Journey Home.* (Charles Robinson, Illus.). New York: Macmillan, 1978.

**Summary:** Yuki, a young Japanese girl, her mother, and father are released from a World War II concentration camp in the Utah desert and return to Berkeley, where they lived before the war. Discrimination fed by mistrust and misunderstandings, the critical support of family and loved ones in times of tragedy, and the importance of forgiveness are all themes in this story about the difficulties of life for the Japanese-American during and following the war.

**Grade Level/Content Area Use:** In grades 3–6, this book fits units on awareness and sensitivity about diversity and discrimination, the conflicts surrounding war, or the history of the western region of the United States.

═══ Van Woerkom, Dorothy. *Becky and the Bear.* (Margot Tomes, Illus.). New York: Putnam's, 1975.

**Summary:** In colonial Maine, a young girl who wants to go hunting with her father and brother is left at home, where she must contend with a bear. She feeds the bear molasses and rum, he falls asleep, and she and her grandmother tie him to a tree until her father gets home.

**Grade Level/Content Area Use:** In a grade 1–3 social studies unit on colonial America, this book provides a good glimpse of colonial life and the bravery of women.

═══ Ziefert, Harriet. *A New Coat for Anna.* New York: Knopf, 1986.

**Summary:** In this World War II story, probably set in England, Anna's mother decides she will trade the few valuables she has left for a winter coat for her growing daughter. She trades a gold watch, a lamp, a garnet necklace, and a teapot to a farmer, spinner, weaver, and tailor, who all help make Anna's coat. Based on a true story, this tale holds a simple lesson about love and patience, how clothing is made, and how hardship can give life to hope.

**Grade Level/Content Area Use:** In K–2 social studies, this book fits a study of how clothing is made, a European community of the past, the problems of wartime, or a mother's love for her daughter.

## *Biography* ═══════════════════════════════

═══ Bains, Rae. *Martin Luther King.* (Hal Frenck, Illus.). Mahwah, NJ: Troll, 1985.

**Summary:** This is the story of a civil rights leader who believed in integration and used nonviolent protest to secure equal rights for blacks. He had a dream of equality for all and his beliefs live on.

**Grade Level/Content Area Use:** This book fits grades 2–4 social studies units on U.S. history, the history of black people, and integration.

═══ Conner, Edwina. *Marie Curie.* (Richard Hook, Illus.). New York: Bookwright Press, 1987.

**Summary:** This is the story of a famous woman scientist—her childhood in Poland, her determination to finish college in France, her marriage to another famous scientist, Pierre Curie, her discovery of radium, her appointment as the first woman professor of physics and receipt of the Nobel Prize twice, her determination to be a good mother, her efforts to get X-ray equipment to soldiers in World War I, the slow deterioration of her health due to exposure to radium, and finally, her death in 1934.

**Grade Level/Content Area Use:** Students in grades 4–6 studying the scientific method, radiation, or influential women in history in social studies enjoy this book about the power of knowledge, determination, and dedication.

═══ Ernst, John. *Escape King: The Story of Harry Houdini.* (Ray Abel, Illus.). Englewood Cliffs, NJ: Prentice-Hall, 1975.

**Summary:** Originally born Ehrich Weiss in 1874 in Hungary, Harry Houdini became a legendary magician who first worked with his brother and then his wife. He possessed special muscular control and litheness that gave him the ability to escape any imprisonment.

**Grade Level/Content Area Use:** Students in grades 4–7 studying health and physical fitness enjoy the story of this man's unbelievable career.

═══ Felton, Harold. *Mumbet: The Story of Elizabeth Freeman.* (Donn Albright, Illus.). New York: Dodd, Mead, 1970.

**Summary:** Mumbet is the nickname of a black slave who in August of 1781 won her freedom in the Massachusetts courts. The book shows her courage and determination in the face of adversity and oppression.

**Grade Level/Content Area Use:** This book fits social studies units in grades 4–6 about slavery, the Constitution, and the revolutionary war.

═══ Fritz, Jean. *Will You Sign Here, John Hancock?* (Trina Schart Hyman, Illus.). New York: Coward, McCann & Geoghegan, 1976.

**Summary:** This is an account of John Hancock's life, including his foibles and virtues, and particularly his role in the colonies' struggle against England. The tone is light and humorous, yet the story is filled with authentic facts and information.

**Grade Level/Content Area Use:** Students in grades 3–6 studying the history of government and colonial life enjoy this story that personalizes history.

═  Fritz, Jean. *And Then What Happened, Paul Revere?* (Margot Tomes, Illus.). New York: Coward, McCann & Geoghegan, 1973.

**Summary:**    Set in Boston in the late 1770s and early 1880s, this story covers the life of Paul Revere from the age of 15, concentrating on his involvement in our fight for freedom against the English.

**Grade Level/Content Area Use:**  For students in grades 4–7, this book fits a social studies unit on U.S. history, geography, and economics.

═  Goffstein, M. B. *A Little Schubert.* New York: Harper & Row, 1972.

**Summary:**  This story takes place many years ago in Vienna and is about the life of a famous composer, Franz Schubert, who lived in a bare room without a fire. It describes how he heard music differently than other people and how he composed by writing his ideas down as quickly as he could.

**Grade Level/Content Area Use:**  For children in grades K–2, this book supports a unit on music, or in social studies a unit on careers.

═  Greene, Carol. *Elie Wiesel: Messenger from the Holocaust.* Chicago: Children's Press, 1987.

**Summary:**  This book is about Elie Wiesel, who survived the Holocaust and dedicated his life to speaking and writing about it. He is the winner of the 1986 Nobel Peace Prize.

**Grade Level/Content Area Use:**  For students in grades 4–8, this book supports a social studies unit on Europe during World War II or the creation of Israel.

═  Greene, Carol. *Mother Teresa: Friend of the Friendless.* Chicago: Children's Press, 1983.

**Summary:**  This is the story of Mother Teresa, the Catholic nun whose work with the poor in India, in response to her understanding of God's will, has made her famous.

**Grade Level/Content Area Use:**  This book fits grades 3–5 social studies units on careers, important women in history, world hunger, Nobel Prize winners, and racial acceptance.

═  Hitz, Demi. *Lu Pan the Carpenter's Apprentice.* Englewood Cliffs, NJ: Prentice-Hall, 1978.

**Summary:**  This is the story of Lu Pan, the greatest of all Chinese artisans, who built great halls, houses, mills, pavillions, observatories, bridges, toy helicopters, and kites, among other things. It takes Lu Pan from his years as a young boy helping his father with carpentry to his days working with the

Master of Carpentry as he refined his skills to his later life when he became a famous architect, engineer, and inventor, whose carpentry manual is still used in China today.

**Grade Level/Content Area Use:** In grades 4–8, this book fits a social studies unit on the Chinese culture or a study of careers.

Lasker, David. *The Boy Who Loved Music.* (Joe Lasker, Illus.). New York: Viking, 1979.

**Summary:** This is the story of Joseph Haydn's time as music director at the summer palace of Prince Esterhazy in eighteenth-century Austria, and of a young boy named Karl who is a horn player in the Prince's orchestra. When the Prince stays at his summer palace far into the fall and does not seem interested in returning to Vienna where his musicians long to be, Haydn composes the *Farewell* symphony with a surprise ending that persuades the Prince to return with his court.

**Grade Level/Content Area Use:** In grades 2–4, this book enriches a music appreciation unit, a study of men in the arts, or provides social studies background for a study of the history of Europe.

Lauber, Patricia. *Lost Star: The Story of Amelia Earhart.* New York: Scholastic, 1988.

**Summary:** This is the story of one of America's first female fliers, who had a singular vision about herself and the airplane. Black and white photographs accompany this story of Amelia Earhart's life from the time she was seven years old and jumping fences in Kansas until her death at age 40.

**Grade Level/Content Area Use:** In grades 3–7, this book supports a social studies unit on transportation or aviation, World War I, careers, or women as explorers and leaders.

Lee, Betsy. *Judy Blume's Story.* Minneapolis, MN: Dillon, 1985.

**Summary:** This is the story of the life of one of the most popular authors of juvenile fiction today, from her days as a young girl growing up during World War II to the present. Major emphasis is on her experiences and feelings during her pre-teen and teen years, and it also contains some descriptions of Jewish customs.

**Grade Level/Content Area Use:** In grades 4–12, this book fits a study of biographies and social studies units on the World War II period or Jewish culture.

Meltzer, Milton. *Betty Friedan: A Voice for Women's Rights.* (Stephen Marchesi, Illus.). New York: Viking Penguin, 1985.

**Summary:** This is the story of Betty Friedan's life, from her birth in 1921 to the present day. It documents Betty's desire to do something with her life and the thinking that resulted in her most famous book *The Feminine Mystique* and the establishment of the National Organization for Women.

**Grade Level/Content Area Use:** In grades 3–7 social studies, this book fits a unit on the history of women and the women's rights movement. The book provides young girls with a strong role model, and without glossing over her faults, Friedan is presented as a free thinker with an inner fire.

Norman, Gertrude. *Johnny Appleseed.* (James Caraway, Illus.). New York: Putnam's, 1960.

**Summary:** This is the story of John Chapman (Johnny Appleseed), set in the wilderness of colonial America, from his childhood as a boy of seven or eight years old to an elderly man.

**Grade Level/Content Area Use:** This book fits science units in grades 1–2 on the interdependence between humans and their environment or the growth cycle.

Powers, Mary Ellen. *Our Teacher's in a Wheelchair.* Niles, IL: Albert Whitman, 1986.

**Summary:** Brian Hanson, a daycare teacher who is partially paralyzed and uses a wheelchair, is the subject of this biography. His life story includes the injury that caused the paralysis and his many accomplishments.

**Grade Level/Content Area Use:** In grades K–3, this book fits a social studies unit on careers and can help children accept and understand people with handicaps.

Sabin, Louis. *Patrick Henry: Voice of the American Revolution.* (Bill Ternay, Illus.). Mahwah, NJ: Troll, 1982.

**Summary:** This story focuses on Patrick Henry's youth in the colony of Virginia. His persuasive oratory, fairness, sound education, sense of humor, love of music and the violin, affinity for the freedom he felt when he was close to nature, and his ability to debate are some of the skills and character traits the book describes.

**Grade Level/Content Area Use:** For students in grades 3–6, this book fits a social studies unit on the American Revolution or life in the early colonies.

Stevens, Bryna. *Deborah Sampson Goes to War.* (Florence Hill, Illus.). Minneapolis: Carolrhoda Books, 1984.

**Summary:** This book is about the early life of Deborah Sampson, who disguised herself as a man and went to fight as a soldier in the American Revolution. Despite her illnesses and injuries, no one learned of her identity until near the end of the war.

**Grade Level/Content Area Use:** In grades 2–6, this book supports a study of the revolutionary war or women in U.S. history.

Sufrin, Mark. *George Bush: The Story of the Forty-first President of the United States.* New York: Dell, 1989.

**Summary:** This book documents George Bush's life from his birth to his election as President, including the many different jobs he has held, from navy pilot to businessman, ambassador, head of the CIA, and Vice President. His roles as husband and father are also discussed.

**Grade Level/Content Area Use:** In grades 3–6 social studies, this book fits units on government, political leaders, or current events.

Weil, Lisl. *I, Christopher Columbus.* New York: Atheneum, 1983.

**Summary:** This is the story of an Italian explorer who faced many obstacles and made many voyages, which resulted in his discovery of America for Spain. He never accomplished his goal of reaching the Far East by sailing west and so did not repay with riches those who financed his trips; instead, he brought back American Indians as slaves.

**Grade Level/Content Area Use:** For students in grades 2–4 who are studying the history of North America or slavery, or who are using maps and globes, this book is helpful.

*Poetry* ═══════════════════════════════════════════════════════════

Agree, Rose. *How to Eat a Poem and Other Morsels.* (Peggy Wilson, Illus.). New York: Random House, 1967.

**Summary:** This is a collection of poems about all sorts of foods by poets such as Lewis Carroll, Walter de la Mare, John Ciardi, Phyllis McGinley, and Randall Jarrell. Noodles, fish, fries, paella, pudding, chicken soup with rice, and the origins of foods are all subjects for poems in this collection.

**Grade Level/Content Area Use:** Enjoyed by all in K–6, this book fits a science unit on nutrition or social studies unit on taking care of oneself through proper diet.

Armour, Richard. *All Sizes and Shapes of Monkeys and Apes.* (Paul Galdone, Illus.). New York: McGraw-Hill, 1970.

**Summary:** Written in the form of rhymed poetry, this book gives the reader facts and information about 10 different kinds of monkeys and apes.

**Grade Level/Content Area Use:** These poems are appropriate for children in grades 2–4 studying animal needs, communities, dependencies, behavior, and the food chain in science, or poetry in language arts and reading.

Blishen, Edward. *The Oxford Book of Poetry for Children.* (Brian Wildsmith, Illus.). New York: Peter Bedrick Books, 1984.

**Summary:** Various poems, some well known and some less well known, on a variety of topics and characters, from a baby in a cradle to apples in an orchard; randomly illustrated.

**Grade Level/Content Area Use:** This collection of poems enriches a range of science and social studies topics in grades 2–6.

Bloom, Suzanne. *We Keep a Pig in the Parlor.* Middletown, CT: Weekly Reader Books, 1988.

**Summary:** This rhymed text is about a pig who is unhappy with his life in the barn, where he must eat unpopped corn and sleep on straw. He is allowed to come indoors to sleep on the settee in the parlor, where he eats popcorn and watches TV and comes to live with a young boy and his family.

**Grade Level/Content Area Use:** In grades K–3, this story-poem complements a unit on farm animals or a unit on nonsense or narrative poetry.

Cole, Joanna. *A New Treasury of Children's Poetry.* Garden City, NY: Doubleday, 1984.

**Summary:** An anthology of more than 200 old and new poems, light verse, riddle rhymes, and limericks that will delight children's senses.

**Grade Level/Content Area Use:** These poems foster an appreciation for poetry and language, a knowledge of concepts, and identification with characters and situations for children in PreK–6. These poems serve as good models to imitate as children write their own poetry.

de Regniers, Beatrice Schenk, Moore, Eva, White, Mary Michaels, & Jan Carr. *Sing A Song of Popcorn.* (Marcia Brown, Leo and Diane Dillon, Richard Egielski, Trina Schart Hyman, Arnold Lobel, Maurice Sendak, Marc Simont, and Margot Zemach, Illus.). New York: Scholastic, 1988.

**Summary:** This collection contains 128 poems, ranging from traditional to contemporary, with full-color illustrations by nine Caldecott Medal–winning artists. The poems, which are humorous, touching, profound, and nonsensical, are divided into nine themed sections: Fun with Rhymes; Mostly Weather; Spooky Poems; Story Poems; Mostly Animals; Mostly People; Mostly Nonsense; Seeing, Feeling, Thinking; and In a Few Words.

**Grade Level/Content Area Use:** Children in PreK-3 enjoy these short poems that complement the study of poetry and rhyme in language arts, or the study of animals, weather, other cultures, and self-awareness in science and social studies.

— Fisher, Aileen. *But Ostriches* . . . . (Peter Parnall, Illus.). New York: Crowell, 1970.

**Summary:** This is a book of contrasts that compares the oddities of the ostrich with its bird cousins in humorous rhyme. It contains predictable information about a particular bird, followed by "but ostriches . . . " and then contrasting information about ostriches.

**Grade Level/Content Area Use:** Children in K-4 studying adaptations, birds, or habitats in science enjoy this book, and it could serve as a model for writing similar kinds of books.

— Fleischman, Paul. *Joyful Noise: Poems for Two Voices.* (Eric Beddows, Illus.). New York: Harper & Row, 1988.

**Summary:** A collection of poems about insects for reading by two voices that is a companion to *I Am Phoenix,* a collection about birds for two voices. It is told from the point of view of the insects and includes the rhythm and sounds of the insect world.

**Grade Level/Content Area Use:** In grades 1-6, this book can be used for choral speaking in language arts, or in science as an enrichment for a unit on the insect world.

— Frost, Robert. *Stopping by Woods on a Snowy Evening.* (Susan Jeffers, Illus.). New York: Dutton, 1978.

**Summary:** The quiet, haunting, magical delights of winter are evident as the poet stops his horse at the edge of the woods on the darkest night of the year to watch the snow. He remembers that he cannot stay because he has "promises to keep."

**Grade Level/Content Area Use:** In grades 3-6, this poem fits a science unit on winter, a language arts unit on poetry, or an art unit on pencil drawings.

— Grossman, Bill. *Donna O'Neeshuck Was Chased by Some Cows.* (Sue Truesdell, Illus.). New York: Harper & Row, 1988.

**Summary:** A story told in rhyming, five-line verse in which Donna gives pats on the head to cows, a policeman, a boy on a bike, and other animals and people, who all chase after her for more.

**Grade Level/Content Area Use:** Children in PreK–3 enjoy this poem that can introduce narrative poetry and serve as a model for writing it.

≡ Harnden, Ruth. *Wonder Why.* (Elaine Livermore, Illus.). Boston: Houghton Mifflin, 1971.

**Summary:** This is a collection of poems that answers questions commonly asked by children about familiar experiences of childhood, for example, how a child feels about a new baby or why a beach is different sizes at different times of the day.

**Grade Level/Content Area Use:** Grades K–5 children enjoy this poetry that reinforces the science curriculum. Through it, children can develop the ability to solve problems creatively and hypothesize about problems and solutions.

≡ Kuskin, Karla. *Any Me I Want to Be.* New York: Harper & Row, 1972.

**Summary:** This collection of 30 poems covers a variety of subjects: an ant, a dog, a kite string, a witch's broom. The poems are sometimes explicitly about an object or character and sometimes the subject must be guessed.

**Grade Level/Content Area Use:** In grades 1–2, this collection can reinforce a variety of topics in science or social studies and can introduce poetry effectively to children since they can be easily involved with guessing who some of the poems are about.

≡ Larrick, Nancy. *Cats Are Cats.* (Ed Young, Illus.). New York: Philomel, 1988.

**Summary:** This is a collection of 42 poems about cats of various descriptions and dispositions.

**Grade Level/Content Area Use:** Because the images of cats are so realistic these poems enrich a science unit on animals or a language arts unit on poetry in grades 3–9.

≡ Lewis, Richard. *Out of the Earth I Sing: Poetry & Songs of Primitive Peoples of the World.* New York: Norton, 1968.

**Summary:** This is a collection of poems and songs by primitive people from all over the world. Represented are the Sioux, Zulu, Iroquois, Winnebago, Inca, Aztec, Maori, Apache, Bantu, Chippewa, Bushmen, Eskimo, Borneo, Aboriginal, Pygmy, Pawnee, Papago, Navaho, Dakota, and Hawaiian. Common themes are morning, children, hunting, prayer, animals, and love.

**Grade Level/Content Area Use:** Students in grades 3–6 studying communities and cultures of the world in social studies enjoy these poems that enrich their understanding of primitive people the world over.

= Merriam, Eve. *Blackberry Ink.* (Hans Wilhelm, Illus.). New York: Morrow, 1985.

**Summary:** This is a mixture of 24 one-page rhythmic poems, some rhymes, some silly verses, and some bedtime poems, with topics like pizza, weather, rain, snow, baths, Halloween, caterpillars, and monsters.

**Grade Level/Content Area Use:** In PreK–1, these poems enrich a social studies unit on the family and the everyday world of the community.

= Oliver, Robert. *Cornucopia.* New York: Atheneum, 1978.

**Summary:** These poems use the alphabet as a foundation for describing animals and insects in amusing and informative ways.

**Grade Level/Content Area Use:** In science units on living things, these poems provide information on many familiar and not so familiar animals and insects for grades 1–3.

= Prelutsky, Jack. *Read-Aloud Rhymes for the Very Young.* (Marc Brown, Illus.). New York: Knopf, 1986.

**Summary:** This is a collection of over 200 short poems, written by both traditional and contemporary poets, that appeal to young children with short attention spans. The poems deal with children's concerns such as waking, animals, bedtime, seasons, holidays, special events, and play and show children that life is happy and fun.

**Grade Level/Content Area Use:** Children in K–3 enjoy these poems as part of a language arts unit on poetry or a social studies unit on the community.

= Prelutsky, Jack. *The New Kid on the Block.* (James Stevenson, Illus.). New York: Greenwillow, 1984.

**Summary:** These poems are written about an assortment of odd characters, creatures, animals with human likenesses, and "whatevers" invented by the author, from Stringbean Small to the Gloppy Gloopers.

**GradeLevel/Content Area Use:** In grades 2–6, these poems are enjoyed for their humor and craziness. They support a unit on poetry appreciation and writing and stimulate vocabulary growth and use of the imagination.

= Seuss, Dr. *I Am Not Going to Get Up Today.* (James Stevenson, Illus.). New York: Random House, 1987.

**Summary:** In this example of rhyming narrative poetry, a young boy decides he is going to sleep in and convinces others to leave him alone. The story describes numerous ways to wake the boy up.

**Grade Level/Content Area Use:** Children in grades PreK–2 enjoy this poem that stimulates creative thinking and discussion of the effects of doing something unusual.

Silverstein, Shel. *Where the Sidewalk Ends.* New York: Harper & Row, 1974.

**Summary:** A collection of brief, humorous poems about everyday things that communicate the author's creative eye and tongue.

**Grade Level/Content Area Use:** Students in grades 1–6 enjoy these poems that can be shared for their pure enjoyment and as examples of how a writer uses common, seemingly unimportant topics that he has observed carefully to write about.

Thayer, Lawrence. *Casey at the Bat: A Ballad of the Republic.* (Wallace Tripp, Illus.). New York: Coward, McCann & Geoghegan, 1978.

**Summary:** This is a ballad in which a baseball team of the 1800s, called the Mudville 9, finds itself losing the game. When Casey, one of the animal players, comes to the plate the fans are encouraged, suspense builds, and hopes run high, but Casey strikes out.

**Grade Level/Content Area Use:** In grades 3–6 language arts, this poem introduces children to the ballad and can be used as a model for writing one. It is appropriate as a poem about springtime or sports.

Viorst, Judith. *If I Were in Charge of the World and Other Worries.* New York: Macmillan, 1981.

**Summary:** This book of 41 poems, most of which rhyme and are humorous, reveals the worries, wishes, and secret thoughts that everyone may have.

**Grade Level/Content Area Use:** This book appeals to children in grades K–6 and promotes appreciative listening, a discussion of feelings, or the writing of personal essays or individual poems on the same topic, which can be collected in a class book.

## *Information Books*

Aliki (Brandenberg). *Corn Is Maize: The Gift of the Indians.* New York: Crowell, 1976.

**Summary:** This is a Let's-Read-and Find-Out Science Book that takes a kernel of corn from planting to harvesting and grinding by machines. It includes the place of corn in different cultures throughout history and is accompanied by green and yellow drawings.

**Grade Level/Content Area Use:** Students in grades 2–3 who are studying American Indians in social studies or foods and nutrition in science enjoy this informative and factual book.

Ashabranner, Brent. *The Vanishing Border: A Photographic Journey along our Frontier with Mexico.* (Paul Conklin, Illus.). New York: Dodd, Mead, 1987.

**Summary:** This Notable 1987 Children's Trade Book in Social Studies documents an author-photographer team as they meet and interview individuals and families along the U.S.-Mexican border. Issues such as illegal aliens, smuggling, the relationship between twin border cities, and Indian populations are discussed and enhanced with black and white photos.

**Grade Level/Content Area Use:** Students in grades 4–9 studying Mexico and/or the southern United States profit from this look at the problems and realities of the border between these two countries. This text develops understandings of our linkages with Mexico, the diverse racial and ethnic groups, and the economies of both countries.

Baron, Nancy. *Getting Started in Calligraphy.* (Michael Shelley, Photog.). New York: Sterling, 1979.

**Summary:** This is a guide to "beautiful writing" for both children and adults. Its illustrations, photos, and text exercises give step-by-step instructions and lessons in how to write in five different calligraphic styles. It includes an assortment of posters, poems, placards, greeting cards, and invitations as samples of special calligraphy projects.

**Grade Level/Content Area Use:** This book fits a social studies unit on the history of writing and the alphabet, or supports the improvement of legibility in handwriting in general in grades 4–7.

Brown, Laurene Drasny, & Brown, Marc. *Dinosaurs Divorce: A Guide for Changing Families.* New York: Atlantic, 1986.

**Summary:** After a table of contents and glossary of terms come sections on reasons why parents divorce, possible repercussions and reactions, dealing with visitations, living in two homes, celebrating holidays, and adjusting to parent dating, remarriage, and step-siblings. Humor and sensitivity distinguish this book and the dinosaur characters allow children to distance themselves emotionally from the characters yet identify with the issues.

**Grade Level/Content Area Use:** This book fits nicely into the family life segment of a social studies curriculum in grades K–4.

═ Dorros, Arthur. *Ant Cities.* New York: Crowell, 1987.

**Summary:** Named an Outstanding Science Trade Book for 1987, this book is an introduction to ants and the observation of them. It includes information about types of ants, urban and rural ant habitats, and instructions on how to build a simple ant city.

**Grade Level/Content Area Use:** For children in grades 1-3, this book supplements a science unit on investigating the insect world, ecosystems, and living things.

═ Gibson, Michael. *The Energy Crisis.* Vero Beach, FL: Rourke Enterprises, 1987.

**Summary:** This book examines the inadequacy of America's supply of energy resources. The text, with colored photographs, discusses the political and economic ramifications of a growing dependency on foreign countries for energy. It explores the problem of developing new sources of energy while protecting the environment.

**Grade Level/Content Area Use:** This book is appropriate for a study of energy and the environment in grades 5-8. It also provides background for forming opinions on economic and social issues such as nuclear energy, fossil fuel conservation, and the balance of trade.

═ Goennel, Heidi. *Seasons.* Boston: Little, Brown, 1986.

**Summary:** *Seasons* provides an introduction to how the world changes during a year, with descriptions of things seen and felt during each season.

**Grade Level/Content Area Use:** Grades PreK-1 use this book to support a science unit on the cycle of seasons or weather.

═ Gomi, Taro. *Bus Stops.* San Francisco: Chronicle Books, 1985.

**Summary:** A bus on its daily route in a Japanese community stops at such places as a beach, downtown, baseball field, church, home, restaurant, and marketplace.

**Grade Level/Content Area Use:** Grades PreK-1 children enjoy this book that fits with a social studies unit on the community, community workers, or transportation. Similarities in communities around the world can be shown.

═ Hirschi, Ron. *City Geese.* (Galen Burrell, Illus.). New York: Dodd, Mead, 1987.

**Summary:** This book follows a flock of Canada geese, which has established itself in a North American city, through a year in an urban environment. It describes nesting and raising young in the spring, molting during summer, feeding flights in autumn, and forming new pairs in winter. The text is accompanied by full-color photographs.

**Grade Level/Content Area Use:** This book is appropriate for students in grades 4–7 studying the natural world, birds, and adaptations of animal life to the environment.

═══ Irvine, Joan. *How to Make Pop-Ups.* (Barbara Reid, Illus.). New York: Morrow Junior Books, 1987.

**Summary:** This book gives step-by-step instructions for making pop-up cards, books, sculptures, and other objects out of paper and other materials found at home. Detailed pen-and-ink drawings of many different types of paper art make this book usable by children as well as adults.

**Grade Level/Content Area Use:** Although the book is probably written for grades 3–6 to read, pop-ups can be made by children in K–6. The activities in this book can accompany any content-area unit and many writing lessons.

═══ Jasperson, William. *Ice Cream.* New York: Macmillan, 1988.

**Summary:** The reader is taken on a tour of Ben and Jerry's ice-cream plant in Waterbury, Vermont, to explain where and how ice cream is made. It includes a description of how to run a successful company.

**Grade Level/Content Area Use:** Children in grades 2–4 studying food and nutrition in science, or the economics of running a business, or the New England economy in social studies enjoy this story.

═══ John, Naomi. *Roadrunner.* (Peter and Virginia Parnall, Illus.). New York: Dutton, 1980.

**Summary:** This story is set in the desert of the Southwest and is about a day in the life of a roadrunner, who is both predator and prey.

**Grade Level/Content Area Use:** For students in grades 4–6 studying habitats, specifically the desert, or predator/prey relationships, or a unit on birds.

═══ Langley, Andrew. *Passport to Great Britain.* New York: Franklin Watts, 1986.

**Summary:** This book provides facts about the land, people, government, economy, and home life of the British. It is a collection of photographs, maps, graphs, charts, and diagrams, with key facts listed separately. It is one of a series of "Passport" books.

**Grade Level/Content Area Use:** Students in grades 3–6 studying modern Western Europe in social studies or the effect of environment on populations and communities in science enjoy this book that also supports the study of graphs and maps.

Lauber, Patricia. *Volcano: The Eruption and Healing of Mount St. Helens.* New York: Bradbury, 1987.

**Summary:** In this Newbery Honor book, which is a full-color photographic essay, Lauber explains the most destructive volcanic eruption in the history of the United States. With the help of scientists and naturalists and the careful eye of her camera, she describes and shows the return of life to the mountain's barren landscape.

**Grade Level/Content Area Use:** This book fits science units in grades 2-9 on the earth's changing surface, animals, and plants.

Macaulay, David. *Castle.* New York: Trumpet, 1977.

**Summary:** This book traces the step-by-step planning and construction of a castle and a town, from the hiring of a skilled master engineer to the actual test of castle defenses when hundreds of Welsh soldiers launch a direct attack. The pen-and-ink drawings that accompany the text won this book a Caldecott Honor award and ALA Notable Book award.

**Grade Level/Content Area Use:** This book fits grades 3-6 social studies units on early European history, or careers, specifically architects, civil engineers, and city planners.

MacDonald, Golden. *The Little Island.* (Leonard Weisgard, Illus.). New York: Scholastic, 1974.

**Summary:** This is the story of the flora, fauna, and ecology of an island in the middle of the ocean as it experiences the four seasons.

**Grade Level/Content Area Use:** Children in grades 1-3 studying the seasons or environmental ecology in science enjoy this book.

McLaughlin, Molly. *Earthworms, Dirt, and Rotten Leaves: An Exploration in Ecology.* (Robert Shetterly, Illus.). New York: Atheneum, 1986.

**Summary:** This book examines the earthworm and its environment and suggests experiments to introduce basic ecological concepts, as demonstrated by the earthworm's survival in its habitat. Survival, the life cycle, and the interdependence of plants and animals are concepts taught in this book, which enhances a problem-solving, hands-on approach to learning science.

**Grade Level/Content Area Use:** This book fits grades 2-7 life science studies of living things and their effects on the environment and the scientific method.

═══ Morris, Campbell. *The Best Paper Aircraft: New and Expanded.* New
York: Perigee, 1986.

**Summary:** This book includes easy-to-follow instructions and drawings of
28 flyable paper airplane models, including super loopers, a kamikaze water
bomber, the space shuttle, jump jets, and more.

**Grade Level/Content Area Use:** Students in grades 3–6 enjoy this how-to
book that enriches a science unit on rocketry or space exploration and helps
teach the principles of lift and aerodynamics.

═══ Musgrove, Margaret. *Ashanti to Zulu: African Traditions.* (Leo and
Diane Dillon, Illus.). New York: Dial, 1976.

**Summary:** This is an ABC book about African traditions of 26 different peoples. It includes a custom important to each people and gives a feeling of the
vastness of Africa, its varied peoples, and how important tradition is in Africa.

**Grade Level/Content Area Use:** This book fits with grades 3–6 social studies units on world communities or cultures. In science it provides examples
of how people cope with nature and how environmental conditions influence populations.

═══ Petty, Kate. *Build Your Own Space Station.* (Louise Nevett, Illus.). New
York: Franklin Watts, 1985.

**Summary:** This book contains step-by-step directions and drawings for
space station projects that can be done unaided by children with common
everyday household materials.

**Grade Level/Content Area Use:** Children in grades 1–4 studying space exploration in science or model making in an art unit can easily use this book.
It promotes hands-on active involvement in science and art.

═══ Pryor, Bonnie. *The House on Maple Street.* (Beth Peck, Illus.). New
York: Morrow, 1987.

**Summary:** In this Notable Children's Trade Book in Social Studies for 1987,
the 300-year history of a house at 107 Maple Street is described, with all the
changes and development that have occurred. The two little girls who live
there now have a tiny china cup and an arrowhead as remnants of the
house's past.

**Grade Level/Content Area Use:** Students in grades 2–4 who are studying
the history of their community learn much from this easy to understand book
that documents the changes and people who once lived on or near this
property.

— Wakefield, Pat A., with Carrara, Larry. *A Moose For Jessica.* (Larry Carrara, Photog.). New York: Trumpet, 1987.

**Summary:** An Outstanding Science Trade Book for Children for 1987, this full-color photographic essay documents the 76-day visit of a moose to the Shrewsbury, Vermont, farm of Lila and Larry Carrara. Through the moose's courtship of Jessica, a young Hereford cow, the authors delve into the habits and life-style of the North American moose and include a powerful environmental message about man's interference with nature.

**Grade Level/Content Area Use:** Students in grades 3–7 enjoy this true account of a quirk of nature. Science units on animals, reproduction, and environmental concerns are strengthened with this current, high-interest story.

## *Teacher Resources*

The following resources include textbooks, handbooks, computer software, and a journal in which you will find further information about literature and semantic webbing.

— Bosma, B. (1987). *Fairy Tales, Fables, Legends, and Myths: Using Folk Literature in Your Classroom.* New York: Teachers College Press.

In this readable paperback, three chapters are of special interest to the teacher who wants to weave literature into the curriculum. "Learning to Write with Folk Literature," "Creative Activities with Folk Literature," and "A Fifth Grade Class Uses Folk Literature" all contain good ideas for integration.

— Cooper, C. R. (Ed.). (1985). *Researching Response to Literature and the Teaching of Literature: Points of Departure.* Norwood, NJ: Ablex.

This book has chapters contributed by Rosenblatt, Purves, Petrosky, Applebee, Squire, Cooper, and others who discuss and explore a wide range of issues surrounding response to literature and ways of researching this complex area. A major premise of the book is that understanding how to describe and measure the reading and response process will help us teach it better.

— Cullinan, B. E. (Ed.). (1987). *Children's Literature in the Reading Program.* Newark, DE: International Reading Association.

This is a readable book about literature and its place in teaching reading. A variety of experts contribute their beliefs and ideas, and the suggestions are practical and easily used in the classroom.

— Cullinan, B. E. (1989). *Literature and the Child* (2nd ed.). New York: Harcourt Brace Jovanovitch.

In this comprehensive text on children's literature, useful examples and explanations of webs and webbing are included.

Heimlich, J. E., & Pittelman, S. D. (1986). *Semantic Mapping: Classroom Applications.* Newark, DE: International Reading Association.

This 48-page paperback contains several practical classroom suggestions about the use of semantic mapping. Five applications and numerous examples make it immediately useful to classroom teachers.

Huck, C. S., Helper, S., & Hickman, J. (1987). *Children's Literature in the Elementary School* (4th ed.). New York: Holt, Rinehart & Winston.

In this comprehensive volume, children's literature is covered and ideas for using webs and webbing to integrate children's literature with the curriculum are found.

Huck, C. S., & Hickman, J. (Eds.). *The Web.* (The Ohio State University, Room 200 Ramseyer H, 29 West Woodruff, Columbus, OH 43210.)

This quarterly magazine for teachers contains reviews of new books and helpful webs showing possibilities for integrating literature into the curriculum.

Jalongo, M. R. (1988). *Young Children and Picture Books: Literature from Infancy to Six.* Washington, DC: National Association of the Education of Young Children.

This 120-page paperback is a practical source for early childhood educators who wish to give literature a central position in their programs. It provides help in the selection and use of some of the best picture books from which to develop children's enjoyment and early literacy acquisition.

Johnson, T. D., & Louis, D. R. (1987). *Literacy Through Literature.* Portsmouth, NH: Heinemann.

This book shares classroom-tested practices that can build children's literacy through the use of real books.

Lamme, L. L., Cox, V., Matanzo, J., & Olson, M. (1980). *Raising Readers: A Guide to Sharing Literature with Young Children.* New York: Walker.

This book provides concrete ideas for parents and teachers about sharing books as well as annotated bibliographies of books for infants, toddlers, prereaders, and beginning readers.

Lukens, R. J. (1990). *A Critical Handbook of Children's Literature* (4th ed.). Glenview, IL: Scott, Foresman.

This well-written and thoughtful book examines character, plot, setting, theme, point of view, style, tone, and the genres of children's literature using examples of children's books. Reading it gives one a better vantage point from which to make judgments about quality in literature.

Norton, D. E. (1987). *Through the Eyes of a Child: An Introduction to Children's Literature* (2nd ed.). Columbus, OH: Merrill.
In this comprehensive text on children's literature, webs and the webbing process using children's literature are explained.

Pearson, P. D., & Johnson, D. J. (1978). *Teaching Reading Comprehension.* New York: Holt, Rinehart & Winston.
Chapter 3 contains a long section on the use of semantic maps as a way of organizing concepts. It includes several examples that illustrate how maps improve comprehension.

Pehrsson, R. S., & Denner, P. R. (1989). *Semantic Organizers: A Study Strategy for Special Needs Learners.* Rockville, MD: Aspen.
This book is about teaching students to organize their ideas and improve memory and learning through semantic webbing. It is divided into two parts—(1) theory and practice and (2) practical applications to school subjects. Readers will find extremely helpful the examples of many different types of webs used to represent specific content and concepts since they can be easily adapted to the elements of story.

Purves, A. C., & Monson, D. L. (1984). *Experiencing Children's Literature.* Glenview, IL: Scott, Foresman.
This is a handbook for teachers on using children's literature. It explores Louise Rosenblatt's transactional theory of literature use, which strikes a balance between purely literary considerations and the response of the reader. It is full of basic information about the genres, yet includes examples of specific books and discussions of poetry, evaluating and selecting books, and the design and evaluation of literature programs.

Sinatra, R., Geisert, G., & DeMeo, V. (1985). *Thinking Networks for Reading and Writing.* New York: Thinking Networks.
This is a set of computer-based reading and writing materials for reading levels 2-9. It uses semantic mapping to help the learner move from reading to restructuring, then rewriting and preorganizing, and finally into original composition. It uses maps to teach episodes as one structure of story organization and themes as a way of organizing prose and report writing.

Taylor, D., & Strickland, D. (1986). *Family Storybook Reading.* Portsmouth, NH: Heinemann.
This easy-to-read paperback for parents discusses the whys and hows of storybook reading. It explores ways to make storybook reading an important part of family life and the ways that storybook sharing helps children learn to read and write.

# Awards for Quality in Children's Books

## The Caldecott Medal and Honor Books

The Caldecott Medal, named in honor of nineteenth-century English illustrator Randolph Caldecott, is awarded annually by the Association for Library Service to Children, a division of the American Library Association, to the artist of the most distinguished American picture book for children.

1990    *Lon Po Po: A Red Riding Hood Story From China*, by Ed Young, Philomel
        **Honor Books**
        *Hershel and the Hanukkah Goblins*, by Eric Kimmel, illustrated by
        Trina Schart Hyman, Holiday House
        *The Talking Eggs*, by Robert D. Sans Souci, illustrated by Jerry Pinkney, Dial
        *Bill Peet: An Autobiography*, Houghton Mifflin
        *Color Zoo*, by Lois Ehlert, Lippincott

1989    *Song and Dance Man*, by Karen Ackerman, illustrated by Stephen Gammell,
        Knopf/Random House
        **Honor Books**
        *The Boy of the Three Year Nap*, by Dianne Snyder, illustrated by Allen Say,
        Houghton Mifflin
        *Free Fall*, by David Wiesner, Lothrop
        *Goldilocks and the Three Bears*, by James Marshall, Dial
        *Mirandy and Brother Wind*, by Patricia C. McKissack, illustrated by Jerry Pinkney,
        Knopf/Random House

1988    *Owl Moon*, by Jane Yolen, illustrated by John Schoenherr, Philomel
        **Honor Book**
        *Mufaro's Beautiful Daughters*, by John Steptoe, Lothrop

1987    *Hey, Al*, by Arthur Yorinks, illustrated by Richard Egielski, Farrar
        **Honor Books**
        *The Village of Round and Square Houses*, by Ann Grifalconi, Little, Brown
        *Alphabatics*, by Suse MacDonald, Bradbury
        *Rumpelstiltskin*, retold and illustrated by Paul O. Zelinsky, Dutton

1986    *The Polar Express*, by Chris Van Allsburg, Houghton
        **Honor Books**
        *The Relatives Came*, by Cynthia Rylant, illustrated by Stephen Gammell, Bradbury
        *King Bidgood's in the Bathtub*, by Audrey Wood, illustrated by Don Wood, Harcourt

1985    *Saint George and the Dragon*, retold by Margaret Hodges, illustrated by
        Trina Schart Hyman, Little, Brown
        **Honor Books**
        *Hansel and Gretel*, retold by Rika Lesser, illustrated by Paul O. Zelinsky, Dodd, Mead
        *Have You Seen My Duckling?*, by Nancy Tafuri, Greenwillow
        *The Story of Jumping Mouse*, retold and illustrated by John Steptoe, Lothrop

1984    *The Glorious Flight: Across the Channel with Louis Blériot*, by Alice and
        Martin Provenson, Viking
        **Honor Books**
        *Little Red Riding Hood*, retold and illustrated by Trina Schart Hyman, Holiday House
        *Ten, Nine, Eight*, by Molly Bang, Greenwillow

1983    *Shadow*, by Blaise Cendrars, translated and illustrated by Marcia Brown, Scribner
        **Honor Books**
        *A Chair for My Mother*, by Vera B. Williams, Greenwillow
        *When I Was Young in the Mountains*, by Cynthia Rylant, illustrated by Diane Goode,
        Dutton

1982    *Jumanji*, by Chris Van Allsburg, Houghton
        **Honor Books**
        *Where the Buffaloes Begin*, by Olaf Baker, drawings by Stephen Gammell, Warne
        *On Market Street*, words by Arnold Lobel, pictures by Anita Lobel, Greenwillow
        *Outside Over There*, by Maurice Sendak, Harper
        *A Visit to William Blake's Inn: Poems for Innocent and Experienced Travelers*,
        by Nancy Willard, illustrated by Alice and Martin Provenson, HBJ

1981    *Fables*, by Arnold Lobel, Harper
        **Honor Books**
        *The Bremen-Town Musicians*, retold and illustrated by Ilse Plume, Doubleday
        *The Grey Lady and the Strawberry Snatcher*, by Molly Bang, Four Winds
        *Mice Twice*, by Joseph Low, McElderry/Atheneum
        *Truck*, by Donald Crews, Greenwillow

1980    *Ox-Cart Man*, by Donald Hall, pictures by Barbara Cooney, Viking
        **Honor Books**
        *Ben's Trumpet*, by Rachel Isadora, Greenwillow
        *The Garden of Abdul Gasazi*, by Chris Van Allsburg, Houghton
        *The Treasure*, by Uri Shulevitz, Farrar

1979    *The Girl Who Loved Wild Horses*, by Paul Goble, Bradbury
        **Honor Books**
        *Freight Train*, by Donald Crews, Greenwillow
        *The Way to Start a Day*, by Byrd Baylor, illustrated by Peter Parnall, Scribner

1978    *Noah's Ark*, by Peter Spier, Doubleday
        **Honor Books**
        *Castle*, by David Macaulay, Houghton
        *It Could Always Be Worse*, retold and illustrated by Margot Zemach, Farrar

1977    *Ashanti to Zulu: African Traditions*, by Margaret Musgrove, pictures by Leo and
        Diane Dillon, Dial
        **Honor Books**
        *The Amazing Bone*, by William Steig, Farrar
        *The Contest*, retold and illustrated by Nonny Hogrogian, Greenwillow
        *Fish for Supper*, by M. B.Goffstein, Dial
        *The Golem*, by Beverly Brodsky, Lippincott
        *Hawk, I'm Your Brother*, by Byrd Baylor, illustrated by Peter Parnall, Scribner

1976    *Why Mosquitoes Buzz in People's Ears*, retold by Verna Aardema, pictures by Leo and
        Diane Dillon, Dial Books for Young Readers
        **Honor Books**
        *The Desert Is Theirs*, by Byrd Baylor, illustrated by Peter Parnall, Scribner
        *Strega Nona*, retold and illustrated by Tomie de Paola, Prentice

1975    *Arrow to the Sun,* by Gerald McDermott, Viking
**Honor Book**
*Jambo Means Hello,* by Muriel Feelings, illustrated by Tom Feelings, Dial

1974    *Duffy and the Devil,* retold by Harve Zemach, pictures by Margot Zemach, Farrar
**Honor Books**
*Three Jovial Huntsmen,* by Susan Jeffers, Bradbury
*Cathedral,* by David Macaulay, Houghton

1973    *The Funny Little Woman,* by Arlene Mosel, illustrated by Blair Lent, Dutton
**Honor Books**
*Anansi the Spider,* adapted and illustrated by Gerald McDermott, Holt
*Hosie's Alphabet,* by Hosea, Tobias and Lisa Baskin, illustrated by Leonard Baskin, Viking
*Snow-White and the Seven Dwarfs,* translated by Randall Jarrell, illustrated by Nancy Ekholm Burkert, Farrar
*When Clay Sings,* by Byrd Baylor, illustrated by Tom Bahti, Scribner

1972    *One Fine Day,* by Nonny Hogrogian, Macmillan
**Honor Books**
*Hildilid's Night,* by Cheli Duran Ryan, illustrated by Arnold Lobel, Macmillan
*If All the Seas Were One Sea,* by Janina Domanska, Macmillan
*Moja Means One,* by Muriel Feelings, illustrated by Tom Feelings, Dial

1971    *A Story A Story,* by Gail E. Haley, Atheneum
**Honors Books**
*The Angry Moon,* by William Sleator, illustrated by Blair Lent, Atlantic/Little
*Frog and Toad Are Friends,* by Arnold Lobel, Harper
*In the Night Kitchen,* by Maurice Sendak, Harper

1970    *Sylvester and the Magic Pebble,* by William Steig, Windmill Books
**Honor Books**
*Goggles,* by Ezra Jack Keats, Macmillan
*Alexander and the Wind-Up Mouse,* by Leo Lionni, Pantheon
*Pop Corn & Ma Goodness,* by Edna Mitchell Preston, illustrated by Robert Andrew Parke, Viking
*Thy Friend, Obadiah,* by Brinton Turkle, Viking
*The Judge,* by Harve Zemach, illustrated by Margot Zemach, Farrar

1969    *The Fool of the World and the Flying Ship,* retold by Arthur Ransome, illustrated by Uri Shulevitz, Farrar
**Honor Book**
*Why the Sun and the Moon Live in the Sky,* by Elphinstone Dayrell, illustrated by Blair Lent, Houghton

1968    *Drummer Hoff,* adapted by Barbara Emberley, illustrated by Ed Emberley, Prentice-Hall
**Honor Books**
*Frederick,* by Leo Lionni, Pantheon
*Seashore Story,* by Taro Yashima, Viking
*The Emperor and the Kite,* by Jane Yolen, illustrated by Ed Young, Philomel

1967    *Sam, Bangs & Moonshine,* by Evaline Ness, Holt
**Honor Book**
*One Wide River to Cross,* by Barbara Emberley, illustrated by Ed Emberley, Prentice-Hall.

1966    *Always Room for One More*, by Sorche Nic Leodhas, illustrated by Nonny Hogrogian, Holt
        **Honor Books**
        *Hide and Seek Fog*, by Alvin Tresselt, illustrated by Roger Duvoisin, Lothrop
        *Just Me*, by Marie Hall Ets, Viking
        *Tom Tit Tot*, by Evaline Ness, Scribner

1965    *May I Bring a Friend?*, by Beatrice Schenk de Regniers, illustrated by Beni Montresor, Atheneum
        **Honor Books**
        *Rain Makes Applesauce*, by Julian Scheer, illustrated by Marvin Bileck, Holiday
        *The Wave*, by Margaret Hodges, illustrated by Blair Lent, Houghton
        *A Pocketful of Cricket*, by Rebecca Caudill, illustrated by Evaline Ness, Holt

1964    *Where the Wild Things Are*, by Maurice Sendak, Harper
        **Honor Books**
        *Swimmy*, by Leo Lionni, Pantheon
        *All in the Morning Early*, by Sorche Nic Leodhas, illustrated by Evaline Ness, Holt
        *Mother Goose and Nursery Rhymes*, illustrated by Philip Reed, Atheneum

1963    *The Snowy Day*, by Ezra Jack Keats, Viking
        **Honor Books**
        *The Sun Is a Golden Earring*, by Natalia M. Belting, illustrated by Bernarda Bryson, Holt
        *Mr. Rabbit and the Lovely Present*, by Charlotte Zolotow, illustrated by Maurice Sendak, Harper

1962    *Once a Mouse*, by Marcia Brown, Scribner
        **Honor Books**
        *The Fox Went Out on a Chilly Night*, illustrated by Peter Spier, Doubleday
        *Little Bear's Visit*, by Else Holmelund Minarik, illustrated by Maurice Sendak, Harper
        *The Day We Saw the Sun Come Up*, by Alice E. Goudey, illustrated by Adrienne Adams, Scribner

1961    *Baboushka and the Three Kings*, by Ruth Robbins, illustrated by Nicholas Sidjakov, Parnassus
        **Honor Book**
        *Inch by Inch*, by Leo Lionni, Astor-Honor

1960    *Nine Days to Christmas*, by Marie Hall Ets and Aurora Labastida, Viking
        **Honor Books**
        *Houses from the Sea*, by Alice E. Goudey, illustrated by Adrienne Adams, Scribner
        *The Moon Jumpers*, by Janice Udry, illustrated by Maurice Sendak, Harper

1959    *Chanticleer and the Fox*, adapted from Chaucer, illustrated by Barbara Cooney, Crowell
        **Honor Books**
        *The House that Jack Built*, by Antonio Frasconi, HBJ
        *What Do You Say, Dear?*, by Sesyle Joslin, illustrated by Maurice Sendak, Scott
        *Umbrella*, by Taro Yashima, Viking

1958    *Time of Wonder*, by Robert McCloskey, Viking
        **Honor Books**
        *Fly High, Fly Low*, by Don Freeman, Viking
        *Anatole and the Cat*, by Eve Titus, illustrated by Paul Galdone, McGraw

1957    *A Tree Is Nice*, by Janice Udry, illustrated by Marc Simont, Harper
        **Honor Books**
        *Mr. Penny's Race Horse*, by Marie Hall Ets, Viking
        *1 Is One*, by Tasha Tudor, Walck
        *Anatole*, by Eve Titus, illustrated by Paul Galdone, McGraw
        *Gillespie and the Guards*, by Benjamin Elkin, illustrated by James Daugherty, Viking
        *Lion*, by William Pène du Bois, Viking

1956    *Frog Went A-Courtin'*, retold by John Langstaff, illustrated by Feodor Rojankovsky,
        HBJ
        **Honor Books**
        *Play with Me*, by Marie Hall Ets, Viking
        *Crow Boy*, by Taro Yashima, Viking

1955    *Cinderella*, by Charles Perrault, translated and illustrated by Marcia Brown, Scribner
        **Honor Books**
        *Book of Nursery and Mother Goose Rhymes*, illustrated by Marguerite de Angeli,
        Doubleday
        *Wheel on the Chimney*, by Margaret Wise Brown, illustrated by Tibor Gergely,
        Lippincott
        *The Thanksgiving Story*, by Alice Dalgliesh, illustrated by Helen Sewell, Scribner

1954    *Madeline's Rescue*, by Ludwig Bemelmans, Viking
        **Honor Books**
        *Journey Cake, Ho!*, by Ruth Sawyer, illustrated by Robert McCloskey, Viking
        *When Will the World Be Mine?*, by Miriam Schlein, illustrated by Jean Charlot, Scott
        *The Steadfast Tin Soldier*, by Hans Christian Andersen, illustrated by Marcia Brown,
        Scribner
        *A Very Special House*, by Ruth Krauss, illustrated by Maurice Sendak, Harper
        *Green Eyes*, by A. Birnbaum, Capitol

1953    *The Biggest Bear*, by Lynd Ward, Houghton
        **Honor Books**
        *Puss in Boots*, by Charles Perrault, illustrated and translated by Marcia Brown,
        Scribner
        *One Morning in Maine*, by Robert McCloskey, Viking
        *Ape in a Cape*, by Fritz Eichenberg, HBJ
        *The Storm Book*, by Charlotte Zolotow, illustrated by Margaret Bloy Graham, Harper
        *Five Little Monkeys*, by Juliet Kepes, Houghton

1952    *Finders Keepers*, by Will Lipkind, illustrated by Nicolas Mordvinoff, HBJ
        **Honor Books**
        *Mr. T. W. Anthony Woo*, by Marie Hall Ets, Viking
        *Skipper John's Cook*, by Marcia Brown, Scribner
        *All Falling Down*, by Gene Zion, illustrated by Margaret Bloy Graham, Harper
        *Bear Party*, by William Pène du Bois, Viking
        *Feather Mountain*, by Elizabeth Olds, Houghton

1951    *The Egg Tree*, by Katherine Milhous, Scribner
        **Honor Books**
        *Dick Whittington and His Cat*, by Marcia Brown, Scribner
        *The Two Reds*, by Will Lipkind, illustrated by Nicolas Mordvinoff, HBJ
        *If I Ran the Zoo*, by Dr. Seuss, Random
        *The Most Wonderful Doll in the World*, by Phyllis McGinley, illustrated by
        Helen Stone, Lippincott
        *T-Bone, the Baby Sitter*, by Clare Newberry, Harper

1950     *Song of the Swallows*, by Leo Politi, Scribner
         **Honor Books**
         *America's Ethan Allen*, by Stewart Holbrook, illustrated by Lynd Ward, Houghton
         *The Wild Birthday Cake*, by Lavinia Davis, illustrated by Hildegard Woodward,
         Doubleday
         *The Happy Day*, by Ruth Krauss, illustrated by Marc Simont, Harper
         *Bartholomew and the Oobleck*, by Dr. Seuss, Random
         *Henry Fisherman*, by Marcia Brown, Scribner

1949     *The Big Snow*, by Berta and Elmer Hader, Macmillan
         **Honor Books**
         *Blueberries for Sal*, by Robert McCloskey, Viking
         *All Around the Town*, by Phyllis McGinley, illustrated by Helen Stone, Lippincott
         *Juanita*, by Leo Politi, Scribner
         *Fish in the Air*, by Kurt Wiese, Viking

1948     *White Snow, Bright Snow*, by Alvin Tresselt, illustrated by Roger Duvoisin, Lothrop
         **Honor Books**
         *Stone Soup*, by Marcia Brown, Scribner
         *McElligot's Pool*, by Dr. Seuss, Random
         *Bambino the Clown*, by George Schreiber, Viking
         *Roger and the Fox*, by Lavinia Davis, illustrated by Hildegard Woodward, Doubleday
         *Song of Robin Hood*, edited by Anne Malcolmson, illustrated by Virginia Lee Burton,
         Houghton

1947     *The Little Island*, by Golden MacDonald, illustrated by Leonard Weisgard, Doubleday
         **Honor Books**
         *Rain Drop Splash*, by Alvin Tresselt, illustrated by Leonard Weisgard, Lothrop
         *Boats on the River*, by Marjorie Flack, illustrated by Jay Hyde Barnum, Viking
         *Timothy Turtle*, by Al Graham, illustrated by Tony Palazzo, Welch
         *Pedro, the Angel of Olvera Street*, by Leo Politi, Scribner
         *Sing in Praise: A Collection of the Best Loved Hymns*, by Opal Wheeler, illustrated by
         Marjorie Torrey, Dutton

1946     *The Rooster Crows*, by Maud and Miska Petersham, Macmillan
         **Honor Books**
         *Little Lost Lamb*, by Golden MacDonald, illustrated by Leonard Weisgard, Doubleday
         *Sing Mother Goose*, by Opal Wheeler, illustrated by Marjorie Torrey, Dutton
         *My Mother Is the Most Beautiful Woman in the World*, by Becky Reyher, illustrated by
         Ruth C. Gannett, Lothrop
         *You Can Write Chinese*, by Kurt Wiese, Viking

1945     *Prayer for a Child*, by Rachel Field, illustrated by Elizabeth Orton Jones, Macmillan
         **Honor Books**
         *Mother Goose*, illustrated by Tasha Tudor, Walck
         *In the Forest*, by Marie Hall Ets, Viking
         *Yonie Wondernose*, by Marguerite de Angeli, Doubleday
         *The Christmas Anna Angel*, by Ruth Sawyer, illustrated by Kate Seredy, Viking

1944     *Many Moons*, by James Thurber, illustrated by Louis Slobodkin, HBJ
         **Honor Books**
         *Small Rain: Verses from the Bible*, by Jessie Orton Jones, illustrated by
         Elizabeth Orton Jones, Viking
         *Pierre Pigeon*, by Lee Kingman, illustrated by Arnold E. Bare, Houghton
         *The Mighty Hunter*, by Berta and Elmer Hader, Macmillan
         *A Child's Good Night Book*, by Margaret Wise Brown, illustrated by Jean Charlot,
         Scott
         *Good Luck Horse*, by Chin-Yi Chan, illustrated by Plao Chan, Whittlesey

1943    *The Little House*, by Virginia Lee Burton, Houghton
        **Honor Books**
        *Dash and Dart*, by Mary and Conrad Buff, Viking
        *Marshmallow*, by Clare Newberry, Harper

1942    *Make Way for Ducklings*, by Robert McCloskey, Viking
        **Honor Books**
        *An American ABC*, by Maud and Miska Petersham, Macmillan
        *In My Mother's House*, by Ann Nolan Clark, illustrated by Velino Herrera, Viking
        *Paddle-to-the-Sea*, by Holling C. Holling, Houghton
        *Nothing at All*, by Wanda Gàg, Coward

1941    *They Were Strong and Good*, by Robert Lawson, Viking
        **Honor Book**
        *April's Kittens*, by Clare Newberry, Harper

1940    *Abraham Lincoln*, by Ingri and Edgar Parin D'Aulaire, Doubleday
        **Honor Books**
        *Cock-a-Doodle Doo*, by Berta and Elmer Hader, Macmillan
        *Madeline*, by Ludwig Bemelmans, Viking
        *The Ageless Story*, illustrated by Lauren Ford, Dodd

1939    *Mei Li*, by Thomas Handforth, Doubleday
        **Honor Books**
        *The Forest Pool*, by Laura Adams Armer, Longmans
        *Wee Gillis*, by Munro Leaf, illustrated by Robert Lawson, Viking
        *Snow White and the Seven Dwarfs*, by Wanda Gàg, Coward
        *Barkis*, by Clare Newberry, Harper
        *Andy and the Lion*, by James Daugherty, Viking

1938    *Animals of the Bible*, by Helen Dean Fish, illustrated by Dorothy P. Lathrop, Lippincott
        **Honor Books**
        *Seven Simeons*, by Boris Artzybasheff, Viking
        *Four and Twenty Blackbirds*, by Helen Dean Fish, illustrated by Robert Lawson, Stokes

## The Newbery Medal and Honor Books

Named in honor of John Newbery (1713–1767), the first English publisher of children's books, this medal has been given annually (since 1922) by the American Library Association's Association for Library Service to Children. The recipient is recognized as author of the most distinguished book in children's literature published in the United States in the preceding year. The award is limited to citizens or residents of the United States.

The Association for Library Service to Children (ALSC) is one of eleven divisions of the American Library Association, the oldest and largest library association in the world. The members of ALSC include librarians in public libraries, school media centers, and hospitals; college and university faculty and students; authors, editors, critics and others who are interested in and support quality library service for children.

1990    *Number the Stars,* by Lois Lowry, Houghton Mifflin
        **Honor Books**
        *Afternoon of the Elves,* by Janet Taylor Lisle, Orchard
        *Shabanu, Daughter of the Wind,* by Suzanne Fisher Staples, Knopf
        *The Winter Room,* by Gary Paulson, Orchard

1989    *Joyful Noise: Poems for Two Voices,* by Paul Fleischman, Harper & Row
        **Honor Books**
        *In the Beginning: Creation Stories from Around the World,* by Virginia Hamilton, Harcourt Brace Jovanovitch
        *Scorpions,* by Walter Dean Myers, Harper & Row

1988    *Lincoln: A Photobiography,* by Russell Freedman, Clarion
        **Honor Books**
        *After the Rain,* by Norma Mazer, Morrow
        *Hatchet,* by Gary Paulsen, Bradbury

1987    *The Whipping Boy,* by Sid Fleischman, Greenwillow
        **Honor Books**
        *A Fine White Dust,* by Cynthia Rylant, Bradbury
        *Volcano,* by Patricia Lauber, Bradbury
        *On My Honor,* by Marion Bauer, Clarion

1986    *Sarah, Plain and Tall,* by Patricia MacLachlan, Harper & Row
        **Honor Books**
        *Commodore Perry in the Land of the Shogun,* by Rhoda Blumberg, Lothrop
        *Dogsong,* by Gary Paulsen, Bradbury

1985    *The Hero and the Crown,* by Robin McKinley, Greenwillow
        **Honor Books**
        *Like Jake and Me,* by Mavis Jukes, Knopf
        *The Moves Make the Man,* by Bruce Brooks, Harper
        *One-Eyed Cat,* by Paula Fox, Bradbury

1984    *Dear Mr. Henshaw,* by Beverly Cleary, Morrow
        **Honor Books**
        *The Sign of the Beaver,* by Elizabeth George Speare, Houghton
        *A Solitary Blue,* by Cynthia Voigt, Atheneum
        *Sugaring Time,* by Kathryn Lasky, Macmillan
        *The Wish Giver,* by Bill Brittain, Harper

1983    *Dicey's Song,* by Cynthia Voigt, Atheneum
        **Honor Books**
        *The Blue Sword,* by Robin McKinley, Greenwillow
        *Dr. De Soto,* by William Steig, Farrar
        *Graven Images,* by Paul Fleischman, Harper
        *Homesick: My Own Story,* by Jean Fritz, Putnam
        *Sweet Whispers, Brother Rush,* by Virginia Hamilton, Philomel

1982    *A Visit to William Blake's Inn: Poems for Innocent and Experienced Travelers,* by Nancy Willard, Harcourt
        **Honor Books**
        *Ramona Quimby, Age 8,* by Beverly Cleary, Morrow
        *Upon the Head of a Goat,* by Aranka Siegal, Farrar

1981   *Jacob Have I Loved,* by Katherine Paterson, Crowell
       **Honor Books**
       *The Fledgling,* by Jane Langton, Harper
       *A Ring of Endless Light,* by Madeleine L'Engle, Farrar

1980   *A Gathering of Days: A New England Girl's Journal, 1830–32,* by Joan Blos,
       Scribner's
       **Honor Book**
       *The Road from Home: The Story of an Armenian Girl,* by David Kherdian,
       Greenwillow

1979   *The Westing Game,* by Ellen Raskin, Dutton
       **Honor Book**
       *The Great Gilly Hopkins,* by Katherine Paterson, Crowell

1978   *Bridge to Terabithia,* by Katherine Paterson, Crowell
       **Honor Books**
       *Anpao: An American Indian Odyssey,* by Jamake Highwater, Lippincott
       *Ramona and Her Father,* by Beverly Cleary, Morrow

1977   *Roll of Thunder, Hear My Cry,* by Mildred D. Taylor, Dial
       **Honor Books**
       *Abel's Island,* by William Steig, Farrar
       *A String in the Harp,* by Nancy Bond, Atheneum/McElderry

1976   *The Grey King,* by Susan Cooper, Atheneum/McElderry
       **Honor Books**
       *The Hundred Penny Box,* by Sharon Bell Mathis, Viking
       *Dragonwings,* by Lawrence Yep, Harper

1975   *M. C. Higgins, the Great,* by Virginia Hamilton, Macmillan
       **Honor Books**
       *Figgs & Phantoms,* by Ellen Raskin, Dutton
       *My Brother Sam Is Dead,* by James Lincoln Collier & Christopher Collier, Four Winds
       *The Perilous Gard,* by Elizabeth Marie Pope, Houghton
       *Philip Hall Likes Me, I Reckon Maybe,* by Bette Greene, Dial

1974   *The Slave Dancer,* by Paula Fox, Bradbury
       **Honor Book**
       *The Dark Is Rising,* by Susan Cooper, Atheneum/McElderry

1973   *Julie of the Wolves,* by Jean George, Harper
       **Honor Books**
       *Frog and Toad Together,* by Arnold Lobel, Harper
       *The Upstairs Room,* by Johanna Reiss, Crowell
       *The Witches of Worm,* by Zilpha Keatley Snyder, Atheneum

1972   *Mrs. Frisby and the Rats of NIMH,* by Robert C. O'Brien, Atheneum
       **Honor Books**
       *Incident at Hawk's Hill,* by Allan W. Eckert, Little
       *The Planet of Junior Brown,* by Virginia Hamilton, Macmillan
       *The Tombs of Atuan,* by Ursula K. Le Guin, Atheneum
       *Annie and the Old One,* by Miska Miles, Atlantic/Little
       *The Headless Cupid,* by Zilpha Keatley Snyder, Atheneum

1971    *Summer of the Swans*, by Betsy Byars, Viking
        **Honor Books**
        *Kneeknock Rise*, by Natalie Babbitt, Farrar
        *Enchantress from the Stars*, by Sylvia Louise Engdahl, Atheneum
        *Sing Down the Moon*, by Scott O'Dell, Houghton

1970    *Sounder*, by William H. Armstrong, Harper
        **Honor Books**
        *Our Eddie*, by Sulamith Ish-Kishor, Pantheon
        *The Many Ways of Seeing: An Introduction to the Pleasures of Art*, by Janet Gaylord
        Moore, World
        *Journey Outside*, by Mary Q. Steele, Viking

1969    *The High King*, by Lloyd Alexander, Holt
        **Honor Books**
        *To Be a Slave*, by Julius Lester, Dial
        *When Shlemiel Went to Warsaw and Other Stories*, by Isaac Bashevis Singer, Farrar

1968    *From the Mixed-Up Files of Mrs. Basil E. Frankweiler*, by E. L. Konigsburg, Atheneum
        **Honor Books**
        *Jennifer, Hecate, Macbeth, William McKinley, and Me, Eilzabeth*, by E. L. Konigsburg,
        Atheneum
        *The Black Pearl*, by Scott O'Dell, Houghton
        *The Fearsome Inn*, by Isaac Bashevis Singer, Scribner's
        *The Egypt Game*, by Zilpha Keatley Snyder, Atheneum

1967    *Up a Road Slowly*, by Irene Hunt, Follett
        **Honor Books**
        *The King's Fifth*, by Scott O'Dell, Houghton
        *Zlateh the Goat and Other Stories*, by Isaac Bashevis Singer, Harper
        *The Jazz Man*, by Mary H. Weik Atheneum

1966    *I, Juan de Pareja*, by Elizabeth Borten de Trevino, Farrar
        **Honor Books**
        *The Black Cauldron*, by Lloyd Alexander, Holt
        *The Animal Family*, by Randall Jarrell, Pantheon
        *The Noonday Friends*, by Mary Stolz, Harper

1965    *Shadow of a Bull*, by Maia Wojciechowska, Atheneum
        **Honor Book**
        *Across Five Aprils*, by Irene Hunt, Follett

1964    *It's Like This, Cat*, by Emily Cheney Neville, Harper
        **Honor Books**
        *Rascal*, by Sterling North, Dutton
        *The Loner*, by Esther Wier, McKay

1963    *A Wrinkle in Time*, by Madeleine L'Engle, Farrar
        **Honor Books**
        *Thistle and Thyme*, by Sorche Nic Leodhas, Holt
        *Men of Athens*, by Olivia Coolidge, Houghton

1962    *The Bronze Bow*, by Elizabeth George Speare, Houghton
        **Honor Books**
        *Frontier Living*, by Edwin Tunis, World
        *The Golden Goblet*, by Eloise McGraw, Coward
        *Belling the Tiger*, by Mary Stolz, Harper

1961     *Island of the Blue Dolphins*, by Scott O'Dell, Houghton
        **Honor Books**
        *America Moves Forward*, by Gerald W. Johnson, Morrow
        *Old Ramon*, by Jack Schaefer, Houghton
        *The Cricket in Times Square*, by George Selden, Farrar

1960     *Onion John*, by Joseph Krumgold, T. Crowell
        **Honor Books**
        *My Side of the Mountain*, by Jean George, Dutton
        *America Is Born*, by Gerald W. Johnson, Morrow
        *The Gammage Cup*, by Carol Kendall, Harcourt

1959     *The Witch of Blackbird Pond*, by Elizabeth George Speare, Houghton
        **Honor Books**
        *The Family Under the Bridge*, by Natalie S. Carlson, Harper
        *Along Came a Dog*, by Meindert DeJong, Harper
        *Chucaro: Wild Pony of the Pampa*, by Francis Kalnay, Harcourt
        *The Perilous Road*, by William O. Steele, Harcourt

1958     *Rifles for Watie*, by Harold Keith, T. Crowell
        **Honor Books**
        *The Horsecatcher*, by Mari Sandoz, Westminster
        *Gone-Away Lake*, by Elizabeth Enright, Harcourt
        *The Great Wheel*, by Robert Lawson, Viking
        *Tom Paine, Freedom's Apostle*, by Leo Gurko, T. Crowell

1957     *Miracle on Maple Hill*, by Virginia Sorensen, Harcourt
        **Honor Books**
        *Old Yeller*, by Fred Gipson, Harper
        *The House of Sixty Fathers*, by Meindert DeJong, Harper
        *Mr. Justice Holmes*, by Clara Ingram Judson, Follett
        *The Corn Grows Ripe*, by Dorothy Rhoads, Viking
        *Black Fox of Lorne*, by Marguerite de Angeli, Doubleday

1956     *Carry on, Mr. Bowditch*, by Jean Lee Latham, Houghton
        **Honor Books**
        *The Secret River*, by Marjorie Kinnan Rawlings, Scribner's
        *The Golden Name Day*, by Jennie Lindquist, Harper
        *Men, Microscopes, and Living Things*, by Katherine Shippen, Viking

1955     *The Wheel on the School*, by Meindert DeJong, Harper
        **Honor Books**
        *The Courage of Sarah Noble*, by Alice Dalgliesh, Scribner's
        *Banner in the Sky*, by James Ullman, Lippincott

1954     *. . . and now Miguel*, by Joseph Krumgold, T. Crowell
        **Honor Books**
        *All Alone*, by Claire Huchet Bishop, Viking
        *Shadrach*, by Meindert DeJong, Harper
        *Hurry Home Candy*, by Meindert DeJong, Harper
        *Theodore Roosevelt, Fighting Patriot*, by Clara Ingram Judson, Follett
        *Magic Maize*, by Mary and Conrad Buff, Houghton

1953     *Secret of the Andes*, by Ann Nolan Clark, Viking
        **Honor Books**
        *Charlotte's Web*, by E. B. White, Harper
        *Moccasin Trail*, by Eloise McGraw, Coward
        *Red Sails to Capri*, by Ann Weil, Viking
        *The Bears of Hemlock Mountain*, by Alice Dalgliesh, Scribner's
        *Birthdays of Freedom*, Vol. 1, by Genevieve Foster, Scribner's

1952    *Ginger Pye,* by Eleanor Estes, Harcourt
        **Honor Books**
        *Americans Before Columbus,* by Elizabeth Baity, Viking
        *Minn of the Mississippi,* by Holling C. Holling, Houghton
        *The Defender,* by Nicholas Kalashnikoff, Scribner's
        *The Light at Tern Rock,* by Julia Sauer, Viking
        *The Apple and the Arrow,* by Mary and Conrad Buff, Houghton

1951    *Amos Fortune, Free Man,* by Elizabeth Yates, Aladdin
        **Honor Books**
        *Better Known as Johnny Appleseed,* by Mabel Leigh Hunt, Lippincott
        *Gandhi, Fighter Without a Sword,* by Jeanette Eaton, Morrow
        *Abraham Lincoln, Friend of the People,* by Clara Ingram Judson, Follett
        *The Story of Appleby Capple,* by Anne Parrish, Harper

1950    *The Door in the Wall,* by Marguerite de Angeli, Doubleday
        **Honor Books**
        *Tree of Freedom,* by Rebecca Caudill, Viking
        *The Blue Cat of Castle Town,* by Catherine Coblentz, Longmans
        *Kildee House,* by Rutherford Montgomery, Doubleday
        *George Washington,* by Genevieve Foster, Scribner's
        *Song of the Pines,* by Walter and Marion Havighurst, Winston

1949    *King of the Wind,* by Marguerite Henry, Rand
        **Honor Books**
        *Seabird,* by Holling C. Holling, Houghton
        *Daughter of the Mountains,* by Louise Rankin, Viking
        *My Father's Dragon,* by Ruth S. Gannett, Random
        *Story of the Negro,* by Arna Bontemps, Knopf

1948    *The Twenty-One Balloons,* by William Pène du Bois, Viking
        **Honor Books**
        *Pancakes-Paris,* by Claire Huchet Bishop, Viking
        *Li Lun, Lad of Courage,* by Carolyn Treffinger, Abingdon
        *The Quaint and Curious Quest of Johnny Longfoot,* by Catherine Besterman, Bobbs
        *The Cow-Tail Switch, and Other West African Stories,* by Harold Courlander, Holt
        *Misty of Chincoteague,* by Marguerite Henry, Rand

1947    *Miss Hickory,* by Carolyn Sherwin Bailey, Viking
        **Honor Books**
        *Wonderful Year,* by Nancy Barnes, Messner
        *Big Tree,* by Mary and Conrad Buff, Viking
        *The Heavenly Tenants,* by William Maxwell, Harper
        *The Avion My Uncle Flew,* by Cyrus Fisher, Appleton
        *The Hidden Treasure of Glaston,* by Eleanore Jewett, Viking

1946    *Strawberry Girl,* by Lois Lenski, Lippincott
        **Honor Books**
        *Justin Morgan Had a Horse,* by Marguerite Henry, Rand
        *The Moved-Outers,* by Florence Crannell Means, Houghton
        *Bhimsa, The Dancing Bear,* by Christine Weston, Scribner's
        *New Found World,* by Katherine Shippen,Viking

1945    *Rabbit Hill,* by Robert Lawson, Viking
        **Honor Books**
        *The Hundred Dresses,* by Eleanor Estes, Harcourt
        *The Silver Pencil,* by Alice Dalgliesh, Scribner's
        *Abraham Lincoln's World,* by Genevieve Foster, Scribner's
        *Lone Journey: The Life of Roger Williams,* by Jeanette Eaton, Harcourt

1944    *Johnny Tremain*, by Esther Forbes, Houghton
        **Honor Books**
        *These Happy Golden Years*, by Laura Ingalls Wilder, Harper
        *Fog Magic*, by Julia Sauer, Viking
        *Rufus M.*, by Eleanor Estes, Harcourt
        *Mountain Born*, by Elizabeth Yates, Coward

1943    *Adam of the Road*, by Elizabeth Janet Gray, Viking
        **Honor Books**
        *The Middle Moffat*, by Eleanor Estes, Harcourt
        *Have You Seen Tom Thumb?*, by Mabel Leigh Hunt, Lippincott

1942    *The Matchlock Gun*, by Walter D. Edmonds, Dodd
        **Honor Books**
        *Little Town on the Prairie*, by Laura Ingalls Wilder, Harper
        *George Washington's World*, by Genevieve Foster, Scribner's
        *Indian Captive: The Story of Mary Jemison*, by Lois Lenski, Lippincott
        *Down Ryton Water*, by Eva Roe Gaggin, Viking

1941    *Call it Courage*, by Armstrong Sperry, Macmillan
        **Honor Books**
        *Blue Willow*, by Doris Gates, Viking
        *Young Mac of Fort Vancouver*, by Mary Jane Carr, T. Crowell
        *The Long Winter*, by Laura Ingalls Wilder, Harper
        *Nansen*, by Anna Gertrude Hall, Viking

1940    *Daniel Boone*, by James Daugherty, Viking
        **Honor Books**
        *The Singing Tree*, by Kate Seredy, Viking
        *Runner of the Mountain Tops*, by Mabel Robinson, Random
        *By the Shores of Silver Lake*, by Laura Ingalls Wilder, Harper
        *Boy with a Pack*, by Stephen W. Meader, Harcourt

1939    *Thimble Summer*, by Elizabeth Enright, Rinehart
        **Honor Books**
        *Nino*, by Valenti Angelo, Viking
        *Mr. Popper's Penguins*, by Richard and Florence Atwater, Little
        *"Hello the Boat!"*, by Phyllis Crawford, Holt
        *Leader by Destiny: George Washington, Man and Patriot*, by Jeanette Eaton, Harcourt
        *Penn*, by Elizabeth Janet Gray, Viking

1938    *The White Stag*, by Kate Seredy, Viking
        **Honor Books**
        *Pecos Bill*, by James Cloyd Bowman, Little
        *Bright Island*, by Mabel Robinson, Random
        *On the Banks of Plum Creek*, by Laura Ingalls Wilder, Harper

1937    *Roller Skates*, by Ruth Sawyer, Viking
        **Honor Books**
        *Phebe Fairchild: Her Book*, by Lois Lenski, Stokes
        *Whistler's Van*, by Idwal Jones, Viking
        *Golden Basket*, by Ludwig Bemelmans, Viking
        *Winterbound*, by Margery Bianco, Viking
        *Audubon*, by Constance Rourke, Harcourt
        *The Codfish Musket*, by Agnes Hewes, Doubleday

1936    *Caddie Woodlawn*, by Carol Brink, Macmillan
        **Honor Books**
        *Honk, The Moose*, by Phil Stong, Dodd
        *The Good Master*, by Kate Seredy, Viking
        *Young Walter Scott*, by Elizabeth Janet Gray, Viking
        *All Sail Set*, by Armstrong Sperry, Winston

1935    *Dobry*, by Monica Shannon, Viking
        **Honor Books**
        *Pageant of Chinese History*, by Elizabeth Seeger, Longmans
        *Davy Crockett*, by Constance Rourke, Harcourt
        *Day on Skates*, by Hilda Van Stockum, Harper

1934    *Invincible Louisa*, by Cornelia Meigs, Little
        **Honor Books**
        *The Forgotten Daughter*, by Caroline Snedeker, Doubleday
        *Swords of Steel*, by Elsie Singmaster, Houghton
        *ABC Bunny*, by Wanda Gàg, Coward
        *Winged Girl of Knossos*, by Erik Berry, Appleton
        *New Land*, by Sarah Schmidt, McBride
        *Big Tree of Bunlahy*, by Padraic Colum, Macmillan
        *Glory of the Seas*, by Agnes Hewes, Knopf
        *Apprentice of Florence*, by Anne Kyle, Houghton

1933    *Young Fu of the Upper Yangtze*, by Elizabeth Foreman Lewis, Winston
        **Honor Books**
        *Swift Rivers*, by Cornelia Meigs, Little
        *The Railroad to Freedom*, by Hildegarde Swift, Harcourt
        *Children of the Soil*, by Nora Burglon, Doubleday

1932    *Waterless Mountain*, by Laura Adams Armer, Longmans
        **Honor Books**
        *The Fairy Circus*, by Dorothy P. Lathrop, Macmillan
        *Calico Bush*, by Rachel Field, Macmillan
        *Boy of the South Seas*, by Eunice Tietjens, Coward
        *Out of the Flame*, by Eloise Lownsbery, Longmans
        *Jane's Island*, by Marjorie Allee, Houghton
        *Truce of the Wolf and Other Tales of Old Italy*, by Mary Gould Davis, Harcourt

1931    *The Cat Who Went to Heaven*, by Elizabeth Coatsworth, Macmillan
        **Honor Books**
        *Floating Island*, by Anne Parish, Harper
        *The Dark Star of Itza*, by Alida Malkus, Harcourt
        *Queer Person*, by Ralph Hubbard, Doubleday
        *Mountains Are Free*, by Julia Davis Adams, Dutton
        *Spice and the Devil's Cave*, by Agnes Hewes, Knopf
        *Meggy Macintosh*, by Elizabeth Janet Gray, Doubleday
        *Garram the Hunter*, by Herbert Best, Doubleday
        *Ood-Le-Uk the Wanderer*, by Alice Lide and Margaret Johansen, Little

1930    *Hitty, Her First Hundred Years*, by Rachel Field, Macmillan
        **Honor Books**
        *Daughter of the Seine*, by Jeanette Eaton, Harper
        *Pran of Albania*, by Elizabeth Miller, Doubleday
        *Jumping-Off Place*, by Marian Hurd McNeely, Longmans
        *Tangle-Coated Horse and Other Tales*, by Ella Young, Longmans
        *Vaino*, by Julia Davis Adams, Dutton
        *Little Blacknose*, by Hildegarde Swift, Harcourt

1929    *The Trumpeter of Krakow,* by Eric P. Kelly, Macmillan
        **Honor Books**
        *Pigtail of Ah Lee Ben Loo,* by John Bennett, Longmans
        *Millions of Cats,* by Wanda Gàg, Coward
        *The Boy Who Was,* by Grace Hallock, Dutton
        *Clearing Weather,* by Cornelia Meigs, Little
        *Runaway Papoose,* by Grace Moon, Doubleday
        *Tod of the Fens,* by Elinor Whitney, Macmillan

1928    *Gayneck, The Story of a Pigeon,* by Dhan Gopal Mukerji, Dutton
        **Honor Books**
        *The Wonder Smith and His Son,* by Ella Young, Longmans
        *Downright Dencey,* by Caroline Snedeker, Doubleday

1927    *Smoky, The Cowhorse,* by Will James, Scribner's
        **Honor Books**—No Record

1926    *Shen of the Sea,* by Arthur Bowie Chrisman, Dutton
        **Honor Book**
        *Voyagers,* by Padraic Colum, Macmillan

1925    *Tales from Silver Lands,* by Charles Finger, Doubleday
        **Honor Books**
        *Nicholas,* by Anne Carroll Moore, Putnam
        *Dream Coach,* by Anne Parrish, Macmillan

1924    *The Dark Frigate,* by Charles Hawes, Atlantic/Little
        **Honor Books**—No Record

1923    *The Voyages of Doctor Dolittle,* by Hugh Lofting, Lippincott
        **Honor Books**—No Record

1922    *The Story of Mankind,* by Hendrik Willem van Loon, Liveright
        **Honor Books**
        *The Great Quest,* by Charles Hawes, Little
        *Cedric the Forester,* by Bernard Marshall, Appleton
        *The Old Tobacco Shop,* by William Bowen, Macmillan
        *The Golden Fleece and the Heroes Who Lived Before Achilles,* by Padraic Colum,
        Macmillan
        *Windy Hill,* by Cornelia Meigs, Macmillan

# index

The following figures were adapted from the work of the following teachers:
Mary Bonner (Figures 2.4 and 2.6)
Yvonne Caravaglia (Figures 7.7, 7.8, 7.11, 7.32, 7.51)
Carol Cedarholm (Figures 7.1, 7.2, 7.25, 7.26, 7.37, 7.38)
Chris Czarnecki (Figure 4.5)
Charlotte DeAlmeida (Figures 7.13, 7.22, 7.24, 7.33, 7.55)
Kris deVente (Figures 7.36, 7.56)
Suzanne French (Figures 2.7, 7.5, 7.54)
Kate Giblin (Figures 2.5, 7.37, 7.41, 7.47)
Liz Harris Ginrich (Figures 2.5, 7.35, 7.41, 7.47)
Helen Hermann (Figure 7.40)
Stephanie Horowitz (Figures 7.41, 7.50)
Wendy Hughes (Figures 1.3, 1.5)
Mary Johnson (Figures 7.3, 7.6, 7.19, 7.28, 7.30, 7.48)
Terri Judge (Figures 3.1, 5.6, 6.1, 6.2, 7.8, 7.14, 7.19, 7.21, 7.28, 7.30, 7.31, 7.32, 7.35)
Jeffrey Long (Figures 5.6, 5.7, 5.8)
Regina Mardex (Figures 2.2, 4.1, 7.7, 7.8, 7.9, 7.31)
Lisa Milano (Figures 7.1, 7.2, 7.4, 7.12, 7.16, 7.17, 7.18, 7.27, 7.31, 7.39, 7.42, 7.45, 7.49, 7.52, 7.53)
Valerie Myers White (Figure 1.4)
Mary Stratton (Figure 7.14, 7.21)
Jill Zavelick (Figure 7.1, 7.2, 7.34, 7.44)